The
WRITER'S
COMPASS

FROM STORY MAP TO FINISHED DRAFT IN 7 STAGES

NANCY Ellen DODD

WD

WRITER'S DIGEST
BOOKS

Writer's Digest Books
An imprint of Penguin Random House LLC
penguinrandomhouse.com

Printed in the United States of America

ISBN 978-1-59963-197-4

Edited by Scott Francis
Designed by Terri Woesner

ABOUT THE AUTHOR

Nancy Ellen Dodd is a writer, university instructor, and an editor with two master's degrees in writing from the University of Southern California. She currently teaches screenwriting at Pepperdine University and has studied with a number of award winning authors.

Photo © Aaron Peterson

table of
CONTENTS

part three the End:
LIVING A WRITER'S LIFE

INTRODUCTION
ABOUT *THE WRITER'S COMPASS*

SOME THINGS YOU SHOULD KNOW BEFORE YOU BEGIN

Most of us will never be Ernest Hemingway or Jane Austen or Lillian Hellman or John Grisham or ... well, you get the picture. However, many of us have a story or stories we long to tell—if we only knew how. We search for insights into the following questions:

- How do I write a story out of this one idea?
- How do I turn all those pages that gushed out from an idea into a complete story?
- When am I telling and not showing?
- What is my story missing?
- Which critiques from my friends or other writers should I accept?
- Should I follow my own instincts?
- How do I know what is working and what doesn't work?
- When do I know I've edited enough?
- How many drafts does it take to finish a story?
- Can I succeed as a writer?

Most books or instructors cannot answer these questions because the answer lies within you—the individual. *The Writer's Compass* guides you, as a writer, to find your own answers by thinking through what you are writing, why you are writing it, and what you want to say—setting the compass for your work. Once you find true north for your ideas, it is easier to stay the course and write the story you have dreamed of telling, even when you aren't sure what that story might be.

How *The Writer's Compass* is Organized
The Writer's Compass is set up like a three-act structure with Acts I, II, and III represented as *Beginning, Middle,* and *End.* Some stories also contain a prologue (which explains backstory or information that won't be in the actual story or that flashes forward in an attempt to hook the reader. In this book the prologue is the *Introduction*.

In the *Introduction* you will learn both how this book is organized and how to use the book to get the most benefit for your writing.

In *Part I*, the *Beginning*, you prepare your life for writing by developing a writing time, space, and mind-set. This section has ideas that will help you focus and prepare for *Part II*, the *Middle*, which is the story's development.

The *Middle* is the heart of *The Writer's Compass*. This section explains story mapping, the 7-Stage process, and the obstacles one must work through to create a strong story. The *Middle* includes:

- The Story Map
- Stage 1—Forming Stories and Developing Ideas
- Stage 2—Building Strong Structures
- Stage 3—Creating Vibrant Characters
- Stage 4—Structuring Scenes, Sequences, and Transitions
- Stage 5—Increasing Tension and Adjusting Pacing
- Stage 6—Enriching the Language and Dialogue
- Stage 7—Editing the Hard Copy and Submitting

Charting the key elements of storytelling with your ideas across a *story map* lays the foundation for your story. Progressing systematically through each stage helps you develop your story with the least number of revisions. Working through the story map and the stages together creates a stronger story that will evolve organically and that says what you want it to say.

Each of the 7 Stages addresses an area of storytelling that tends to need more development. Much like constructing a house, the 7 Stages are based on developing the story foundation, then adding the structure, the roof, the walls, the flooring, painting, and designer touches, and finally moving in. Each stage adds another level of breadth and depth to the story across the entire structure chart.

Stage 1 discusses how ideas are formed and the act of brainstorming. The evolution of writing stories takes many forms and starts at many different points on the structure chart, but this stage shows the writer how to use that evolution to an advantage in forming ideas for writing the story. This process allows for the different ways writers write.

Stages 2 through *6* focus on the process of story development, but also continue to expand ideas. Each of these stages addresses a specific area of development in a system that builds rather than crisscrosses efforts. In other words, when relying on "just reading through" to reveal story weaknesses, the writing process is inefficient, and there is a crossover of efforts with multiple passes of the same material. When a story is developed strategically using the 7-Stage process, your writing is stronger and does not have to be revised as many times. For example, *Stage 6* is "Enriching the Language and Dialogue." If this task occurs before the structure is in place or the characters are developed, the writer finds herself needing to rewrite but not wanting to "disturb" the writing that has already been perfected. Because of this, she may hold on to scenes or bits of dialogue that do not work. In other words, it is easier to set aside what doesn't work when the writer hasn't invested a significant amount of time or fallen in love with the language in that material.

By waiting until a later development stage to work on the language, the story is already richer and fuller and nearer completion. Therefore, the time spent on language at this later stage is far more efficient. Compare this concept to a potter focusing on the intricate design around the outside of a pot before shaping the pot from the inside out. The efforts put into the artwork now become distorted or are ruined during the attempt to shape the pot.

Stage 7 is the final stage of editing, submitting, and continuing to write. Each of the stages grows progressively shorter, like a pyramid, as more writing of the story is completed and less writing and revision needs to be done.

The *End*, as in stories, is the shortest section of the book and addresses the importance of setting goals, quality writing, and how to map the writer's lifestyle.

How to Use *The Writer's Compass*

Developing the structure chart and learning to create the story map will help you hone your internal writing compass as you work through the 7-Stage process. As you develop your story, the map will guide you in moving material around, seeing the weaknesses and holes, and developing a stronger story. You will note as you work through the elements of the structure chart that I use a number of words interchangeably. Because so many instructors and authors use different words, the sense is that these are all different models for writing or different elements to include in writing a story. The truth is that various instructors are often saying the same things using different terminology. There aren't as many elements for good storytelling as all of the terminology implies; there are just several words that help to clarify the meaning of each element. For example, the opening lines of a story can be referred to as the opening, opening action, attention grabber, or a hook. These are not different elements in the opening, they are different ways to describe the opening. This will become clearer as you work through the structure diagram and the examples.

The 7-Stage process of *The Writer's Compass* includes several series of questions designed to stimulate your thinking and guide you through the process of creating and structuring your writing. These questions help you think about the details, events, logic, and development of a good story that may not otherwise occur to you or that someone might suggest in a critique but be unable to articulate. If you've ever taken a psychological test or a personality test, that asks you questions a dozen different ways to help get the real answer out of you, then you are familiar with this process. The questions help you to get to the truth of the story. Answer them simply, and if they seem repetitive, answer them again anyway, but try to think through the answer from a different perspective or lens.

Although some questions sprinkled throughout are rhetorical, the questions you should stop to think about and answer will be obvious. I suggest maintaining a notebook or file and writing out these answers so that you can easily refer back for quick facts about your story. When I work through this process, I answer the questions on 5x8 inch index cards that I carry with me. Using index cards of any size is a tradition in writing. The cards are used for ideas, notes, or writing brief synopses of scenes that are then laid out or put on a bulletin board to give the writer an overview of the story. They are easily rearranged to create a new way for the story to be told.

Getting a Handle on Your Story

Although any size index cards work, I like 5x8 cards for two reasons:

- I can capture as much or as little information on one card as needed for an idea
- I can put them through a printer when I break my stories down for revisions

When using an index card, I know that I'm making a note or capturing an idea, and I don't have to worry about grammar, punctuation, or spelling. I just put the idea down as completely as I can as soon as I can after I have it. If the idea requires more than one card, I number them. I also add the date and the story's working title and where or how the idea came to me so I can re-create that inspiration if I need to recall my feelings and thoughts. It's also a good way to capture several ideas for different stories that I may have when I'm in a situation where I can't use a computer or I don't want to use several sheets of paper to write only a single or a few lines. Because I love color, I often use colored pens to write my ideas.

When I have enough of these ideas, I start writing my story. The best part of index cards is that I can sort through them and rearrange them to develop a stronger structure and coordinate them when I draw my story map. Cards also make it much easier to see ideas that are weak and to pull them out of the stack before I've spent time working on them in a typed draft. Once they are in a draft, it's much harder to hit delete. And, after all, you aren't throwing the card away, you are just culling it from this group.

After every revision of my story, I break it up into beats, which are small segments of writing that need to hang together and only make sense within this particular context. I then print out the beats of the story on 5x8 cards, if possible on a color printer, using a different color for each revision. (Yes, I sometimes buy 5x8 cards by the case. I also turn them over and reuse them.)

Here's the best part: When I have a stack of index cards, I can hold them in my hands. In other words, I can put my hands around my story to get a handle on it. I can shuffle ideas and play with the order to find a better sequence that strengthens the structure. I can include new handwritten ideas. I can readily see where I've unnecessarily duplicated beats or where I've included the same idea in multiple ways—and if I have done this, I should pay attention, as the idea is apparently very important to me. All of this occurs before I spend too much time working on developing scenes I may have to cut later. This is one of the ways I focus on the story and the structure before I worry about grammar and language. I also use index cards to type revisions, which I will explain more about when we discuss tools.

This is not a book of rules. Answering the questions gives you a direction when you feel blocked. If you find a question too vague or unclear, and you are unsure how to answer, remember the purpose is to cause you to *think* about your work from many perspectives, to help you focus on what you want to say, and to ultimately clarify what you want to convey to the reader. The only correct answer is the one that satisfies you.

As you get more deeply involved in the structure of your work, certain ideas and themes might form that are different from your original ones. This is part of the organic writing process for coming to know and understand what you are writing about and who your characters are and what their dilemma is. Defects and weaknesses will also become more obvious. When I add new material, I generally date the input and changes in some manner, like a tracking sheet, to help me keep track of changes and to search for inconsistencies, which is especially helpful if I have to leave the material for a period of time and may forget changes I've made.

Story Tracking Sheet

For keeping notes about a particular story, I use what I call a "tracking sheet." The purpose of the tracking sheet is to help you identify how your work is progressing and to aid you if you need to attach a time frame to changes or editing. On it I note the date, time frame I wrote, and what work I did or changes that I made or notes about new changes to make or research or new scenes I want to write. I have found this very helpful in tracking what I've done and which version or what date I did the work or confirming what I haven't completed. This is particularly useful if you lose track and need to see if your current version includes recent changes. Or if you need to check whether you followed up. Sometimes I make a change in a story and then discover that I need to either undo that change or refer back to when I originally made the change to clarify in my mind why I made the change or other associated changes. This is much easier to do if you've logged the work you've done in each writing session.

I also update the name of my computer file with the current date so that my log and the date on my tracking changes match. This makes it much easier to go back and undo something or to retrieve something from a previous version. It also helps because if your file becomes corrupted, you have something pretty recent and complete to go back to. Yes, it takes more digital space, but I find it worth the effort and much safer as far as viruses and other computer anomalies or mishaps.

If you find any section or question blocks you, move on. The response will develop at a later time as your work progresses, or it may be that that particular question is not meaningful to your story. But remember, by disciplining yourself to think through the answers, you will discover new ideas and depth to your writing and be more willing to make changes before you get set in a path that is rutted with structural flaws.

Stage 3, on *characterization*, is a large section. The questions keep you focused on the main characters' goals, agendas, and conflicts. The questions also help build interesting lifelike characters. On your first pass, you may choose to only sketch in the obvious details because some answers may not be apparent until you get further along in the rough draft.

There is no one right way to work through this book. Although the book is constructed so that you can follow chronologically in a way that builds the story, you may prefer to jump around as ideas come to you or as you address particular issues in your story. Every writer is stimulated to write, organize, and develop their work in their own unique manner. The purpose of *The Writer's Compass* is to enhance that process—not inhibit it—and to shorten the time it takes to reach a final draft by being more efficient.

What if you already have a rough draft or even a completed manuscript? The process of *The Writer's Compass* is to help you create work that you can get your hands around, much like the potter's lump of clay, and then to show you how to shape it into a finished product. By applying the process from *The Writer's Compass* to your manuscript, you will be able to identify the story's strengths and weaknesses. Once you recognize problem areas, you will structure stronger scenes, and editing and revising will be easier and potentially faster and more fruitful. Instead of going through your manuscript twenty-five times to move commas and sentences around, you will see an increase in ideas for your story and significant development that helps you achieve a higher level in your writing.

As you read through *The Writer's Compass*, there will be indicators for when to stop and apply the process to your own story. Whenever story ideas occur to you, stop and write them down. The whole point of a writing book is to help you write, so don't let reading take precedence over writing. In each stage we will discuss how to develop and organize these writing ideas.

PART I

The Beginning

BUILDING A WRITING LIFE

chapter 1

SIMPLIFYING
THE WRITING PROCESS

The Writer's Compass is about transforming simple ideas, or the pages that gush out like a geyser, into a fully developed story. This method uses a proven process of mapping the story across a structure chart, creating a picture map with images that help you visualize your story, asking questions, and working through a system of revisions that teaches you to turn your ideas into the story you want to tell—in 7 Stages.

In other words, this book takes the most important elements of how you tell a story and breaks them down into simple concepts that are then mapped on a structure chart. The 7-Stage process then takes the writing to another level by addressing effective writing and the most efficient ways to examine your work to get the most out of every revision. By approaching your writing in logical steps and putting the analytical side of your brain to work being creative, your writing focus—and your writing process—becomes more developed, more attuned to storytelling, and will evolve more quickly. This creates less work for you and translates into less overall time to finish the final draft.

The most time-consuming part of writing is actually thinking it through and sounding out the depths of your story. *The Writer's Compass* is organized in the same way you tell a story. The *Beginning, Part I*, introduces the book and sets up the ways in which you begin a writer's life. The *Middle, Part II*, is the longest part of the book, just as is the middle of your story, and focuses on development and revision. The *End* is the shortest part of the book and discusses living the writer's life.

The seven stages are broken into topics so that you can start anywhere, just as you can in your writing. However, to get the most out of this book I suggest starting at the *Beginning* and working through the *End*. But please remember I would never suggest you should write from the beginning to the end in developing your story. Your ideas should flow naturally in whatever manner they come. The 7-Stage process will help you to increase the flow of ideas and show you how to develop them into a stronger story.

THE LEARNING PROCESS

Within these pages, *The Writer's Compass* simplifies for you more than two decades of my study of writing. For more than twenty-five years I have attended workshops, seminars, and lectures. I have studied multiple forms and formats of writing through two graduate degrees: a Master's of Professional Writing with an emphasis in dramatic and screenwriting, and a Master's of Fine Arts in playwriting. I took copious notes, listened to hundreds if not thousands of lectures on writing, and read innumerable books, trying to discover the secret to becoming a successful storyteller.

All of the authors and lecturers I looked to for the answer seemed to have a different approach that they believed was key to successful writing. Often they had contradictory opinions and ideas about writing, using different terminology. For example, a plot point might be called a *turning point, inciting incident, catalyst, setting up the main character's goal, outer or inner problem, external or internal conflict, apparent or implied or actual conflict, rising action, end of Act I, beginning of Act II*, and other terms I've forgotten. But how many of these plot points did I need to use? Where did these plot points belong on a three-act structure? The answers seemed illusive.

Apparently, whatever these teachers believed must have worked for them, or they wouldn't be lecturing or writing a book on the topic. Yet, none of them seemed able to share the secret. I'm not sure if they even found an answer to that secret or if they just found what worked for them. But many of them did seem to have one thing in common: Aristotle.

What Does Aristotle Have to Do With Contemporary Writing?

Aristotle was a Greek philosopher in the fourth century B.C. His life and work influenced many important areas in western civilization, from the sciences to logic and ethics to government to rhetoric. Taught by Plato, he wrote on many subjects, among them poetry, theatre, and music. Aristotle developed his ideas for what he believed comprised good storytelling by studying the tragedies and literature of his day. He wrote what is referred to as *The Poetics* about the structure and elements of telling a good story as it related to Greek drama. While some of his ideas no longer fit contemporary storytelling, the basic structure and elements still apply. Either he was a genius for figuring it all out so long ago, or he actually developed what western civilization would come to see as the organic way to tell good stories.

Barbara F. McManus, Professor of Classics Emerita at the College of New Rochelle, distills Aristotle in an "Outline of Aristotle's Theory of Tragedy in the *POETICS*." Basically, Aristotle considered tragedy (drama) to be an important medium for "showing" what could happen in the world as opposed to history, which "tells" the past. He determined the following to be the six basics of good drama listed in their order of priority: plot, character, thought (theme), diction (dialogue and metaphor), chorus (music), and spectacle (spectacular effects). Also important is the catharsis at the end, which purges or brings release to the viewer, specifically for Aristotle's audience from pity and fear.

Unfortunately, what he left behind became fragmented over the centuries, much of it lost, and somewhat complicated for most of us to decipher. For over two millennia, writers and writing instructors have translated, interpreted, and reinterpreted what Aristotle had to say. Those who have studied his work have refined it, and others have built on that refinement. Somewhere along the way someone developed what is considered to be the correlating three-act structure diagram, shown below. There have been several variations on this diagram. We now have many versions of what constitutes good storytelling that can be traced back to Aristotle and *The Poetics*.

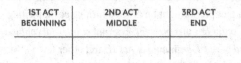

(1.1) *Basic Three-Act Structure*

In 1863 Gustav Freytag, a German critic, editor, poet, novelist, playwright, publicist, and soldier, wrote a book titled *Die Technik des Dramas* (*The Technique of the Drama*, translated in 1895 by Elias J. MacEwan), which was his study of Aristotle and the great dramatists. He created a diagram that expanded Aristotle's ideas, which is called Freytag's Pyramid or Freytag's Triangle. He described the parts of the drama as: a) introduction, b) rise, c) climax, d) return or fall, e) catastrophe.

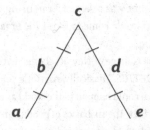

(1.2) *Freytag's Pyramid (Freytag's Triangle)*

As with Aristotle, there have been many versions and evolutions of Freytag's model. A basic modification is shown in the next column.

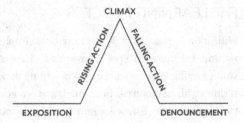

(1.3) *Modified Freytag's Pyramid (Freytag's Triangle)*

The Secret to Great Writing

As I continued studying, it all seemed very confusing to me, and I never seemed to be focused on whatever the current instructor thought was the most important aspect of writing or the right approach. In frustration, I began organizing what I had learned, hoping to find some sort of clarity. I wrote out the ideas that had evolved over the years into a workbook for writers. I called it *Following Through* because it was a way to approach a story from many directions that led to a completed manuscript. I also chose this title because I was notorious for rewriting rather than submitting, never feeling quite finished with a manuscript.

One day, while attending a graduate class at the University of Southern California taught by James Ragan, former director of the Master of Professional Writing program and international poet, and after once again observing someone diagram and discuss his own progression of development on Aristotle's and Freytag's structures, a halogen light bulb turned on in my head. The final piece of the puzzle fell into place. I realized that all these lectures and books were saying the same things—but using different terminology. I began a study of comparing these variations and finally realized I had figured out the secret. What it took me decades to learn, turned out to be elementary, "my dear Watson."

THE DEVELOPMENT OF THE MAP AND THE 7-STAGE PROCESS

At that point, I started looking at the diagram of a three-act structure as a road map, an informal visual outline, and I began to evolve it. First, I drew the three-act diagram and charted on it all the terminology I could think of that other writing teachers and authors used. I placed the terminology approximately where it should fall on the three-act structure as an element of storytelling. My thought was that if I could create the order on the three-act structure where *all* of these different elements fell, I could follow them as a guide to writing my stories and not miss anything important. To my surprise, much of the terminology fell on or near the same points on the chart and I realized that much of it was repetitious. It all began to make sense. I also realized that what one instructor thought critical, another ignored or considered arbitrary. When I grouped the terminology into concepts, I discovered that instead of many elements of good storytelling, there were really only a few—which took me back to Aristotle's basic concepts.

Then I drew the diagram again, this time mapping my ideas for a particular story by correlating them with an essential storytelling element and overlaying the idea on the structure chart where that element belonged. Now when I looked at my ideas on what had become a story map, I could see where my story was weak, where it was strong, where I needed to move an idea from an opening to an obstacle or a revelation, or when the climactic moment was really the turning point in the plot. I could also see which elements I had not yet figured out. Practically overnight the structure of my stories became stronger and more organic. As I continued to study the writing process, the terminology and the diagram evolved.

From the *Following Through* workbook I had developed a few years earlier, I selected material and rearranged those ideas into the 7-Stage process. Each stage addresses an important component of story creation that needs to be considered during revisions. Now I had a map to use as a guideline for organizing/laying out my story and stages of revisions to apply in a logical development. The map went hand-in-hand with the 7 Stages. When I shared my stories in writing groups, after completing Stage 2, which focuses on structure, I would get comments on how strong my structure was, but my characters seemed a little weak. After completing Stage 3, on characterization, the comments would be about how strong my characters and structure were. While working on a play already nearly completed, I decided to rework it using my new system of mapping and stages. When I took the play into class, the story had dramatically improved, and my professor commented, "I'm amazed that you were able to come up with new ideas this late in the story's development."

That is what *The Writer's Compass* is all about—developing ideas, organizing them, and evolving them into a stronger story. Once I knew this process worked, I began teaching it to others. The model works whether you are starting with a single strong idea or working on a story already being developed. Before long I had fellow graduate students asking me to teach them my system. *The Writer's Compass* is the method I evolved from years of writing instruction and includes explanations, questions, and processes:

- To help you formulate your ideas
- To help you determine which ideas work

- To help you revise in more efficient stages
- To help you find your internal compass and develop your intuition so that you write the story you want to tell
- To help you realize when the feedback others are giving you is telling their story and not yours
- To give the analytical side of your brain a problem to solve that allows it the opportunity to be creative

There are some who believe that whatever comes from the heart is perfect just as it flows and should not be edited or revised, but in order for that to work, you have to be a writing genius. Unfortunately, most of us aren't geniuses. We have to work hard to get it right—to make our message understandable, palatable, and exciting. It's especially tough when the competition for publishing and producing is so stiff. We have to be good storytellers so that a reader or viewer will want to take the time to leave their world and step into the world we've created.

It's Not a Formula—It's Immersing Yourself in the Story

As I taught my university students this method, I feared they would think I was teaching them rules and a linear structure—that it may come across as being formulaic, when it is not formulaic at all. The purpose of this process is to immerse you, the writer, in your story and help you make sense of your ideas. The 7-Stage process encourages free-form development, and there is ample room for changing ideas. In fact, as the story and characters grow and evolve, ideas and events should develop organically, which means that you will probably follow where the story or the characters are leading you and not in the original direction you planned to take. The 7-Stage process allows for that moment when the characters and events take over the story. When those moments come, you will be prepared to go with them.

There Are No Rules—Well, Maybe Two

It was not completely true when I said that there are no rules. I have two.

- **Rule 1:** Never, never follow anyone's advice to remove an idea or a scene or any bit from your writing if it goes against your gut intuition to do so. What may be bad writing to someone else could be the heart of the story to you—you just may not have discovered why it is there yet. Once you figure out why it is important, you will be able to develop the idea and replace this bit of poorer writing—or "placeholder," as I like to call it—with something stronger, perhaps even remarkable. When the original idea has served its purpose, you will no longer need that placeholder.
- **Rule 2:** If you want to be a writer, you have to write ... and write ... and write ... and write ... and ...

There are many types of writers, from the ones who have no writing skills, but are innate storytellers, to the geniuses whose every word is treasured. Most of us are somewhere in the middle, climbing that mountain, trying to find our peak, clinging to every boulder for support, working very hard to learn how to be good storytellers. *The Writer's Compass* is the process that will teach you how to write the story you want to tell—in seven stages.

So let's start.

chapter 2

BECOMING A WRITER

There are geniuses whose every word is golden and their phrases are repeated as universal truths long after their deaths. Then there are the rest of us who work hard studying writing, struggling with concepts and terminology that appear contradictory, confusing, and unnecessarily complicated. In the end, most of us only get a glimpse of the mountain peak where the successful storytellers stand. However, it is a tall, broad mountain, and from whatever your vantage point, you can succeed as a writer—having written the story you want to tell. And if that story is filled with universal truths, ideas, and themes that others also relate to and that readers love stories about, then your opportunities for sharing that work will be multiplied.

This chapter discusses becoming a writer and how to build a life and a perspective that encourages writing.

> When a man understands that he is a herald, you will find an urgency in his message ... A herald's job is to go into the throne room of the king every day to see what message he has and then to take it out into the streets and give it to the people. If you're a herald, be a herald—don't be [just] a dreamer.
>
> Alistair Begg, "Truth for Life" 3/18/04
> Los Angeles Radio Station KKLA 99.5

Although this quote doesn't refer specifically to writers, it certainly applies to them. I like to say, "Those who must, write."

As you work through *The Writer's Compass*, try the following:

- Listen to that inner voice and turn off the "I can't," "I'm not any good," and "Someday when I have time" messages. Save the editor in you for when you are editing.

- Let your creative flow guide you. Write scenes when the muse inspires you, and when it doesn't, answer the questions and fill in the blanks to help you focus and to challenge the analytical side of your brain to be creative.
- Be disciplined. Determine a time and environment that helps you to write on a consistent basis.
- *Be passionate about your writing.*

You can be a storyteller without knowing a lot about writing. But if you want to be a writer, you need to know and understand the craft of writing. Writing is a journey, not a destination. Just like developing characters in a novel, writing is a process of growth and development. The more you know about writing, the more you enhance that journey. Take advantage of workshops, seminars, books, and magazines. Read, read, read, especially in areas that interest you. You'll find every piece you write will automatically improve. Familiarize yourself with many types of writing to expand your knowledge and help you find ways to crossover ideas that will enrich your work. In the Professional Writing program at the University of Southern California, I studied all forms of writing, and from each I learned a technique that made other areas of my writing stronger.

Practice, practice, practice. Make mistakes and learn from those mistakes, and do it better the next time, and the next time, until you are a true expert, a true artist, a writer who is able to deliver a message with style and impact.

If you want to sell, then you have to write with your reader in mind. Go beyond what satisfies you to giving your readers the best you have to offer. Think about what will be meaningful and entertaining and thought provoking to them. Develop richness and texture in your writing, show them interesting characters facing life-altering challenges. Write stories that say something about values, and you will find an audience.

DO YOU WANT TO WRITE OR JUST TALK ABOUT WRITING?

The biggest difference between published writers and wannabe writers is that published writers write, and wannabe writers only dream about writing. If you want to be a writer, you have to commit to writing. It's that simple. You don't need a degree. You don't need to be hired to write. You don't need to have a career in writing. You don't need anyone to say, "You have met the requirements, you are now a writer." You don't even have to be any good. You just need to write—that is what makes you a writer.

"But what will make me a good writer?" you ask. The answer is the same. If you want to be a good writer, you have to write and write and write and ... There is no secret formula, there is no fairy dust, there is no magic potion. Only two things make you a good writer: being born with the talent to be a great writer, or experience. Experience comes in writing just like in any other physical or intellectual endeavor. You do it, you make mistakes, you learn from your mistakes and correct them, you do it again and again. You grow into becoming a marathon runner or a pole vaulter or a computer programmer—step by step, day by day, just as you grow into becoming a good, or even great, writer.

If you really want to be a writer, or if you want to grow as a writer, you have to start somewhere. In this section of *The Writer's Compass,* we will look at your writing world and how to find your internal compass so that you can write the story you want to write. As I said earlier, I have only two rules for writing. One of those rules is this: If you want to succeed as a writer, you must write!

Writer's Block—Really?

I don't believe in writer's block. I believe in procrastination. I believe in being afraid to write and being afraid of not being good enough. I believe in being too overwhelmed by life or career or stuff to write. There are times when we are afraid of failure, success, being wrong, making a mistake, facing "The End," rejection, and fear of criticism, whether justified or unjustified. These are all legitimate fears. Most writers have them, but serious writers don't allow those fears to stop them—they use those fears to motivate them or to find a deeper emotional level in their writing.

There are also times when we are percolating answers to the story questions bouncing off the neurons in our brain. During those times we may be doing more internal writing and less external writing—but don't let that stop you from continuing to work it out on paper or on the computer.

Too often we don't write because we haven't taught ourselves self-discipline or made a commitment to write to a certain daily or weekly goal. However, I do have a cure for what we all tend to call writer's block.

Put your pen to the paper and push!

That's it. Pressing the tip against a page and knowing ink or lead is going to come out tends to cause you to either write or doodle (in which case, maybe you really want to be an artist). It doesn't have to make any sense, it doesn't have to be going anywhere, it can start with what is on your mind or an idea you've been toying with, but if you give yourself a chance, you'll probably find there is a subconscious thought trying to form and surface. And one thought usually follows another ...

Some people advocate daily journal writing, which can be very helpful. It's another way to discipline yourself to sit down and write. By calling it a journal you are free to write anything that comes to mind, including events about the day, your philosophy of life, rants, dreams, and stories. The pages you compile might be a memoir or may be a place from which you can excerpt bits and pieces of life.

Creating Your Writing Time and Space

Almost every writer deals with the problem of getting into the creative zone. Our attention is on many different events and subjects at any one moment. Unfortunately, we are too easily diverted by people and media and the noise of life and the attraction of distractions. It can take minutes to nearly an hour before you shift gears out of the everyday world and into the writing mode. It is especially difficult when you know you are facing a blank page and aren't sure how you are going to fill it. (In Stage 1 we will discuss ways to fill the page.)

That's why, when we think about sitting down to write, we often have a sudden urge to do anything else, even things we hate to do: clean a room, vacuum the car, mow the yard, start a new exercise program.

When I have many responsibilities pressing on me, I have a hard time switching off those concerns to focus on writing, even though writing can be an escape. When I'm having a great writing session, I have a hard time shifting away to return to other aspects of my life. What you need is a transition that clears your mind and feelings to move you from the everyday world of your life to the world of creating stories and back again. It is important to establish an environment that stimulates you to turn on the writing mode sooner. When you step into this arena or create a writing ritual, your brain shifts gears and knows this is your writing time.

Some people use music, some nature, some read poetry, or spend time meditating or concentrating on some form of art. Others sit in a favorite chair or use a certain pen or color of paper. The environment you create should feel safe. You want it to open the door to creativity. When I leave the writing world, although my mind may still be abuzz, I reallocate my thoughts to work in my subconscious so that I can pick up next time where I left off. As you go through the day, or before going to sleep, spend some time thinking about your writing dilemmas and let your subconscious go to work solving the problems so that you are prepared to sit down and write at the appointed time.

One of my favorite spots to write is in bed. After all, that's where dreams happen. Add to that a tray with chocolates and hot tea, and I'm in writer's heaven. However, don't trap yourself into believing, "I can only write in this particular setting" or "with this particular pen or paper or computer." Keep in mind that sometimes a writer needs to be able to work in less than ideal or in unexpected circumstances. I've actually written in the dark with only moonlight and the glow of the laptop, in the backseat of a car during a fourteen-hour drive, while children talked and napped all around me. I recharged my laptop battery in restaurants. When I'm in the zone, I can write anytime, anywhere. Getting in the zone—aye, there's the rub. It can take some time to actually get your butt in the seat and your fingers wrapped around a pen or tapping keys on the keyboard.

When those moments of distraction keep you from writing, you have to remind yourself, time is precious and there is little enough of it for writers. If you waste it, you lose it. Like everyone, I sometimes dawdle and think I'll just do a quick check of my email and handle a few items before I start writing, maybe a fast game of FreeCell to warm me up. Just about the time I settle down to actually write is when my family knocks on the door with needs that I have to meet. My time is gone, spent elsewhere, and now I have to wait for my next opportunity to write. If this happens very often—you cease to be a writer—you become a wannabe or a "has written."

I also surround myself with things that inspire me: certain books, a blue tin cup that another writer gave me symbolizing the memory I evoked in him through one of my stories, souvenirs from my play and film productions, and a life-size wooden nutcracker that feeds my whimsical side and stands guard over my muse.

Be sure to minimize distractions. Find your time or moments to write and protect them—mostly from yourself and idle interests that keep you from your goal. Or give it up and spend the time you could have been writing doing what you really enjoy. Believe me, that's much easier, less painful, and certainly less guilt inducing.

What to Consider When Choosing Your Space

Do you need a consistent place to put you in the right frame of mind? What needs to be in that space? What are your writing implements? I like to have at hand *The Synonym Finder* and my favorite dictionary. Do you need coffee, tea, a snack? I like music—different types for different stories. Do you have a way to play music if you need it? Are there images that inspire you, or objects? I have a wonderful reproduction, which I retrieved from a trash bin, that my family and friends call "The Flying Aztec." To them it's junk, to me it represents something magical. I also have a binder filled with pictures and images that stimulate my imagination.

At the University of Southern California I had the opportunity to learn from Pulitzer prize–winning playwright and author Paul Zindel. The first day of class Paul brought in a huge suitcase full of objects—puppets and cultural finds from his travels that had stories behind them—that were inspirational to him and helped him to write. If you like having objects to inspire you, make sure that you don't waste writing time managing them (i.e., buying, cleaning, organizing, finding space to keep them).

Your writing space doesn't have to be elaborate. A big room with a big desk and comfy chair, a view, and an expansive library doesn't mean you will spend any more time writing than if you had a laptop or notebook and pen at the kitchen table that you have to clear away before meals. I knew someone who threw a giant bean bag into a corner with a CD player at arm's reach for music and that became her writing space.

Think it through. The space you are creating is an important part of your creativity. You must treat it with respect. It should contain whatever elements you need to write and whatever inspires you. However, keep it simple and uncluttered so that you aren't distracted with the need to clean up. Make sure you have handy the tools you need just as you would for your job. Don't delude yourself into thinking you need the latest technology. Paper or a notebook and pen work just as well if that's all you have. I like colored gel pens to use on my 5x8 cards. That's all I need when I'm in the development stage, and I can carry them everywhere.

One tip: Don't spend a lot of money to set up your writing space and materials. Start with what you have—just the basics—add what you need at a minimal cost, and earn your way up. If the reason you aren't writing has nothing to do with your computer, then replacing it with the latest, most expensive one on the market won't get you writing. If Grandma's ladder-back chair inspires you, use it. An image you can put on a shelf or a picture on the wall may be all you need to remind you this is your writing space and time. Find a corner near a window with a view, or avoid having a view, move the music a little closer or turn it off, and write.

When I moved to Los Angeles to attend graduate school at the University of Southern California, I had very little money. I lived in a no-frills apartment building, and for the first year I slept on an air mattress (yes, I continued to write in bed). For the best room flow, I placed my air mattress under the high, wide window. When I wrote, I stared across the room at a blank wall. One day, desperately needing a change, I disrupted the flow and moved the bed across the room against the blank wall. I got the shock of my life the next morning when I woke up and started to write. There was a beautiful tree out my bedroom window where squirrels played, and beyond that, the trees of a park. While I knew the trees were there, I hadn't realized how meaningful that setting would be. Suddenly the apartment I disliked became an apartment with an inspiring view of nature (albeit occasionally I awoke to a tree trimmer sitting in the boughs, sawing away limbs). I stayed there for five years. One morning I left the room to prepare for work, and when I returned, I was shocked to find the tree missing. It had been cut down to make room for a building that would block my view of the park. I moved shortly afterward to an apartment with an ocean view from almost every window and several great writing spots. However, I found that in this ideal setting I had too many options, and I struggled to find *my* writing spot. I'm one of those writers who likes a nest to settle in. Of necessity, I've trained myself to write anywhere.

If you can write anywhere, and anywhere is your "writing spot," then limit what you need to the bare essentials. Keep a tote bag or messenger bag handy with pens and tablets or your laptop ready to grab and go, and travel to the places that feed your writing. The main point is to enter a space or have implements at hand that make your body say, "Okay, I'm here now," and your inner writer responds, "Good, let's get to work."

Keep it simple.

Keep it functional.

Keep it inspirational.

Creating Story Boxes

Keep your ideas and stories organized. I used to keep my writing projects in a file cabinet. However, I found that sometimes I acquired things for a story that didn't neatly fit into a folder (audio tapes, pictures or objects, various revisions of thick manuscripts or notes and tablets, 5x8 cards, and story maps). Quite frankly, I don't like regular file cabinets—I hate the way tightly packed folders nick my cuticles when I go through them. And to be honest, sometimes my papers and manuscripts got mixed in with the day's paperwork and bills, and were accidentally stored in unmarked boxes.

One day I came upon the idea of story boxes. I find attractive boxes of all sorts and sizes and use them to hold my stories. I have everything from boot boxes, which I've covered with attractive gift or Christmas wrapping paper, to the heavy cardboard storage boxes that come with metal handles and preprinted designs (plastic bins and tubs also work). I put stories with lots of material in the larger ones and newer stories in the smaller ones, and as they grow I move them into bigger boxes. I even have a few tiny boxes where I keep children's stories.

I keep my story boxes easy to reach and easy to find (because they're labeled). One box contains everything important to me about that story, which means no wasted time searching for accompanying material.

But When Am I Going to Find the Time?

"I want to be a writer, and every day I plan to write, but somehow the day gets away from me and ..." This is a big problem for most of us. To use a cliché: No one said it would be easy. I have a tendency to pack my days and then struggle to meet all the obligations. If you want to write, you have to carve out that writing time and allow nothing but a dire, life-threatening, one-time event get in the way. You've already decided what you are willing to sacrifice—this is when you put that decision into action. If you are freshest in the morning, write first thing in the morning. This may require some planning: What do you have to do the night before so that you can get up early enough to have writing time? Go to bed earlier? Turn the TV off earlier? Wind down earlier so you can go to sleep and wake up with enough time to actually write? How much do you need to lower your caffeine consumption so that you can go to sleep earlier and wake up sooner?

If nighttime is your best time, what gets in the way of your writing then? If your best time is 3:00 A.M., but you have to be at work at 7:00 A.M., then find time to nap. What can you change about your lifestyle—yes, if you want to be a writer, you have to make some lifestyle changes and some sacrifices. You may have to pick a second-best time to write.

I'm not suggesting neglecting your family or other important facets of your life. However, you do have to prioritize, and you have to set those priorities using reason about what your life includes or the future holds. If your best writing time is 6:00 A.M., and the baby wakes up at 6:12 A.M., or you have to be out the door by 6:30 A.M., then you will have to choose your second-best time to write or get up earlier. If the baby's bottle is at 2:00 A.M., or you don't get home from work until 8:00 P.M., or have events and need dinner and time for home chores and to unwind and you can't get to bed until midnight, then maybe the best you can do is fifteen or thirty minutes of writing time. Or maybe your best bet is to write during a salad or sandwich at lunchtime. Your best writing time may not be conducive to your lifestyle, just like your best working hours may not be the hours you are scheduled.

If you can write anytime, anywhere, have your material ready and organize writing into your day. I once committed to writing at least fifteen minutes every day before I could go to sleep. At the time I had a houseful of kids and a full-time job, plus church, and I was attending a local university. Some nights I would be falling asleep as I typed. I'd jar awake to discover I'd typed something really bizarre. Other times I would be able to sneak in four hours. At the end of two years I had written over six hundred pages for the first draft of a novel. Even small amounts of time can add up to a major project if you are prepared and get right to work.

The following exercise was designed to help you think about what you need to write.

The Journalist's Dilemma Exercise

Character:	Your main character is a successful journalist with a perfect place for writing in his home. He is on deadline to complete an editorial for a national magazine. However, he hasn't started yet because of an unexpected opportunity for a skiing trip.
Question:	What does this journalist's ideal writing space look like?
Goal:	The journalist plans to ski for three days and then knuckle down to finish the article by Friday.
Question:	What is the topic of the editorial?
Obstacle:	A blizzard strands the journalist at the ski resort. He also sprained his arm on a steep downhill slope and can only write for short periods of time.
Questions:	How will the journalist meet the deadline?
	What will the journalist do to create a writing space?
Application:	What prevents you from writing?
Questions:	How will you overcome this obstacle?
	If money and location were not an issue, what would your ideal writing space and time look like?
Actions:	How can you modify that image to fit your circumstances today?
	What can you change to improve your writing discipline?

Charting Your Energy Flow

A few years back I worked for a company that used circular charts that metered oil-production flow for twenty-four hours over seven days. One day I decided to use one of these meters to chart my own energy flow, which actually gave me some insight into how I use my time and my high and low energy periods during the day. Using this chart is a good way to see whether you are spending the high energy part of your day on the right priorities. Below is a sample chart for you to use.

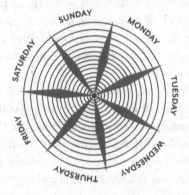

(2.1) *7-Day Energy Flowchart*

The outer circle is the time of day when you have your highest energy peak. The center dot represents the time when you have your lowest energy level, presumably when you go to sleep. Between the outer and inner circles are your available hours. If your peak energy time is 7:00 A.M., and that's when you awake, start the outer circle at 7:00 A.M. If your low energy time is at 7:00 A.M., put that time in the inner circle. If your peak energy time is during the middle of the day, start the outer circle at that time. Color in the hours of the day when you have scheduled activities. At a glance you should be able to tell whether you have overscheduled your life and how much time you are losing to unimportant events.

- What are the hours you have left?
- Are you using your peak energy hours efficiently?

- Can you schedule your writing time during your peak hours?
- What in your schedule can you rearrange?
- Are you scheduling enough sleep?
- Are you scheduling time for personal care and for exercise?

My peak time is early in the morning, and my priorities dictate that I spend part of that time for my devotional and part of it for my writing. However, some days I have early work meetings, so everything either shifts or I lose that writing time.

Deconstructing Bad Writing Habits

Your time is scheduled, your writing space and accoutrements are set. You sit in the chair, turn on your computer, and spend the next forty-eight minutes on the Internet. You sit in a comfy chair with your favorite inspirational objects nearby, you pick up a pen, and start writing your grocery list or you make that quick phone call to your friend about dinner Friday night. You haven't created a writing time and space, you've created an Internet time or a place to make shopping lists or phone calls.

Go back to the drawing board and start over. This time, stay away from the computer or your favorite spot. Shake up your routine. If you use a computer to write, switch to a pad and pen. If you use a pad and pen, try using a computer. If you can write only using that method, then make notes instead. I developed a bad habit of using my writing time for miscellaneous computer activities. When I started making notes on 5x8 cards, it changed my process. When I sat down at the computer, my note cards gave me someplace to start, and I easily moved into the writing mode.

Create a new routine before you start to write. I know one famous screenwriter who does a series of stretches and exercises before sitting down to write. Create a ritual that only takes a few minutes but that you only do before you write. When you do this routinely, your mind will know you are getting ready for some serious writing.

Guilt

With most hobbies or careers, the point is to produce something. With writing, getting to the point of having something finished can take a long time, and with all the revisions, doesn't necessarily look like you are moving forward. When people ask you what you've been doing, you either drive them away with your storytelling or you say, "I've been writing," and maybe hold up a sheaf of papers. You may get the response, "You aren't finished with that yet?"

What's that all about? Where's the product you should have to show for all of your efforts? It's just not as tangible to say you've been writing. Most people think it's a frivolous waste of time. Quite frankly, to me writing sometimes feels very self-indulgent. I crawl inside my head and run around having all sorts of adventures and dramas and find funny things and interesting characters, and I talk to them and I talk to myself. I'm there all alone ignoring everyone and everything else. We aren't supposed to do that. We're supposed to be engaging in life rather than making up our own world. First, there is the writing, then the exhilaration from feeling good about writing, then the guilt for the time spent writing when there are a dozen other obligations that should be met. So what's the appeal? Why torture yourself?

The appeal is that you are burning to say something, to express yourself, to make someone feel happy or sad or angry or just laugh. The appeal is that you believe what you have to say can make a difference in someone's life, and you just might reach a bigger audience and impact several lives. You are the only one who can say what you have to say in just your way. And if it's something powerful, something that can improve humanity or bring insights or change the world, or make people think or laugh—then why feel guilty? What are you waiting for? Get busy writing.

Discovering Personal Motivation

I've written indoors, outdoors, for only five minutes, and for sixteen hours straight. The one thing that typically gets in my way is not the setting or time constraints, it's a lack of motivation.

It's important to spend time thinking through your writing process, understanding how you create, what inspires you, and what de-motivates you. We have already looked at your best writing times, but what are your distractions, and how can you avoid them? If you understand that, you can more readily prepare yourself to find the best writing situation that will motivate you to write and avoid the draws away from writing.

Most writers discover that after a good writing session, the writing doesn't stop just because you've turned off the computer or put down your pen. If your next activity is a shower or exercise or drive or any activity that leaves part of your brain able to continue to write, you will continue to have ideas. Find a way to capture those ideas while they are fresh. Use a tape recorder or a small tablet or my favorite—index cards—to capture those ideas as soon as possible. These ideas give you momentum to start your next writing session.

For most of us, a strong motivator is a deadline. Since you may not have publishing deadlines, you will have to create artificial deadlines. Unfortunately, these are easy to move and to break, which is okay if there's a good reason. Sometimes I look at a project and figure out a timeline for it, and then I break the work up and set smaller goals to meet that deadline. However, since it's an artificial deadline, I've also been known to break those and allow a significant amount of time to pass without completion.

I've had more luck by setting larger life goals and including a writing life as a part of those. Set some life goals that are important for you to reach, and include your realistic writing goals. I say realistic because if you are creating goals that don't make sense for your life, then you have sunk yourself before you've even started. I then set ancillary goals to meet my obligations and responsibilities. For example, I am an academic editor of an online journal for a business school at a university; I also teach screenwriting and management communications at that university. I have a family, I have a religious life, and I have friendships, plus my writing, plus my consulting. Then there are all the things people have to do just to function like taxes, bill paying, household obligations, and the occasional vacation.

A couple of months before starting work on *The Writer's Compass*, I had an epiphany. At the time I had too many commitments on my plate, and I had just returned from a very stressful vacation. I was also in the process of changing car insurance companies. What had started out as a quick business transaction turned into a nightmare. I learned that there was a ding on my driving record that implied I could have had a serious accident while possibly intoxicated with possible multiple injuries. What had actually happened was a couple years earlier I was rear-ended at a stop sign in a very minor accident, but the other car took off and because it was a hit-and-run by a car with government plates, I reported it. I spent several hours of the final days of my vacation on the phone and taking numerous trips to the local police station to straighten out my driving record. It turned out that the officer who took the report checked the wrong box on the form—that was all there was to it. A letter from the police department cleared everything up.

However, while searching for paperwork, in the midst of a profusion of boxes in the garage and listening to novels on CD, it occurred to me how much I love stories. That was my dream—to write stories and to teach! *What happened to that dream?* I was so busy helping everyone else fulfill their dreams, and I had so filled my life with busy work, there was no energy left for my writing. I immediately started canceling consulting jobs and rearranging my time. I looked at my life goals and made new choices, and figured out steps to finish projects to give me the time I needed to write. By rediscovering my dream and making it important in my life goals, I motivated myself to a new level of commitment to my writing. A couple of months later I was working on the proposal for this book with an agent and soon had a contract. After evaluating my life goals, I set the forces in my life in motion to move me toward them. As a religious person, I believe God blessed me with this opportunity—but I had to be ready to take advantage of it. You have to be ready to take advantage of the opportunities that will come to you.

If writing is important to you, you have to look at your goals and make sure it has an appropriate place in your priorities. Set goals for what you need to complete and get off your plate so that you can raise the priority of your writing goals. Look at your obligations and say, "If I want to write, these have to go." Let's face it, we can do a lot, but we can't do it all.

Every time I have gone through the process of setting life goals, I've found that my life actually does move in the direction I want to go, rather than my being carried along by currents of the circumstances in which I live. Setting life goals becomes a personal motivator that works on a different level than setting artificial deadlines. Using the process of setting life goals, you can move toward your life as a writer, rather than drifting in happenstance ever further away.

Developing an Internal Compass

Developing your internal compass is an integral part of learning to write successfully. How many times has someone given you writing criticism or advice that you knew was correct, and you ended up feeling frustrated because you hadn't seen it for yourself? There will always be an area in your writing where you might have made a better choice, but developing your intuition will give you more confidence in your writing and help you to see when your work is the best it can be.

Through all my years of writing, one of the biggest challenges I've faced is knowing when my ideas were strong enough and when someone else's critiques and ideas were helpful or were leading me away from the story I wanted to tell. In one screenwriting class, with my mentor, television and screenwriter Sy Gomberg, there was a particular scene that was really bad, and I knew it was really bad. After workshopping my pages, Sy had several critiques, one of them being, "And get rid of that scene, it shouldn't be there." I agreed and got rid of the scene. As a result, it was some time before I went back to work on that screenplay. It never felt right again. To this day I'm not happy with the outcome. Even though I had written a bad scene, there was something in that idea that was pertinent to the story I was trying to tell, but I hadn't figured out what that was, yet. When I cut that scene, I deleted a placeholder that I needed to figure out what I really wanted to say.

Sometimes your subconscious writer knows what's important to the story, but your conscious writer doesn't have a handle on the words or imagery—yet. If you get rid of that bit of writing before you figure out why it's there, you may disrupt your story to the point where you can't complete it or that you will never be happy with it.

Trusting and Honing Your Intuition

Go back to my first rule of writing, which is: Never, never get rid of something in your story if your gut tells you it needs to be there. As you come to know your story, you will develop your internal compass, and you will eventually figure out what you are trying to say or show. I have worked with writers whose "bad" writing became some of the best writing in their story, once they figured out its significance and what they wanted to say and show. Once you do, you will find you won't need that bad writing as a placeholder anymore. Until then, hold on to it tenaciously and keep working out what it means to you. This is different from holding on to lines even though they don't really fit or they slow the story down just because you have fallen in love with the words you wrote and the way you expressed yourself. In the end you have to be proud of what you wrote, and it has to be the story you want to tell, the way you want to tell it.

In the *Middle*, Stage 1, we will go over the structure chart. At the bottom of the chart there are three areas we will revisit repeatedly: theme, dramatic question, and where the idea is coming from within you. These are the concepts that will further help you develop your internal compass. Some people start their writing with a theme or a dramatic question they are trying to answer. Others start with a piece of dialogue or an image. As you work the story, as you come to know the characters, the plot, the obstacles, and the background, what you are really trying to say will emerge and develop. You have to keep revisiting and refining the theme and the dramatic question until you know what your point really is and can state it in the clearest and most concise way. Then when someone offers you feedback, you will know whether it will improve your story or lead you away from the story you want to write.

Just as not discarding bits of writing and knowing the theme and dramatic question are important to the story, so is understanding why you are writing this story. Why is it important to you to spend the energy? Why are you willing to take time away from another area of your life to develop this story? What is it you want to say and why? And how? Where is it coming from inside of you? If you understand the answers to those questions, you will have a stronger story, and you will be more readily able to develop the discipline it takes to tell that story. Just remember, you are the only one who can tell this story in just this way.

So how do you develop that ability? One of the ways is by reading books, lots of books, especially in, but not limited to, the genre you write. Because each genre has its own accepted rules and methods, you will develop an intuition for what strengthens your writing and what detracts. Get a feel for what's current by reading the best-selling authors. By reading today's popular books you will see what editors are looking for. By reading older books that are considered classics, you will see the types of stories that intrigue readers. However, don't limit yourself—read broadly.

Should I Listen to Critiques or Follow My Own Instincts?

Sometimes the feedback you get is good and something you hadn't thought about. How it sounds in your head when reading to yourself and how it sounds to someone else may mean you totally missed making your point. There may also be outcomes you hadn't thought of or experiences you don't have that someone else has insight into. Sometimes there are good critiques that would make an incredible story—if that were the story you wanted to write.

There are also some critiques that stink. They are hurtful, insensitive, misinformed, cryptic, or based on someone's viewpoint that in no way relates to your own. There are also ambiguous critiques that give the writer no insight:

"There is something about that character that turns me off."

"What?" you ask.

They respond, "I don't know, I just can't relate."

Or you make changes per the suggestions, only to be told "It was better before. Something seems to be missing now."

And then there are critiquers who do not know how to express themselves, and sensing something is wrong with the writing, they have no clue what it is or how to offer useful feedback. These critiques may lead you to fix something that isn't broken instead of dealing with the real issue. "Your plot just doesn't make sense; I don't buy it." What she or he didn't realize is that the character's motivation was weak, and with some tweaking the plot would be stronger.

You should also expect to get different feedback from writers than you would nonwriters. Writers who know the language, or are familiar with writing terms, should be able to express themselves more clearly when they see a problem. Nonwriters do not usually use the same terminology, and so when they say that something doesn't make sense, they could mean that it doesn't feel organic to the story or that it is illogical or that the way you have worded it isn't clear. You should always ask questions to clarify the comments you get so that you don't rewrite in the wrong direction based on a misinterpretation of the feedback. You may find that different word choices work versus an entire rewrite of a scene.

Writing Organically

We will use the term *organic* frequently in *The Writer's Compass*. It simply means that what occurs feels natural to the story. The characters behave in a natural way—the events progress and evolve from the character's behavior or the circumstances in a natural or believable manner. Being organic to the story does not mean it all has to be predictable behavior or events. To change what would be natural or organic behavior requires setting up motivations or situations in which the character might behave unnaturally or in which the circumstances evolve differently than expected. If set up properly, these unpredictable behaviors become organic. This is good storytelling.

Stories that are contrived and not organic are written for the convenience of the author who does not want to take the time, or does not have the experience, to figure out what would really happen or how to evolve what could happen—the unbelievable into the believable.

The next few pages discuss feedback and how to develop your internal compass so that you can better judge the critiques you get and whether to follow them. However, if several critiques give the same negative comments, that means you need to rethink your approach and fix the problem. By the time you complete *The Writer's Compass*, you will have better tools for accomplishing this.

Bad Criticism—Good Feedback

In one of my graduate programs I was in a nonfiction book class in which the generation gap between me and the other students showed in my choice of topic. One day I brought my pages into class to workshop. After I presented them, the person to my right, a woman diametrically opposed to my view, commented. The bloodletting started, and once there was blood in the water, the shark like feeding frenzy began. By the time the critiques went around the table, I was devastated. No, I don't know why the instructor didn't stop it either. It was so bad that after class she told me I never had to bring anything in to workshop again. I never finished the book. I never want to finish the book. I don't even want to go back and look at the notes for the book.

The point of this story is that my work was not being critiqued, my ideas and beliefs were being attacked. This was neither helpful nor encouraging nor good feedback.

Suggestions that improve the story should be welcomed, but they should not be taken as a dictum. People with comments are often thinking about how they would write the story, especially if the story excites them, but their ideas may not be in concert with how you want to write the story. This is when it is imperative to have your internal compass functioning so that you know the difference between a great idea and an idea that doesn't work for the story you want to write.

You have to keep in mind that sometimes someone will give you a great comment that can help you improve your writing, but often comments are more about the emotional response someone else has based on their own *biases* and *life experiences* and *views about good writing*. Always use those three filters as you respond to comments and allow them to influence your story.

After receiving feedback, think about the comments that were made before you read the notes—the ones that stand out may be the ones that are most meaningful to you, unless you remember them because they were hurtful or lavish praise. Think about how these comments apply and how you might use them to improve your story. Then read the written comments or your notes and think objectively about how they apply to your writing. Just because someone makes a suggestion doesn't mean you have to follow it, nor does it mean that this person is right. And good suggestions aren't always the right suggestion for your story—not if it takes you in a different direction than the story you want to write or causes you to lose your way.

- Were there similar comments about a character or scene or the story?
- Were the comments made because the writing wasn't clear and you didn't get across what you wanted?
- Were the comments made because the logic in the scene or overall story didn't work?
- Were there comments about what felt organic or not organic to the story?
- Were there comments that sounded great but took the story in a different direction than what you wanted to write?

- Did the comments make sense or leave you confused? Can that person provide clarity? (Sometimes they can't and wind up making you more confused or giving you a bad critique.)
- Before doing a major rewrite based on a critique, if you tweaked the writing, would it address the comment?
- Is the person offering you the critique your audience or capable of thinking outside of their own preferences?
- What is your gut reaction to making the change suggested by this comment?
- Were the comments given by someone animated or subdued about your writing?

I have been in critiques where everyone had something to say and were all very animated with both positive and negative suggestions. Generally that means you have a story that evokes or provokes a response in people, which is usually what you want and is far better than no response.

When you find yourself in a situation where you are giving other writers feedback, there are a few things to think about. In my university classes and workshops I do not allow negative critiquing. That doesn't mean that the flaws in another writer's work can't be discussed. It means that the comments and feedback are to be approached with respect for the writer and should be confined to technique and formatting and whether the ideas are solid or where they fall short.

Don't use terminology you can't explain in giving feedback. If the story doesn't seem to be organic, but contrived, then that needs to be explained so that the writer can do something with that information. Many years ago I actually knew a writer who quit writing because someone with more experience told her that her work seemed contrived. The critiquer didn't explain what was meant by contrived or the specific part of the story that felt contrived, and since the writer wasn't clear how her writing was contrived, or how to correct it, feared it was a style of writing that couldn't be overcome.

And giving sarcastic or obtuse reviews doesn't make anyone sound smarter—it just makes him arrogant and rude and demoralizing. If you tend to be a cynic, corral your comments or only join groups with people who have very thick skins and appreciate your point of view. These writers may actually think that you're brilliant or at least give you back as good as they take.

When Do I Share My Work?

As you work through *The Writer's Compass*, if you are part of a writer's group, you can begin sharing as soon as you are ready to receive feedback. Make sure to explain that you are working through your story in stages, and ask for specific feedback on the stages you have completed. Is my structure in place? Are my characters fully developed? Where are there holes? Is the story logical? If not, where did you have problems? Are the events organic to the story? Did something feel out of place or out of sync with the story? By asking specific questions, you will hopefully get more appropriate answers to what you need. If you get feedback on the tension and pacing or word choices or dialogue before you get to that point, you'll know that those don't really apply to this stage of your work but might be helpful later.

It is probably a better idea to wait until after you've reached the later stages to give your work to nonwriting friends and family. Friends and family members may not know what is wrong with your story, only that something is not working for them, and they will be expecting the work to be more complete like the books they buy, which will color how they respond to your level of writing. They will also be unnecessarily kind or brutally frank. Don't get too swept up in their comments except to notice when they all agree about a particular area of the story or make similar overall comments. You may luck out, and one of them may give you a comment that is spot on. Remember, those who really like the story are your audience; those who really don't—aren't.

Let's end this section with an exercise to help you develop your writing skills.

Developing Writing Skills Exercise

By analyzing the published work of writers, you will learn techniques that help you and quickly increase your ability to evaluate your own work. The point is not to imitate other writers but to better understand how certain concepts impact your writing.

Choose several works from the media in which you wish to write, including but not limited to the genre that most interests you. Select the opening and ending pages and at least two to five pages from the middle. Read the pages and analyze the following components. If you aren't sure, try to determine the best answer.

- **Author Intrusion:** This was much more common prior to the twentieth century when the author often made comments directly to the reader, as an aside. Today author intrusion is a subtle tactic the author uses to slip in information his character doesn't know. For example, *Mark didn't know this would be the last time he would ever see Sabrina.* If this is told in Mark's point of view, or you are writing in first person, the "I" voice, how could Mark tell us beforehand what he wouldn't know until after it happened?
- **Distinctive Dialogue:** Can you tell who is speaking just by the tone, word usage, or manner of speech?
- **Point of View (POV):** Who is telling the story? Is it in first person (the main character), a narrator (an observer), third-person (using *she* or *he* to refer to the main character), omniscient (the third-person POV knows everything about everyone), or modified omniscient (the third-person POV knows some things about some people)? Is there more than one point of view?
- **Showing:** Showing the story is using words that are active, visual, and that engage the senses. It is also showing who the characters are and

what they do through imagery. Through description, showing puts visual images in your mind, evokes sounds, smells, or the sensation of touch. Showing does just what it says—it shows the story.

- **Telling:** Telling gives weak images, if any. If the author tells that an event occurred in a Las Vegas casino, the reader may conjure an image from personal experiences. But the author hasn't shown anything. Telling relates incidents, tells the action, explains the characters, relates information. It is exposition and narrative rather than visual. Sometimes there is a reason to tell rather than show. By showing details of lesser importance, the story can become bogged down. The reader can even become confused when the author gives something minor more importance than it should have because of the space devoted to showing it. Worst of all, the reader could become bored and disinterested by too much information.

- **Style and Voice:** All authors have their own way of telling stories through their use of language. Lots of (or minimal) description, using lots of metaphors or few, long or short sentences, point of view, and the voice of the characters are all a part of style. The genre's multitude of ways of approaching a topic—vernacular, pacing, attitude, word choice, and the message the story tells—are all a part of style and voice. Some writers have the same style throughout all their work; others use different styles for different types of stories.

- **Tone:** Tone is the overall feeling the story gives. Is the story dark and somber, comedic and playful, romantic, romantic and comedic or dark and somber, inspirational, cynical, irreverent? Are the characters angry, full of despair, full of fun, political activists?

- **Active and Passive Voice:** Does the author use active or passive verbs? Active verbs are more immediate and create action; passive verbs are those that happened in the past, like *has, had, was, gone, went,* and *is.* A passive sentence seems inactive or promises action. An active sentence creates the feeling that something is happening and makes the story more exciting.

Hæc notula locum
Ophire defignat.

PART II

The Middle

THE STORY MAP AND
THE 7-STAGE PROCESS

chapter 3

CREATING THE STORY MAP

HOW DO YOU KNOW WHERE YOU'RE GOING WITHOUT A MAP?

A road map has many streets, highways, and freeways marked for you to follow. It's up to you to choose which ones you want to travel and in what order. Charting your road map doesn't mean you can't take side trips or go off-road. In fact, you can completely change your mind and go someplace else. You can see whether there are any interesting sights along the way or if you'd rather take a different trip. You don't have to go from Point A to Point D in a linear fashion. You can take twists and turns and circle back around if that creates a more interesting journey. A road map helps you locate the important sights you want to see and the most interesting, fastest, or exciting route to your final destination. Once you know those details, you can plot how you want to get there.

In this section, we'll apply this "road map" concept to your story. You'll learn how to create a map on a structure chart, and how to read it so that you can use it to develop your story, your journey. As you fill out the diagram and map your story, at least three things happen:

- You quickly begin to see what you do and do not know about your story and where the ideas are weak
- You put the analytical side of your brain to work to find creative answers
- You see when you are being too cerebral and telling, not showing your story

Later, on page 59, we will work on what I call a "picture map," which will help you to visualize your story. A picture map uses images to represent people, places, items, or settings across your map, the same way maps have images to represent points of interest. When we discuss the picture map, I will show you how to move the storytelling elements around, which will give you even more insights into moving your ideas in a way that strengthens the structure.

This section of the book contains an overview of structure for creating the maps. In order not to slow you down, we will go into only the essential details we need for clarifying the structure chart. Later, as we work through the 7-Stage process, we will more thoroughly discuss various concepts and how they impact writing. For your convenience, I will note the stage or page numbers where additional information may be found, however it is more efficient to understand the story map first and then to delve into these concepts as they are developed in the 7 Stages.

Drawing the Story Map

When I announce to my students that the midterm exam will be a story map, they get very nervous. I reassure them, as I am reassuring you, there is nothing to be nervous about. There are no right or wrong answers. The purpose of the story map is to help you see what you know about your story and what you have to figure out: Where your story is strong, where it is weak, and what creates excitement and tension will be clear once you can read your story's map.

At this point you may be thinking, "But I don't plan to tell my story in a linear format." The purpose of the story map is to help you lay out the elements that create good stories. Once you know you have those elements, you can move them around as best suits your story. The map actually gives you more flexibility when you know what your story needs to be complete, and from there you can determine a more dynamic arrangement of story ideas.

I will walk you through this process with several examples. Your responses should be written as simply as possible and will come from what you know about your story. There are no grammar rules, no spelling rules—you don't even have to use complete sentences. The purpose of the story map is to help you see where you are in the story's development. Once you have charted the diagram, you will have a road map that shows you what you have or have not figured out and where the holes are located.

This is the basic format for the three-act structure, which has evolved from the basis of Aristotle's and Freytag's structures. You have probably seen this or a similar diagram in other books or lectures or on the Internet.

1ST ACT BEGINNING	2ND ACT MIDDLE	3RD ACT END

(3.1) *Basic Three-Act Structure*

Here is a general overview of the three-act structure:

- The first act sets up the story: the story problem, the story question, and the motivation for the protagonist to take action.
- The second act is usually the longest section of the story and where most of the action takes place, where the protagonist faces most of the obstacles that will keep him from achieving the goal or stop the antagonist from achieving his goal.

- The third act is usually the shortest and starts at or immediately after the climax. It is in the third act that we have a resolution that ends the story, reveals any epiphanies, possibly closes with a question, or ties up loose ends.

1ST ACT	2ND ACT	3RD ACT
The 1st Act is longer than the 3rd Act, but much shorter than the 2nd Act, perhaps as much as ½ as long. This is where the hook and setup engages the reader or viewer.	The 2nd Act is the longest act where the story develops. Most of the action takes place here. The tension builds and rises to a crescendo up to the climax.	The 3rd Act has falling action and is the shortest act. This is where all the loose ends are tied up.

(3.2) *Basic Lengths of the Acts in the Three-Act Structure*

Writing instructors have differing views about the length of the various acts, where each of the storytelling elements should be placed, and what they are called. Screenwriters often use the model of 15–35 pages for Act 1, 50–70 pages for Act 2, and 7–15 pages for Act 3 based on a 90- to 120-page screenplay. Plays, novels, and short stories are less restricted since there is more variation in the number of pages and in story development. Not all stories fall neatly into three acts. In fact, stories vary from one to five acts, and sometimes for television there are seven acts, including the teaser or opening gambit. The teaser is sometimes used as an exciting hook to get the viewer to stay tuned and does not always directly relate to the main story (writing hooks and teasers will be discussed further in Stage 2).

The 6-Scene (or 6-Sequence) Structure Model

There are many structures and many ways to build a story. One simple method of constructing a story uses six scenes. These scenes are a series of scenes, also called a sequence of scenes, and should not be confused with the term "scenes" in a screenplay, which means a change of location or time.

In a lecture I attended at the University of Southern California, Budd Schulberg noted he used a 6-scene method in writing *On the Waterfront*, starring Marlon Brando. Basically, scene 1 sets up the problem, scene 2 solves it, the problem in scene 3 is created by the resolution from scene 2, scene 4 solves scene 3, the problem in scene 5 is created by the solution to scene 4, and scene 6 resolves the entire story.

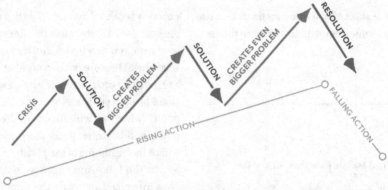

(3.3) *Example of a 6-Scene (6-Sequence) Structure*

As you can see from the diagram, the scenes have "rising action," which means that they grow more intense, and then "falling action" after the climax when the story ends quickly. We will discuss these in more detail in the following pages.

MAPPING THE ELEMENTS OF GOOD STORYTELLING

If you have read books on writing or attended very many lectures, you have probably learned a few writing rules, along with several different terms for describing the elements of good storytelling. As I noted on page 12, I have *only* two rules for writing: 1) Never allow anyone to convince you to cut something from your story that your gut tells you belongs—at least until you know why you wrote it in this story; and 2) If you want to be a writer, you have to keep writing. Using the elements of good storytelling are not rules, they are time-tested components of structure for telling a better story. I am going to show you the simplest way to approach structure and help you make sense of the terminology so that you can easily map your ideas to tell a compelling story.

One of the frustrations I had in studying writing, besides all the differing terminology, was working with teachers who insisted on outlines. I never quite understood what an outline should look like: whether it should be tiered, how detailed it should be, or whether the details should be in sentences or phrases. It especially annoyed me because an outline seemed to impede my writing flow and kept the story from taking off in its own direction as I wrote it. An outline is supposed to tell (better if it shows) what happens next, but the strengths or the weaknesses in the story or what you are missing are not always obvious in an outline.

A story map, on the other hand, tells you exactly that. In a way, it is a type of outline written horizontally instead of vertically. It is more visual and does not need to be written in some sort of chronological flow. Nor does the story map need to be as detailed as an outline, and it has to contain only the essential elements good stories need. If you like outlines, you can still use one to write out the details of your story, but the story map will help you see the strengths and weaknesses in your outline more clearly.

Let's start with the basic three-act structure diagram that has been used for teaching writing for years. This will be the foundation for drawing our map. Remember, our goal is to build on Aristotle's and Freytag's processes and to make sense of all those successful writing methods that use different terminology, but say the same things.

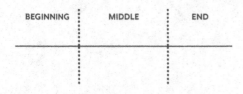

(3.4) *Modified Basic Three-Act Structure*

First of all, note that the acts are changed from *first*, *second*, and *third* to *Beginning*, *Middle*, and *End*. One of the reasons for this change is that there are some stories, especially plays or short films, which are considered to structurally have only one act, and so it is a misnomer to number the sections. However, all stories, whatever the structure, still have a beginning, middle, and end. The change in terminology also allows for the writing to feel more fluid and organic and not confined to the boundaries of acts. Sometimes the elements of good storytelling occur simultaneously and are not easily separated into acts. Note that the vertical lines are dotted to show that they are movable (on your map, you may find it simpler just to draw a solid line). There are no fixed number of pages or a set point for each section or where each element should be placed. Sometimes the "first turning point" (which we will discuss in the following pages) will be earlier in the story; sometimes it will be the beginning of the *Middle*.

In the following pages we will draw the structure chart and place the important story-telling elements on it. However, there will be additional explanations and examples applied as we go through the 7-Stage process.

The Horizontal Line of the Structure Chart

Above and on the horizontal line we will place story elements in the order they occur in a story. Below the horizontal line will be additional space for some of the elements, but it will also contain some notes (in gray) with additional tools and brief concepts to help you develop that element of your story.

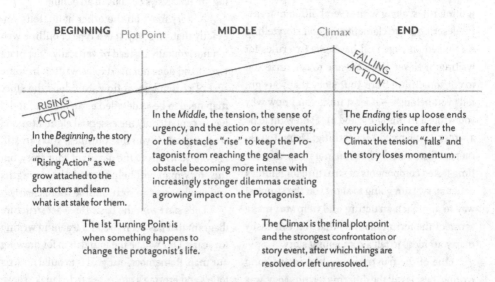

BEGINNING   Plot Point   MIDDLE   Climax   END

RISING ACTION

FALLING ACTION

In the *Beginning*, the story development creates "Rising Action" as we grow attached to the characters and learn what is at stake for them.

In the *Middle*, the tension, the sense of urgency, and the action or story events, or the obstacles "rise" to keep the Pro-tagonist from reaching the goal—each obstacle becoming more intense with increasingly stronger dilemmas creating a growing impact on the Protagonist.

The *Ending* ties up loose ends very quickly, since after the Climax the tension "falls" and the story loses momentum.

The 1st Turning Point is when something happens to change the protagonist's life.

The Climax is the final plot point and the strongest confrontation or story event, after which things are resolved or left unresolved.

(3.5) *Some of the Basic Elements on the Structure Chart With Notes*

Below the horizontal line is also where you will write your theme and dramatic question and clarify why this story matters to you. All of this will become clearer as we work through the diagram. Once you understand the elements of telling a good story, you can rearrange those elements to show your story in the most dynamic progression.

Hook

The next part of drawing the structure chart is to place the elements of good storytelling on the diagram. Let's start with the opening, also referred to as the *hook* or *attention grabber* or *opening image* or *opening lines*, or other names you may have heard used. This means the first moments of your story that have to grab the reader's or audience's attention so that they will want to continue to read or watch your story. For our purposes, we will call this a hook, as we are trying to hook the reader.

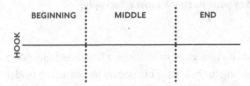

(3.6) *Adding the Hook to the Three-Act Structure Chart*

The hook is the first element on the structure diagram because it comes first in the story and it is critical for capturing your audience's attention. A hook developed for a screenplay or play will be different than one written for a story because imagery in a film, and staging and dialogue in a play, are crucial, but even plays and screenplays are first read before they are produced and seen.

The hook sets the tone for the story. Through the words used, the cadence, the lengths of the first sentences, and the imagery described, the reader is informed about the style and voice of the story. What is written next gives the reader more clues to what the story is about. As you give those clues, you want to further hook your reader by developing a relationship between the reader and the protagonist, which we will discuss more in a few pages. There should also be details about the setting and time frame of the story using the tone and voice of the story (Stages 2 through 6). There are several types of hooks, but the progression of the process will be better served by discussing those in Stage 2.

Setting Up the Story

Starting in or immediately following the hook and before the first turning point, we learn something about the setting, the protagonist (the main character), possibly the antagonist (the person or thing trying to thwart the protagonist), and something about the dilemma or challenge ahead for the protagonist. The dilemma usually involves setting up the "Story Question" and possibly the "theme" (Stage 1). The story setting should evolve into a picture as early as possible so that the reader can visualize where the story takes place: the area, time frame, season, people, story world, or other pertinent information.

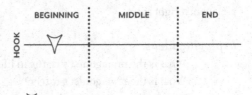

▽ 1st Turning Point—Conflict

Information about the setting, protagonist, dilemma

(3.7) *Adding the First Turning Point and the Setup to the Structure Chart*

Who Are the Characters?

Although we will work more specifically on characterizations in Stage 3, here we will talk about characters as they relate to developing structure. Choice and development of the characters are important aspects of the structure.

Although you may increase or decrease your characters as you develop your story and progress through the stages, think about who you are writing about and who the characters that you really need are. The main characters you need are the protagonist and antagonist, and not even the antagonist if the antagonist is not a person. You could write a story about a single character, although this probably works better as a short story or a play monologue. It's difficult not to have, at the very least, the voices of other characters in a movie—otherwise you have a character talking to himself or silent for one and a half to two hours, which is a tough way to convey a story. Think *Cast Away*. Even Chuck Noland (Tom Hanks) found someone to talk to—Wilson the volleyball. Although Chuck was alone for much of the movie, the movie still sprinkled other characters in to help tell the story and give backstory.

Exploring Ideas:

1. What is the main conflict/disaster of your story?
2. Who is the story about? Whose story is it?
3. Who else is in the work? Who are the important characters and what is their role?
4. Who will tell the story? Whose POV is it told in? Are there multiple points of view? Who can tell the story and convey your purpose most effectively?

Who is the Protagonist?

You want to involve the reader with the protagonist right away so that she will immediately care what happens to the main character and keep reading to find out. This occurs by giving the reader an inkling of who the character really is. Although not all of the following have to be revealed in this section, as many as possible should be used, thereby enabling the audience to relate with the protagonist right away.

Exploring Ideas:

1. What is the protagonist's status in life?
2. What is the protagonist's career?
3. Who is the protagonist when out and about in the world?
4. How does the protagonist behave with family and friends?
5. What does the protagonist think about or do when all alone and no one else sees?
6. What is the protagonist's philosophy of life?

You can show the protagonist's status through their clothing, living conditions, career, car or mode of travel, and food choices. Sometimes these come across as stereotypical, but the reader easily identifies who the character is. Now take it another step and ask yourself "How am I going to show this to readers in a way that connects them and makes them care?" We will continue to discuss this more in Stage 3 as we develop the characters.

While the dilemma may or may not be revealed at this time, the reason the upcoming conflict or challenge will cause a dilemma for the protagonist should be shown. For example, in the opening of one novel, I wrote a beautiful wedding scene and the excitement of the man who was getting married. By showing how important this moment is to him, I'm setting up his perfect world. When things don't work out as expected, we know how this loss influences his dilemma. I chose for the woman to walk out on him in the middle of the ceremony (not a unique choice, other than in the way I used my voice and style to write it). Later the obstacles he faces are colored by this loss of the love of his life. His story question could be "Why did she leave me, and how do I cope with her loss?" or "How does a man reimagine his future without the woman he loves?" Later his dilemma is further complicated when she reappears.

By showing what the character cares about or conversely hates in the setup, you up the emotional level of how the challenges ahead will impact the protagonist.

First Turning Point

The next element of the story is the **first turning point**. It is also called the *inciting incident*, the *catalyst, setting up the main character's goal, creating the conflict, defining moment*, and a *plot point* (plot points are key events that cause the protagonist to take action or the story to take a different direction). It is sometimes called the *prime motivating incident* or *prime motivating force* or the *actual event* or *perceived event*. All of these in some way describe this element.

The main purpose of the first turning point is for something to happen, a conflict or a challenge that will force the protagonist to make a choice as to whether he will take action or not and to provide a challenge the audience can relate to. The protagonist will either accept or try to ignore this challenge. If ignored, there may be a second turning point or plot point. However, the first turning point can be the deciding challenge and can include the protagonist wavering (or not wavering) and then immediately taking action.

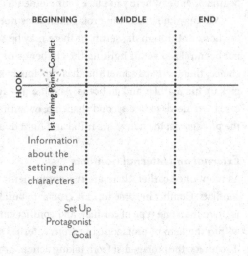

(3.8) *Adding the First Turning Point With Conflict to the Structure Chart*

You will note that this first turning point is a triangle with dashes, because the conflict can be moved along the horizontal line, and because there are two components of conflict to this plot point: internal and external, which we will discuss in the next section. Below the horizontal line is "Set Up Protagonist Goal." Following this point of conflict, we need to know what challenge the protagonist is initially facing,

whether the protagonist will go into battle mode or waver, and what is the initial goal the protagonist has in mind. These story elements can happen just about anywhere in the *Beginning* or even
at the point where the *Beginning* ends and the *Middle* begins (in other words, the beginning of Act
II). Where you place this story element in the structure of the story depends on:

- How long the hook is
- How much of a setup you use to introduce the story
- How quickly the protagonist makes up her mind to face the challenges or
  obstacles ahead or to avoid those obstacles, but finds herself pulled into them
  in spite of best efforts to the contrary

As noted before, the vertical lines are dotted to indicate that they are also movable. There doesn't
have to be a certain point or page number when the first turning point occurs or the *Middle* act
begins or ends. Where you place your elements depends on how you develop your story.

We may know why the protagonist does not want to face the challenge from something in
the hook or through the setup, or there may be something in the backstory (Stage 2), which has
not been related yet. If fighting the challenge or overcoming the obstacle seems like an obvious
choice, then perhaps something has previously happened to the protagonist to cause a desire to
pick up his marbles and go home. And the protagonist may even decide to do just that, in which
case there needs to be a second challenge or conflict or obstacle or event. A second plot point forces
the protagonist to change his mind and fight doubts and fears to face this challenge.

External and Internal Conflicts

As mentioned earlier, there are two components of this plot point: the internal and the external
conflicts. Conflict in some form is crucial to building tension in good storytelling. However, there
is more than one type of conflict, and conflict can come from many directions. It can come from
within the hero or protagonist or from external sources, even friendly sources who are trying to
discourage the protagonist from taking action, or who are encouraging him to take action if we are
talking about a reluctant hero.

There are many reasons why a protagonist would want to accept a challenge that would go
against the character's own best interest or to fight against a challenge that would be in his best
interest. After all, people are complicated, and complicated characters are intriguing to read about or
watch, as long as their behavior is organic and the reader/viewer believes that the character the author
has created would behave in that way or come to behave in that way due to the circumstances.

For our purposes we will talk about the external (overt) conflict, which is the actual event
that happens to create a challenge for the protagonist, and the internal (covert) conflict, which is
what is going on inside the protagonist.

External conflict is the *issue* or *event* or *initial challenge* or *the call to action* or *actual* or *perceived*
event that causes the protagonist to have to decide whether he is going to take action and accept the
challenge or fight against whatever he is facing. Internal conflict is a form of conflict that causes the

protagonist to question whether he should move forward and accept the challenge of the story or walk away—in which case, we don't have a story. However, it is that struggle over indecision that helps create the tension in the story.

External conflict is usually more action- or plot-oriented, and internal conflict is another way for the reader to know the protagonist at a deeper level and feel more connected. Plot-based stories focus on the external conflict. The more important the internal conflict, the more character driven the story becomes.

Exploring Ideas:

1. What are the internal issues this challenge has raised for the protagonist?
2. How does the protagonist feel about the issue?
3. Is there a secret that makes this even harder for the protagonist to deal with?

The secret may actually be revealed later, but by this point there is a clue that a secret exists. Let me include a warning here. Sometimes writers want to keep information close to the vest, planning a big reveal at the end of the story. However, keeping secrets from the audience also keeps them uninformed, disengaged, and frustrated. Secrets should be for the purpose of intriguing the reader and increasing the tension. For this reason, keep the number of secrets to a minimum and continue to reveal some of the secrets so that the reader feels more like an insider to the story than an outsider.

We place the conflict on the structure chart at the first turning point, or plot point, because this is where the protagonist has to choose what she will do next, and we use the triangle as a reminder that we are following two conflicts (internal and external) from one plot point.

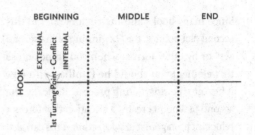

(3.9) *Adding the External and Internal Conflict to the Structure Chart*

Second Plot Point

If the protagonist is reluctant to seek the goal or accept the challenge, or even decides not to do so, a second event (another plot point) may have to happen, at which time the protagonist is forced to decide there is no other choice but to face the challenge. This event then spins the story into the *Middle*.

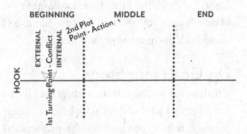

The 1st Turning Point sets up the challenge and the conflicts.

The protagonist decides not to face the challenge.

A second event or challenge forces the protagonist to take action and spins the story into the *Middle*.

(3.10) *Adding the Second Plot Point to the Structure Chart*

Since many books and instructors refer to this second plot point as the "beginning of the second act" or by other terms, when you come across this element you should be familiar with how it fits into the storytelling process. Basically, the second plot point creates a situation that forces a reluctant protagonist to take action. This can also happen in the first turning point. Whether you use a second plot point is dependent on how you develop the *Beginning* of your story, how much character development you draw out, and what event starts the *Middle* and creates the obstacles to thwart the protagonist's efforts to meet the challenge or overcome the antagonist.

For our purposes, we will not add the second plot point to our structure chart since it is not an essential element of storytelling. However, it is a useful element for telling some stories, and you may choose to use it to enhance your story. Later, in "From the First Turning Point to the Middle" (page 46), you will find an example of using both the first and second plot points.

The Goal of the Story

Creating the rising action, adding fuel to the tension, and part of "What's at Stake" come through setting the goal for the protagonist. There are many types of goals—some have to do with coming to a sense of well-being or returning life to what it was before this particular drama and calamity. Sometimes what the protagonist wants and what the protagonist needs create an internal and external conflict within the character. However, making the goal something concrete, like winning the Olympics or the love interest's heart or diffusing the bomb in time, helps the reader identify how close the protagonist or antagonist is getting to the goal and adds to the tension.

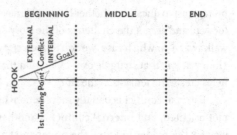

The goal begins as early as the hook but can change as the story develops.

(3.11) *Adding the Goal to the Structure Chart*

It is also imperative to clearly identify both the internal and the external goal for the protagonist and to articulate the character's goals to intrigue the readers and compel them to continue reading.

Exploring Ideas:

Answer the following questions to the best of your ability. There is no right answer, no correct way to interpret the question. The answer should be whatever comes to mind about your story. As you answer the questions and new ideas form, capture them or stop and write as you are inspired and then come back to the questions.

1. What is the protagonist's goal that he wants/needs to achieve? The protagonist's wants/needs and the desire to achieve or fulfill that goal creates the main tension and thread of the story. The more critical the want/need, the more intense the tension.

2. What's at stake if the goal isn't met? If the protagonist does not get what he wants, what are the consequences? What is the price to be paid? If there are no consequences (physical, emotional, economical, existential), it will

be difficult to create dramatic tension or to engage the audience through an entire work.

3. What creates the main tension for the audience to experience vicariously? Does the audience hope the protagonist will achieve the goal? Is there concern for the outcome if the protagonist doesn't achieve the goal? In both cases—achieving the goal or not—should be an equal possibility or achieving the goal grows to be less likely as the story develops.

4. A goal too easily obtained lessens the dramatic tension. What are the obstacles? How do events of the story keep the protagonist from achieving his goal?

5. What are the requirements to get the goal? Will they be spelled out in the beginning, or will they be discovered as the action moves forward? Or will they change as the antagonist places obstacles in the protagonist's way? Will the goal itself change?

Finding the Golden Apple

Choosing what the protagonist must do next usually results in some sort of goal for the protagonist either immediately or after the internal struggle. We will briefly discuss setting goals in the following paragraphs, with more discussion in Stage 3.

There are various types of challenges, conflicts, and goals. Basically, they involve the protagonist wanting to achieve something or to avoid something or to keep the antagonist from achieving something. I call this the "golden apple" approach to goal setting. The golden apple is the object, ideal, or life and death issue that the protagonist and antagonist are fighting over.

Identifying the golden apple may occur after some sort of crisis and a decision as to how to meet that crisis happens, which is often somewhere from your first turning point to the beginning of the *Middle*. However, the goal may be identified as early as the hook, and then that goal is challenged by a crisis or an event. The first turning point occurs once there is a challenge to that goal. The initial goal may also change once the protagonist has been challenged by larger events that make this goal no longer feasible or as meaningful in the larger context of the story. Setting the goal might not occur until the *Middle*, after your protagonist has faced obstacles and has had time to understand and analyze what is happening and then evaluate what the appropriate goal should be.

Golden Apple Goal Setting

In some stories there are basically two leading characters:

- **The Protagonist** is the one the story is about and is considered the hero (or the antihero) of the story.

> · **The Antagonist** is the person—or possibly thing—that opposes the pro-
> tagonist in some way and will attempt to thwart the hero (or potential
> hero) from achieving a specific goal.
>
> BASIC GOALS
>
> · The goal can be something that both the protagonist and the antago-
> nist want and will fight over.
> · The goal can be something the protagonist wants to have, to accom-
> plish, to use to do good—which the antagonist wants to stop.
> · The goal can be something the antagonist wants to use for selfish gain,
> for harm, or to perpetrate evil—which the protagonist wants to stop.

Even if the protagonist is avoiding facing the challenge and is then swept into the events without a goal, you do not want him to be passive. At some point there needs to be a reaction where the protagonist fights back and makes a choice to either win or keep the antagonist from winning. That doesn't mean the protagonist has to win or survive, but if there is no desire to win, the reader may become bored and feel the story is leading nowhere. It is usually boring to read about a passive protagonist who simply won't fight back (not to be confused with a protagonist who doesn't fight back on principle). A passive protagonist is a victim, and if your victim does nothing to change that, well, none of us are too interested in following the behavior of people who are ineffective. (But since there are no rules, someone may accept this as a challenge and write an incredible story about this type of character.)

In *The Divine Conspiracy*, Dallas Willard says, "Each of us must ask ourselves how are we doing it? What, precisely, is our plan? And as teachers of disciples, we must lead everyone we teach into develop-ing his or her own plan." We also do this as writers: We help our characters develop a plan that will either move them toward the light or into the darkness, toward winning or into further conflict.

What's at Stake?

Writers are continually told to create a life-and-death issue for the protagonist, but if every story were a matter of life and death, then all stories would pretty much be the same and at the same intensity. Giving your protagonist a life-and-death struggle does not mean that every protagonist must face death in every story. It means making the stakes as high as you can crank them so that to this protagonist at this time in his life on this day it feels like a life-and-death issue. The serious-ness is not measured by whether the issue is life or death, rather by the intensity of the desire.

Exploring Ideas:

1. What's at stake for your protagonist?
2. How serious is the outcome?

3. Is this the most important issue in the protagonist's life at this time, and will the outcome determine the course of his life to be the best or the worst it can be?

4. Is what's at stake organic to the characters and what really matters for this story?

5. Does what's at stake become more intense when you consider the setting, the people, the circumstances, and the obstacles?

ic event as the potential outcome. How do you develop a sense of urgency in a story without these issues?

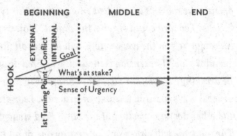

The sense of urgency is another thread that draws the reader through the story. This thread grows in intensity until it is resolved in the climax.

(3.13) *Adding a Sense of Urgency to the Structure Chart*

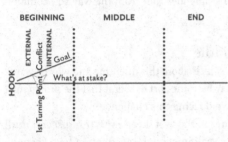

The thread that pulls the reader through the story is knowing what's at stake for the protagonist if he or she fails. ⟶

(3.12) *Adding What's at Stake to the Structure Chart*

Sense of Urgency

There are many components to building tension. One is to make the stakes high enough; another is to have a sense of urgency that increases as the reader moves through the story. An obvious example would be the bomb that is about to detonate if the protagonist can't find it and disarm it in time. This has both the issues of a ticking bomb countdown and a catastrophic event. The television series *24* uses both of these quite effectively.

Not all stories easily lend themselves to a countdown, nor do all stories have a catastroph-

One of the ways is to tighten the story to occur in as short a time period as possible. A story with a quicker pace tends to have more intensity than a slower-paced story. Another way is by the goal you give the protagonist. Is there a time issue in that the goal needs to be accomplished or met by a certain date or time? *If Jerry doesn't arrive in time, his best friend is going to marry the antagonist, who Jerry knows has three other wives.* While this also has a countdown, it is of a different nature than a ticking bomb. Sometimes the countdown is on the antagonist's side. The antagonist needs the unwitting protagonist to be somewhere or do something by a certain time or date to set in motion her own devious goal.

A countdown can also be accomplished by the way things are changing in the world or in the protagonist or in another character. If something doesn't happen to stop the change, it will soon be irreversible. Emotions developing from good to bad to worse can be a type of countdown.

A catastrophic event can be equivalent to what would be catastrophic to your protagonist or your protagonist's world if it happens.

Mary's husband, Leonard, needs brain surgery. This surgery had been impossible before the invention of new robotic laser technology. Her twin brother, Fred, is one of the three brain surgeons trained to operate the robotics and skilled enough to do this type of brain surgery, and the only one of the three who believes Leonard could survive the ordeal. However, since Fred's wife died he's had a drinking problem. Although he's on the wagon now, will he stay on the wagon long enough to perform the surgery and save Leonard's life? The tension is mounting as Fred disappears for days until moments before the surgery. Was he drinking? If Leonard dies, what happens to Mary and Fred's relationship? In this example there are several ways to build a sense of urgency. *Leonard is growing weaker, Mary is growing more desperate, the other doctors rejection of the case, Fred struggling with alcoholism and ruining his unique skills ... The outcome will either save or destroy one or all three of these people.*

The sense of urgency develops not just from a single idea, but from the way you combine those ideas and develop the story.

From the First Turning Point to the Middle

At the first turning point we learn how the protagonist feels about this dilemma and why he wants to face it or to avoid it. As noted previously, there may be some sort of secret that the protagonist is dealing with internally that makes him want to avoid facing this challenge.

New writers often want to hold everything close to the vest, keep everything secret until some big reveal. The problem is that if you aren't revealing enough information to a) keep the reader interested and engaged, and b) keep the tension up by letting the reader know motivations and resolutions, the reader becomes confused or disengaged. Don't resolve the problem of the big reveal by holding back information—create a bigger reveal that comes at the end of several smaller revelations.

The end of the *Beginning* happens when the protagonist is forced to make a choice about facing the challenge or overcoming the obstacle. As noted in the second plot point, this can happen simultaneously with the start of the *Middle*. It can be the same event that reveals the issues of avoidance for the protagonist, or the first turning point can be the event that causes the protagonist to question what she is going to do, maybe even decide she will do nothing. The next event (or second plot point) forces her to take action and begins the *Middle* of the story. There is flexibility and latitude in what precludes the *Middle* of the story and how long it takes the protagonist to figure out what is going on, how she feels about it and what she decides the plan of action will be.

There may not be a plan of action, and the protagonist is swept into events without much thought or introspection. However, there must still be a first turning point, even if it starts in the hook. The protagonist has to face something that she wasn't facing before that now propels her into a series of obstacles or challenges and causes her to create a goal to either overcome these challenges or to put her life back together.

Linda returns home driving down a flood-ravaged street that has ruined her idyllic neighborhood (hook). *She finds that her house, while damaged, is salvageable. Still standing is the rosebush that her husband planted* (mnemonic device, discussed in Stage 2). *Perhaps her husband died while planting this rosebush* (setup and backstory). *The rosebush reminds her of all the dreams they had, which she isn't ready to give up on. She decides that she will rebuild and stay* (initial goal). *Things change when her neighbors come to her and she learns a developer has offered the entire neighborhood a large sum of money to buy their homes, but they all must agree to sell* (first turning point). *The obvious choice for almost everyone else is to take the money, but Linda is not so sure that's what she wants. She is unsure whether staying is worth the challenge and expense of restoring the house, and was this a once-in-a-lifetime flood or could it happen again* (external conflict)? *However, this location, this community, was her life. She and her late husband built this house with their own two hands. The house and the rosebush, maybe a few of his tools that survived, are all she has left of him. She can't bear selling away the dream home he had built for her, and despite the flood, this has been her home for more than two decades. Change isn't easy for Linda; she's afraid of new places and new people and starting over someplace new. But maybe she needs a fresh start* (internal conflict)?

This is Linda's first challenge after the flood. Since the flood and her husband's death occurred before the events we are telling, they are backstory (Stage 2). *Linda makes her decision not to sell. When the developer wreaks havoc against other neighbors who aren't selling, her new goal becomes to thwart the developer's plans* (this is the spin into the *Middle*). *A second plot point would occur if after weighing her choices, she decides she will sell* (first plot point), *until the developer starts creating problems and making threats against other homeowners who are hesitant to sell, and she learns that the developer has plans he hasn't disclosed to the sellers that will forever destroy this community. At this point, she makes a new choice to stand against the developer and fight* (her new goal has changed to stopping the developer), and so we move into the *Middle*.

Rising Action

Stories have a sort of roller-coaster effect, ups and downs and lows and highs as the energy ebbs and wanes—but overall the action, or energy, rises, and the tension increases, until the climax (page 50). After the climax there is falling action (page 50), when the energy quickly falls off, and the story ends shortly thereafter. From the turning point when the protagonist faces the first obstacles after accepting the challenge, until after the climax when the action falls, is the *Middle* of the story. The action rises during the *Middle* of the story and grows more intense. The rising action and the tension are created by obstacles that the protagonist must overcome to achieve a goal.

I'm sure you've listened to or read stories that drone on and on and never seem to go anywhere. These stories may have a number of obstacles or events, but they don't rise in action or seem to lead to a climatic point and therefore do not sustain increasing tension that keeps you on the edge of your seat or, at the very least, engaged with the story.

Obstacles, challenges, or events are what happen to keep the protagonist from reaching his goal and interfering with the outcome he is trying to achieve. These are the events that create tension in a story and develop the rising action. Sometimes obstacles are placed in an order that causes the energy and tension to fall instead of rise. To create rising action, be sure that all of the obstacles in your story grow in intensity and become tougher for the protagonist to overcome. It is easier to see when you chart your obstacles on the story map, as I will show you beginning on page 54. Below is how they appear on the diagram.

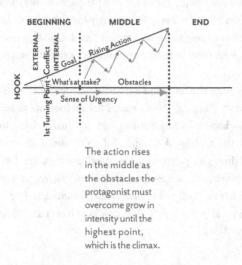

The action rises in the middle as the obstacles the protagonist must overcome grow in intensity until the highest point, which is the climax.

(3.14) *Adding Rising Action and Obstacles to the Structure Chart*

How Many Obstacles Do You Need?

I would say as many as it takes to get your protagonist through the *Middle* to the *Climax*. However, the number depends on the type of story you are telling, its complexity, and how you craft each obstacle—whether they are quick beats or take time to set up. A beat in a written story can be a sentence, paragraph, or more. A beat is a cohesive piece that must be intact to make sense; in a play or screenplay, a beat is each change in the story, or each movement, and is usually a line or very few lines that form a

single thought and must remain intact to make sense. Beats often have the feel of a rhythm in a story. The individual elements on the structure chart are not the same as beats.

A rule of thumb is to write at least three to seven "major" obstacles for a full-length story. Perhaps more if some of the obstacles are smaller or take less time to resolve. If you find yourself with fewer than three, you probably have not fully developed your story, or you may not have enough material to carry a full-length work, in which case you may want to consider a short story, a short one-act play, or a short film. If you have more than seven major obstacles, you may be dragging things out too long, and you may give the reader the sense of a farcical or comedic story. However, three to seven is not a rule, it's an arbitrary number to give you an idea of challenges your protagonist is going to need to meet.

The Resolution of One Obstacle Creates the Next One

The obstacles become more organic and more intense when, instead of having several separate obstacles, the resolution of one obstacle creates the next obstacle. (On page 152, at the end of Stage 3, will be a story map to represent this concept.) Let's look at sequential obstacles that are not necessarily connected.

Marlin is trying to get to the pharmacy to fill his prescription for a specific cold medicine (goal). *It is cold outside and looks like it will snow again any moment* (story setting), *which he doesn't want to be caught in* (sense of urgency). *However, he is really ill, and he needs to recover in time to meet with his boss tomorrow to explain why he just lost the company's biggest client, or he risks getting fired* (what's at stake). *He just called the pharmacist and learned because of a family celebration, they are closing early. He checks his watch; he only has fifteen minutes to get there (sense of urgency with a countdown). He's not overly worried because he's only five minutes away by car. Sneezing and coughing, he makes his way out to the car, slips on the sidewalk (obstacle 1), and lands on his rear. He's lost a minute as he struggles to get up (countdown). He gets in the car, but the battery is dead (obstacle 2), and he loses five minutes trying to start the car. Blowing his nose, he gets out of the car, feels his forehead, and realizes his temperature is going up. He hurries down the sidewalk, watching for ice patches. He is stopped at the corner by a stoplight, and now he's down to seven minutes. As Marlin sneezes and hacks, a stray dog runs up to him, gives him a curious look, then pees on his pant leg (obstacle three). Martin is cold and wet with a leg doused in dog urine. The light changes, he rushes to cross the crosswalk, but ice on the street causes cars to skid past the stop, and he must dodge them to get across the street (obstacle four). He has three minutes left to make a five-minute walk and so he takes off running, skirting around children, shoppers, more dogs, and parents with baby strollers (obstacle five).*

The obstacles are all separate events. This happened and then this happened and then this happened. What connects them is the story thread—Marlin trying to get to the pharmacy for his cough syrup. These are all small events and could actually be part of a smaller scene that would be in a story about a day in the life of Marlin, who is facing the larger issue of whether he's going to get fired and his life end as he currently knows it.

Now let's see how the obstacles could be more interconnected. Same story.

Marlin gets off the phone, sneezes, blows his nose, checks his watch. He glances at his coat rack, but nothing is hanging there (obstacle 1). He jerks his sweater from under the sleeping cat, causing the cat to shriek, not noticing a loose thread caught on the cat's claw, which now dangles below his back. He grabs his car keys and rushes out the door but slips off the steps and falls on his rear onto the sidewalk where he loses his keys in the snow (obstacle 2). It takes him a moment to find the keys, but he finally retrieves them and jumps into the car, slamming the door, not noticing that the thread, which has grown longer, is now caught in the door (foreshadowing—something is obviously coming, but it doesn't keep him from his goal, Stage 2). The car doesn't start (obstacle 3), and his sneezing and coughing continues. He checks the time, gets out of the car, and heads down the street, the yarn from his sweater catching and pulling a little longer from splinters on fences and stems on various bushes. A dog smells the cat on him and chases after Marlin, who makes a run for the corner as more dogs converge toward him. He dodges skidding cars as he runs across the street against the light trying to escape the dogs, and for a moment we think Marlin is done for (obstacle 4, and we see what was foreshadowed play out).

The dogs at his heels, Marlin manages to clear the fence at the park in one hop. He is safe in the park from the dogs who can't get past the fence. Marlin rushes through the trees, glimpsing the pharmacy through the branches across the street. But just before he leaves the stand of trees, a leg emerges on the path in front of him, and Marlin trips over it. He tumbles onto his back and finds himself looking up at a man wearing a ski cap down over his face with holes for his mouth and eyes (obstacle 5). The thief takes Marlin's wallet and watch, but after a second glance at the watch, tosses it back. Marlin has forty-five seconds to finish crossing the park and get to the pharmacy. He gets up, limping, and rushes toward the glass door. Just as snow begins to fall, Marlin emerges from the trees in time to see the closed sign reversed and a hand turn the lock (obstacle 6). Marlin stands in front of the pharmacy and bangs on the glass, partly in frustration, partly hoping one last person is inside. The glass breaks, an alarm goes off, and the neighborhood cop speeds down the block to arrest poor Marlin (obstacle 7).

In this version of the story, the resolution to each obstacle creates the next obstacle. Taking the sweater from under the cat with the dangling thread, which had been the cat's pull toy, led him to being chased by the dogs, then nearly hit by the car. Jumping the fence to escape the dogs led him into the park, where he is attacked by a burglar, which keeps him from getting to the pharmacy on time, but hoping someone is still inside and banging on the pharmacy door leads him to being arrested.

Climax

The climax is generally the biggest moment of the story and the end of the *Middle*. This is the major confrontation between the protagonist and the antagonist, in whatever form the antagonist takes. The climactic moment spins the story into the *End*. For some stories the climax resolves everything in the story by answering who is going to win or allowing the protagonist to achieve his goal, or not, or it creates the moment of defeat for the antagonist. In some stories the climax is a major action moment, but instead of resolving the story, it creates a moment of indecision for the protagonist who must now decide how he is going to respond to the outcome and whether he truly won or lost.

In the climax, all the forces of the story come together at their highest peak, and the tension of the story is the greatest. The entire momentum of this story has been leading to this moment. Because of this being the peak of tension, it is often portrayed by some sort of action scene. In movies and plays an action scene carries a bigger impact than in a novel or short story. Action scenes are not quite as effective in writing as they are visually. Some stories are not action stories; in those the climax is simply the most dramatic moment.

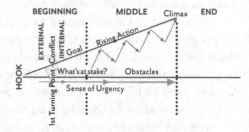

The climax is the most exciting or action-packed moment of the story, which determines the outcome of the story or is the largest event that leads to the final decision for the outcome and ends the *Middle*.

(3.15) *Adding the Climax to the Structure Chart*

Falling Action: Denouement

Once the climactic moment has occurred, the tension falls dramatically, and the story moves toward the ending quickly by resolving what has yet to be resolved and wrapping up loose ends. From this point to the *End* is called the *denouement*.

You will notice that a triangle with dashed lines has been added in the next diagram.

The dashes show that the resolution can occur anywhere from the climax to the final lines of the story. The triangle indicates another plot point, or turning point, which turns the story from the climax to the resolution. In this section you may write a revelation, resolve your story, and give the tag or results, although you don't have to do any of these. Your story could end with the outcome at the climactic moment. Most stories, however, need a resolution with at least one of the three elements below.

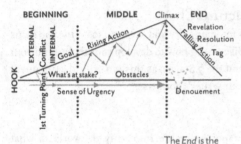

The *End* is the Falling Action, also called the Denouement. This is where final secrets and motivations are revealed, epiphanies occur, the story is resolved, and any story questions are answered and loose threads tied up.

(3.16) *Adding the Falling Action Elements to the Structure Chart*

Revelation

A revelation, also called an epiphany or a reveal, is when one of the characters learns something he didn't know that maybe the audience knew, or the audience learns something they didn't know, which now makes sense of the context of certain events that were puzzling before. However, this type of revelation can occur anywhere in the story.

A revelation can also be when the protagonist or antagonist has a moment of self-discovery or realization about life or your story world. This is where the characters come to understand the truth of your theme or premise. It is also a way to reconcile all the threads in a story and to clarify motivation for the character's behavior.

The first time we learn that Darth Vader is Luke's father, there is a moment of shock and disbelief. Later when Darth Vader dies for his son, it brings poignancy and resolution to the death of the antagonist, and we know that Vader has been under the influence of an even greater antagonist who has been pulling the strings all along.

If a revelation is included in the *End*, it is usually just after the climax and leads to the final resolution.

Resolution

If your story question has not been answered, you will want to answer it in the resolution unless you are writing a story that is left unresolved. Although this used to be a common tactic, most readers and audiences find it very unsatisfying and are less likely to shell out the money for your next book or movie knowing you are the writer who leaves things unresolved. It is my belief that if a story has a good hook, a mediocre middle and a great ending, people will tend to like the story; if the story has a lousy ending, regardless of how great the rest of the book, the story is sunk.

Tag

A tag is the final lines of the story. It is used to either tie up any minor loose ends or resolve any unanswered questions in the story or to give the reader something to think about. The tag gives the impact or the outcome of the story or any results of the story or an indication of what the future for these characters and/or their story world might be. Much like stories about crime, when the story ends before the court drama, the final words on the screen tell us how much prison time the perpetrator got. Or in a romantic comedy we might see the couple kiss and make up as the resolution, but the tag is their driving off with cans and shoes trailing under a "Just Married" sign on their car.

The tag can be used in stories when there is something more to say: a summing up of events or a final morality message. In the tag the writer puts words in one of the character's dialogues or thoughts that sums up something about life or makes a statement that the author, through the characters, wants the reader or audience to remember.

The Last Three Concepts on the Structure Chart

These are elements that are over arching concepts for your story and help you to define the focus of your story. In Stage 1 we will spend more time discussing how to develop your theme and your story question and revisit these concepts throughout the 7 Stages, as this is a critical component of story development and finding true north for your writer's compass.

Theme

Your theme is what you are trying to say—your perspective on life, humanity, the world, or whatever is important to you. It is the over arching message you want your story to convey to your audience. What are the issues you want to raise to stir the audience to think about? The theme can be stated in a phrase and does not have to be a complete sentence. More on writing themes will be discussed in "Tools to Develop Your Writing Skills" at the end of Stage 1 (page 88).

What is the Story or Dramatic Question?

The question the reader wants answered is "How are they going to resolve this problem?" The story question is the overriding dilemma that the character must resolve. Generally, I include the basics of the story within the question so that it embodies what I am writing about and relates to this specific story. Less preferable is an ambiguous question about life. Answering the story question will probably be one of your biggest scenes and will tell the reader whether the payoff was worth the time they spent reading or watching your story and determines whether they will want to read or watch the next one. We will also discuss more about the Dramatic Question in "Tools to Develop Your Writing Skills" at the end of Stage 1 (page 88).

Where is the Story Coming From?

Why are you writing this story? Where is it coming from inside you? In the beginning you may not know the answer, but as time progresses, understanding why you find this story important or how you relate to it will help you to be more honest, more genuine in your writing, and help you create ideas. We will also come back to this in future stages. The following exercise will give you an opportunity to explore this concept.

Philosophy of Life Exercise

If you were a monk living in solitude, and after years of silence you were finally given the opportunity to shout one message into the world, what is the single most important message you would want the world to hear?

Think in images and write a scene with two to three lines of dialogue about your philosophy of life.

The Complete Storytelling Map

Now let's look at the diagram as a whole. In the lower right hand corner there is a heart with the word *Inspiration*. Although not a storytelling element, it is there to remind you to find what inspires you to write this particular story.

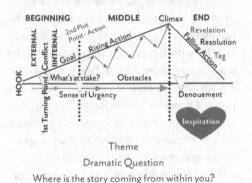

Theme
Dramatic Question
Where is the story coming from within you?

(3.17) *The Completed Structure Chart*

These are the basic elements of good storytelling. Some books and instructors have more items—some less. However, these are the fundamental elements good stories need.

BRAINSTORMING AND MAPPING YOUR STORY

Basically, creating the story map is also a way to brainstorm for ideas. By writing down what you know, you realize what you don't know and recognize the ideas that are weak and not fully developed, and you then set your subconscious to work. Throughout the 7-Stage process you will constantly be led to continue brainstorming. Even in the later stages of writing there will be frequent opportunities to capture and add new ideas. Because you are guided in this process to make the analytical side of your brain creative, you will find your ideas will generally be more organic to the story.

Tips for Creating Your Story Map

Let's take a few minutes to explain how we will create this map. You will need a blank sheet of paper as large as you are comfortable using. Make sure you have plenty of room to work. Paper that works well:

- Large poster-size sheets from easel pads—the type used in workshops and conferences on stands that you can rip pages away from or fold over.
- Easel pads that are sticky across the top and can be pressed against the wall without an easel stand. Turn the paper sideways to have more room. You might want to use a little masking or painter's tape to hold the other side in place.
- 11"x17" copier paper.
- Large sheets of art or construction paper clamped to an art board.

I like to map my stories in color, and I like to change the color combination for different stages. I use a variety of colored pens or markers (if doing this on the wall, make sure they don't bleed through). Use whatever you are comfortable with: pencil, pen, crayons, or markers.

What you want is to feel the experience of drawing your story out. When finished, you will probably want to post your story map next to your writing work space.

So let's begin. Remember, you will use the actual ideas for your story to replace the elements on the structure chart that we have been discussing.

Draw the horizontal and vertical foundation lines, using solid lines if that's easier.

(3.18) *Basic Story Map Layout*

Referring back to the completed diagram (page 53), start filling in what you currently know about your story. It doesn't matter where you start, nor does it matter how much or how little you know. Unlike an outline or a synopsis in which you have to know the basics of the complete story and the order in which it will be told, with the story map you can start by knowing a little or a lot. In fact, you may have already written an idea down, or pages and pages of material. This is just a place to gather your ideas, to see what information you already have, to stimulate new ideas, and to recognize where your story is weak or not developed.

And remember, what you write down isn't set in stone. What you put as the climax this time, you may decide later is a different element of the story, or you may decide it doesn't belong in this story. There are no right or wrong answers. You are just filling in the details you know and giving the analytical side of your brain a chance to work on your story and be creative. As your story develops and you work through the stages, it will all evolve and grow. Be as short and concise as possible. You are just putting down ideas and concepts, not sentences and paragraphs. However, be as descriptive as possible.

For illustration purposes, we'll use an idea I'm creating as I write these instructions.

This is a story about Josh, who quits the job he hates and decides to travel the world as a surfer. At first, that's all I know. What else can I figure out by using the story map?

The obvious seems to be a climax where Josh is injured on a surfboard and nearly drowns. When something is obvious, it may be the same idea everyone else would have. Your goal as a writer is to come up with ideas that are different from what everyone else would write—better yet, something surprising and unexpected, but still organic to the story and true to the characters. However, good writing and good ideas usually come after really getting to know the story and understanding your characters and what you are writing about. Until you get to that point, everything else you write can be considered a placeholder. *So let's put Josh on a surfboard getting injured for now.*

What else do I know about this story, or can I create as a placeholder? What about a sense of urgency? What I just thought of, which I didn't know when I started, was that *Josh's father died before the story begins. Josh was so distraught he missed several days of work and came in with a hangover after the funeral. His boss didn't know what had happened and fired Josh. Josh, being the kind of guy who keeps things to himself, didn't explain the situation to his boss, or maybe his boss is the kind of guy who would have fired him anyway. The reason Josh didn't care about losing his job is that Josh has come to realize all the men in his family die before they hit forty-five and he's twenty-five. If he's only got twenty years or fewer left, he doesn't want to be stuck in this job. He wants those years to be meaningful to him.*

I just made these details up as I typed. Some of it's good, some of it's cliché, some of it's ordinary. But it's a start to a story. I gave the analytical side of my brain, which I've been training for some time, a problem, and it came up with some answers for me. Let's see how this would look on our story map. At any point you can switch to your story map or update it with new ideas. Usually in my own writing I do a new story map at the end of each stage. At that point I reorganize my ideas and move them around because I've now decided an idea would be stronger as a different element, and the story would be better served by rearranging the scenes. I also can see by any internal reticence which elements are still not fully developed.

I have a hook, both the external and internal conflicts, the climax, the sense of urgency, and the revelation. While diagramming this story, I also discovered *Josh has a fear of dying young without having fully lived his life;* however, I added more jeopardy by risking his life in the climax. I also looked at the resolution, and I answered in a way that says I don't know yet, because I haven't decided what type of story this will be. I also haven't decided what's at stake or what the obstacles Josh will face are.

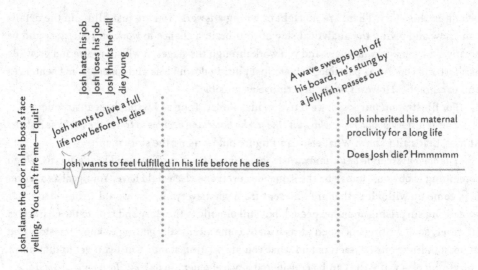

Josh hates his job
Josh loses his job
Josh thinks he will die young

A wave sweeps Josh off his board, he's stung by a jellyfish, passes out

Josh wants to live a full life now before he dies

Josh inherited his maternal proclivity for a long life

Does Josh die? Hmmmmm

Josh wants to feel fulfilled in his life before he dies

Josh slams the door in his boss's face yelling, "You can't fire me—I quit!"

(3.19) Replacing Structure Elements With Ideas on the Story Map

Evaluating the Story Map

In looking at my story map, I see there may be two conflicting elements, which indicates a weak spot. The hook is Josh being fired, but I show the overt conflict as Josh hates his job, which seems to be resolved by his being fired. As I work through the story, I will need to address this and figure out something stronger for one or both of these elements. I could make them work together. However, remember that the more complicated you make your story, the more holes you dig and have to climb out of—this is how a story gets convoluted. Or, I can use as my first obstacle that Josh hates his job, and as the solution he's fired, which creates the next problem—what does he do now? What all of these answers to these conflicting elements say is that there are no rules—you can write the story any way you want as long as it serves the story you want to write and doesn't make the story convoluted.

As we see, this story can evolve many ways. I can spend the time to map out additional ideas, all of which are placeholders and can change as I create stronger, more informed ideas. From this point forward, everything I write will add to my knowledge of the story, whether I eventually use it or not. I can also stop mapping and start capturing this story at any time by writing these ideas into moments or scenes or dialogue or whatever comes to mind. In fact, the whole point is to help you stimulate ideas that you then capture in some format.

Throughout this process, as ideas for events and scenes develop, I write them on index cards with any notes, the setting, time, and date. I usually reorganize these cards in a way that better tells the story every time I create a new structure chart. One of the benefits of using index cards for recording ideas is that they can easily be shuffled around and reordered and arranged and rearranged like pieces of a puzzle or a storyboard. I also number and date them so that I can put them back in the original order if I change my mind or get confused. I find this idea so useful that every time I finish a stage of writing and draw an updated story map, I create a new computer file in which I break up the story into beats and then print the beats out, one per index card, so that I can reorganize the writing to make it stronger.

While creating the story map, you may tend to tell the ideas for what happens, rather than show them. I sometimes have students who think in terms of concepts rather than visual images. This is being too cerebral and can hinder the creation of showing scenes. It is much harder to tell an interesting story (albeit sometimes faster) when it is a cerebral story. I also have students who can create wonderful images, but there is no concept or theme for a story to accompany the image. For now, just write the ideas on the story map as they come to you. As you work through the stages you will see ways to make your story both more visual and have stronger concepts. We will revisit how to develop imagery and the use of metaphors, and showing versus telling, in Stage 3 when we work on characterization.

WHEN TO RESEARCH

What about the research? I know nothing about surfing. Right now I'm constructing the ideas for my story. I don't want to be sidetracked by research. The research can come in a later stage when I need to add more details, find the organic truths for my story that add interest, and enliven the language. I do not want to stop the flow of my story by researching this soon in the process. However, I do know something about the fear of dying by a certain age because my mother died early. I know what it feels like to be in a job or a situation I hate. I can relate to the desire to build a meaningful life. I also know, from observing other's behavior, that frequently after a father's death a son's behavior becomes erratic. Knowing what you are writing about often means understanding the complexities of emotional experiences more than it is about living through certain events. Case in point: science fiction. How many people who write sci-fi have traveled via spaceships to other worlds and battled aliens?

When the need to know becomes problematic, I can study about surfing: learn the terminology, read where the "big waves" are geographically located, and come to know the mechanics. I can interview surfers and get a sense of their lives and experiences. As I do the research, I will probably find new ideas to help my story feel genuine. Or I can change from surfing to another situation, keeping the basic idea of Josh's struggle with his life being finite as he searches for meaning in another context or setting.

As you write you should make note of any details that will need to be researched later. Sometimes I mark my rough draft in such a way that I know how to quickly search and return to the areas I wanted to research. When you do begin the research, set aside specific research time separate from your writing time if at all possible. Jot down places to get information as you find resources. By being organized, knowing specifically what you need to research and potential places to find the information, you will save time. Keep your research data as uncomplicated as possible. I often use an Excel spreadsheet or a table in Word so I can do key-word searches. Or you may choose to use index cards you can quickly sort through or organized file folders. Or you may just rely on your memory, a highlighter, and sticky notes to mark places you think you'll want to return to.

GOOD-VERSUS-EVIL STRUCTURE

Before we leave this section on creating structure charts, I want to introduce you to an additional model: "Man's Inner Conflict with Good vs. Evil." It is a simple way to illustrate a story that can be played out in many ways across many genres of man's battle against his weaknesses to find his strengths. The hook in this story can begin with the man's initial goodness or start with his struggle over a life-changing event that causes him to question whether he is on the right path.

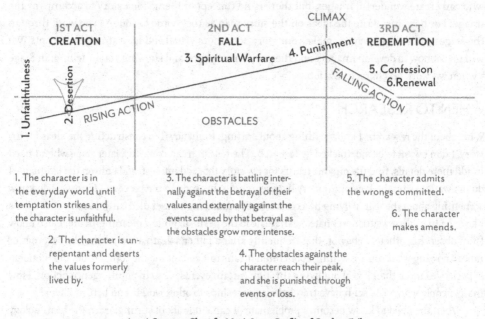

1. The character is in the everyday world until temptation strikes and the character is unfaithful.

2. The character is unrepentant and deserts the values formerly lived by.

3. The character is battling internally against the betrayal of their values and externally against the events caused by that betrayal as the obstacles grow more intense.

4. The obstacles against the character reach their peak, and she is punished through events or loss.

5. The character admits the wrongs committed.

6. The character makes amends.

(3.20) Structure Chart for Man's Inner Conflict of Good vs. Evil

- One story might be about a man who marries his teenage sweetheart. He plans a long and happy life, but then chooses a career that causes him to travel. Eventually he succumbs to the lure of more than one wife living in other cities. Then one day a sick child causes him to rethink the downward spiral his life has become. He then seeks to rectify his wrongs by accepting his punishment and changing his life.
- It could be about a woman who, when her twin dies, questions everything she thought she knew about the goodness in life and decides to go on a wild rampage.
- It could be a spiritual struggle of the good in man against the temptation to do wrong to his fellow man.
- Or it could be man struggling with God or his personal spiritual traditions.

There are many stories in which this structure plays out, and every writer brings their own unique perspective to it. This model can also be used for creating the "B" story, or subplot for the protagonist's internal struggle. We will discuss the subplot in Stage 2.

CREATING THE PICTURE MAP

Because of my concern that students (and that you) do not lose the spontaneity and free form of creativity in your own writing, I used my great artistic skills (not), to draw a picture that overlays the structure chart. The picture map represents the many ways one story can be told. A story example accompanies the picture map that teaches how to move around the ideas on the story map to tell the story in a more engaging manner—the story you want to tell!

Let's go through the picture so that you can see how the story map works with the picture map. While we do so, think about how you can create your own picture map. If you have my artistic talents, you may want to cut pictures from magazines or download clip art that represent elements of your story to create your picture map, as opposed to drawing it.

(3.21) *Picture Map for Ray's Story*

In this story the main protagonist, who we'll call Ray, has made a decision about his life today—about his marriage, his wife, his career, his future. His decision is one of four things: either he's leaving his wife, he's quitting his job, he's doing both, or he's decided not to do either (his thinking about those things would then be the backstory. The hook is his decision. However, if I'm saving that decision to reveal later, the hook is his letting it be known to someone that he'd come to a decision, but not what the decision is.) *Because we are not writing ideas here, but using images to show concepts, I've started Ray in his everyday world.* (I could have put a picture of Ray or a picture of his career or wife or chosen any number of ways to show he had made a choice about his life. I actually don't have the hook represented in this picture map. The hook could place him in his everyday world, or it could be a place where he reveals the decision he's made about his life.)

It's a nice spring day—the sun is shining, flower beds surround the house, soft white clouds float overhead. The swing on the tree indicates this is a family. Ray picks some flowers from the yard and takes them in to his wife (setting). *Inside the house Ray finds his wife crying and learns she heard from her doctor that she has a rare form of cancer* (conflict: external, his wife has cancer; internal: how does this impact his decision?) *Ray is stunned, to say the least* (what's at stake: his wife's life). *Ray begins to research about this rare disease and discovers information about a flower that is rumored to have healing properties, especially effective on this form of cancer. However, this flower only grows three weeks out of the year* (sense of urgency, countdown) *and is some distance away—across the water and on the other side of a mountain, and he could face some treacherous territory if he goes after it. Ray does not want his wife to die, regardless of the decision he's made, and so he sets out on a quest for this flower* (first plot point: He decides to put his previous decision on hold, and his goal is the flower; his decision about his life could have been the first plot point, depending on how the story is set up, and this a second one. Regardless we have spun the story into the *Middle*).

(Rising action) *Ray must navigate a river that has sandbars and currents to get to the mountain, when his boat gets stuck* (obstacle 1) *he has no choice but swim to the mountain, holding his backpack with his equipment above his head* (resolution). *At the edge of the water he is confronted with snakes* (obstacle 2), *he fights against the snakes and just as we think he might lose the battle, he escapes into the woods* (resolution), *where he is finally safe, but lost* (obstacle 3). *In the woods, he is confronted by wolves* (obstacle 4), *which chase him until he manages to escape into some boulders, and up the steep mountain* (resolution 3 and 4). *There is a crevasse, in the mountain which he tumbles into* (obstacle 5), *but fortunately he brought some rock-climbing gear in his backpack and is able to make his way out* (resolution; we will discuss "Taking It With You" on page 116). *Relieved, Ray realizes he is near the top of the mountain and hopes that he will find the flower on just the other side. Then he sees it—a swift river and a waterfall between him and the top of the mountain* (obstacle 6). *He could go back and face all those obstacles again and attempt to come up the other side, or try to cross the river, which doesn't appear too wide. Ray chooses to cross the river.*

Ray discovers a tree that has fallen partway across the river and then some boulders that are positioned almost like giant stepping stones; if he can get from one to the next without falling into the swift current of the river, he'll be okay (resolution). *Step by step he makes it across the tree and jumps to the first boulder. At the second boulder he loses his footing and slips and winds up being held fast by his backpack* (obstacle 7). *He manages to get out of his backpack and onto the boulder, but loses his grip on the backpack, which filled with all of his supplies, goes over the waterfall* (the climactic moment: things are pretty bad, but he's survived) (Falling action). *Ray easily makes it across the*

CREATING THE STORY MAP

last two boulders. At last he is in the area where the flower is supposed to be, he can see a field filled with foliage and flowers and knows this is it, between him and the flower is only a fence that he must climb over (metaphor for the last hurdle and confronting his earlier decision about his life). *At last he gets to the flower. He carefully gathers the flowers and then realizes they are the same flowers that grow in his own yard. Now he realizes that maybe what he's looking for in life has been there all along* (revelation).

What we don't see in my picture map is that he takes a boat home. Ray is now a changed man as he delivers the flowers to his wife. A lab turns the flowers into a drug. We then imagine Ray's wife in a hospital, receiving the drug intravenously, the last detail being Ray sitting beside his wife, holding her hand (tag).

I have put nearly all of the events into my picture that I would have put on the story map; however, now I can look at my picture and see that there are at least a dozen ways I can tell this story. The story could be told in flashbacks or out of order or in any order. I could start with the hook being this disheveled man picking a flower, then realizing it grows in his own yard and his reliving the story, with the ending being what he now chooses to do. I could start the story on the sandbar or with the wolves or in the crevasse. I could choose for the story to be more of a character study, and instead of climbing the mountain, Ray takes the long way around on the water and reflects on his life. If you choose for the resolution to be back in his normal home, then you might start Ray at the flower or beginning the journey. The hook could be his finding the flower and that he thinks going down the mountain is a faster way home—his goal becomes getting the flower to his wife and it's going home he faces all the obstacles and his decision about his life evolves. If you write the wolves as the climactic moment, then the crevasse and the waterfall become the lesser obstacles and should be sooner. (Ray's Story Map can be found on page 175.)

By knowing that you have included the key storytelling elements in your story, you can then organize your story any way that suits your purposes. And it doesn't have to be told in a linear chronology.

How you tell the story depends on what is important to you, how you will write it, what your theme and dramatic question are, and where the story is coming from within you. This is what makes storytelling unique to the storyteller. If you told this story your way, it would most certainly be different from how I would tell it.

How Would You Tell Ray's Story? Exercise

Write a synopsis for a story using the same elements in my picture map. You can add or delete anything you choose and start the story anywhere you like. After you complete the synopsis, write what your hook would be.

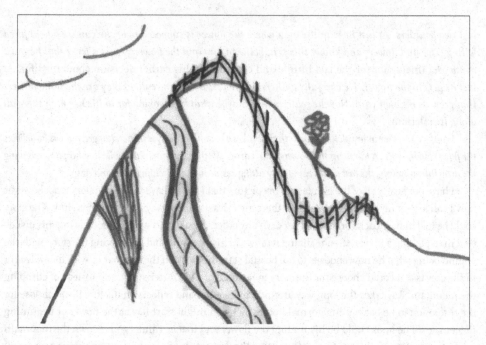

(3.22) How Would You Tell Ray's Story?

Start Your Own Picture Map Exercise

If you have ideas, begin a picture map of your own story. Can you draw? Can you make stick figures? Find images in magazines or use clip art that represents ideas for your story, and put together a picture map. Each of the story elements, as well as the obstacles, can be possible images for your map. Keep it simple, but try to include all of the storytelling elements you know. You will add to the picture map as your story evolves.

If you don't have enough ideas yet, we will begin building them in Stage 1.

chapter 4

STAGE 1—DEVELOPING IDEAS

WHERE DO IDEAS COME FROM?

I have the type of mind that can create a story out of anything. In fact, one of my best stories came from a challenge my engineer, photographer, and writer friend Tim gave me. We were sitting in his loft apartment in downtown Los Angeles playing a game. He would point out something in the room that I would have to make up a story about on the spot. One of the items was his guitar, and I told Tim the story of a woodworker whose love for music was the only way he could reach his special needs child. That story evolved into the play *Guit*.

There are very few stories that haven't been told. It's your unique perspective in how you tell your story and the way you draw and advance your characters that make it more interesting than the thousands of times it was told before. As you develop your ideas, think about ways your story can be more interesting and different from what has been done before—remember that a story must still be organic and remain true to what would happen in this situation with these characters.

There are many ways to come up with stories. Reading newspapers and books often trigger ideas. Dialogue that you overhear between strangers (or sometimes acquaintances) in unexpected places can spark your imagination. Music or art that stirs your soul can inspire a story. Events that happen or the unique way you interpret those events can ignite stories. I remember one of my first writing teachers, Joel Henry Sherman, author of *Corpseman* and *Random Factor*, suggested asking yourself, "What if it didn't happen that way? What if it happened this way?" Since then I've heard many versions of the "What if?" question.

Pulitzer prize-winning playwright and author Paul Zindel came into the first day of class with a suitcase full of items that inspired him. Maybe you have a box or trunk or bookcase with items that inspire you. In a writing group I once read pages with a description of a cabin and my character drinking out of a blue enamel camping cup. One of the members of the group found one of those cups and brought it to me at the next meeting because of the memories it had evoked in him. That cup inspired me to work on that particular series of stories.

A criticism of young writers is that they do not have enough life experience from which to write. They write from what they've seen on television or from things they have experienced vicariously, or from very superficial events. If you can plumb the depths of your own life to find a story, you will be ahead of your peers. Find an event, a defining moment, a turning point, something from your life that is an experience unique to you, and use that as the starting point for creating your story. You don't have to tell us what that event is, and you don't have to write the event as it happened, but you have to be true to the emotional depth of that moment and incorporate that into your story. After I faced a significant health issue with a long, difficult recovery, I'm told the depth of my writing rose to a new level. I was able to take the reader deeper into the characters' story—the human experience—because what I had experienced suffused the stories I told, even when the story had nothing to do with my personal experience. You don't have to have faced life and death to reach that level of writing. You do have to understand the human experience, to empathize with the reader's experiences and depth of feelings, and give those to your characters without contriving or manufacturing emotions.

Good writing is getting to the core of a truth and helping others to understand something more about humanity through understanding that truth. In that way, it is good to write about what you know. That means becoming vulnerable and stripping yourself naked. Not in writing about you, but in writing about what you know to be true with all of its beauty marks and warts. It doesn't have to be factual, in fact, it will probably be much stronger if it is metaphorical because you can then write about it more objectively, and you can get to the deepest, most painful, most vulnerable part of the truth. It's not as much about what you've experienced as it is the depth of that experience and the truths it reveals to you.

Most writers will say there is a grain of truth in their best stories or a piece of them in each of their characters. We've all read stories that were so well written, so honest with emotions and the details so perfect that we've wondered if it really did happen. That's what you want—for the story to feel so real that the audience is willing to "suspend disbelief."

Why Do You Want to Write This Story?

An important part of developing ideas is understanding why a story is important to you. Why do you want to write this story? What are you trying to say? If you understand that, you will be more motivated, more focused on the story, and more attuned to finding ways of writing what you want to say.

Often it takes time to figure out what you are trying to say, and sometimes it changes as the story develops. There may be a moral or message or theme you want to talk about, a point you want to prove, but you only have an ambiguous idea of what you are trying to say or how to say it. In the development questions, I ask over and over again for you to rewrite your premise, your theme, and other important concepts until it may become annoying. However, as you develop your story, each time you answer those questions the message you want to give becomes clearer. It also develops the writer's compass that keeps you from going in the wrong direction. Every question, comment, and critique of your story is countered with you asking yourself: Will this change what I am trying to say? Will it make it stronger? Will it cause me to lose my way?

Exploring Ideas:

1. Why are you writing this story?
2. What matters to you about this story?
3. What purpose do you believe this story serves?
4. Are you writing to express something you believe?
5. Are you writing it just for entertainment?
6. What one important concept or principle is this work about?

The following exercise will help you think about what it is you want to say and may even create a scene you can use in your work.

Message in a Bottle Exercise

You are enjoying yourself on a cruise ship, when an unexpected storm comes up, and a wave washes you overboard. You manage to cling to a life preserver that went over with you and finally float to a small deserted island. You remain alone on the island as the days and weeks and months turn into years. You have now had plenty of time to reflect on your life and the future and things you would like to say if you had anyone to talk to.

One day debris floats to the shore that includes a corked bottle. By now you realize that there is no way you are going to be found or return home. You down the contents of the bottle and carefully peel off the softened label. As it dries you think about what is important to you and what you want to say to the world. You have just enough room to write a single message. You think about who you hope will find that message. When the label is dry you pick up a piece of charcoal and write ...

1. What is your message?
2. Who do you hope will find it?
3. Why that particular person(s)?

Why is This Story Important to You?

The more you understand why you care about writing this story, the longer you'll stick with finishing it, and the closer you will remain to your vision. Perhaps it represents something from your own life that you want to share, but still be able to change the facts. Maybe there is a particular character who intrigues you and who you want to follow to see what the outcome is if you put that character in a particular set of circumstances.

Exploring Ideas:

1. Why do you care about writing this story?
2. What is your purpose for writing this story? Do you have something to say and an idea for expressing it, or are you just cleaning out the garbage in the alleyways of your memories? If it is the latter, you'll need to be sure you have a good plot and interesting characters if you want the reader to make the journey with you.
3. What makes this story interesting?
4. Is the idea funny to you or sad or intriguing? Or does it elicit another emotion?
5. What are you really trying to say?
6. What is the actual event of the story—what is really happening? Is it overt (more external) or covert (more internal)?
7. What is the main conflict/disaster?
8. What is the payoff moment?

Inspiration

Often ideas evolve from what inspires you. Drink deeply from those things that fill your soul. When you've emptied yourself out, either through a good writing session or from the events of a day in your life, find what inspires you and immerse yourself. Top off whenever you can.

I find that daily devotionals are a tremendous inspiration. Some might call this meditation. During my devotionals I take time to be thankful for what I have been blessed with. I pray, and I read from the Scriptures. Sometimes I sing, and often I read inspirational material. I also have around five hundred sayings, thoughts, and stories that I call "Messages of Persistence" printed on, you got it, 5x8 cards. These are bits of wisdom and ideas and motivations that inspire me to be the best I can be and to never give up what I believe I am here to do.

We've talked about music and books and images. Nature has a way of filling us up without a word being spoken. Sometimes movies fill you. I have favorite movie and television characters that inspire me to write. I've also found inspiration in unexpected places. I clearly remember passing the pool in front of my old apartment and climbing the steps, putting the key in the lock, and hearing words that inspired me to write a play called *Pitter-Patter*.

My assignment for a one-week intensive workshop was to write a one-act play. I needed an idea fast. Water has always been my inspiration, and as I passed the pool, the words *pitter-patter* came to me. I asked myself, "What is pitter-patter? What would a story about pitter-patter be about?" The answer: "a big toe stuck in a faucet." I wrote a comedic play that Pulitzer prize-winning Paul Zindel told me verged on genius. Of course, in my exuberance to prove him right, I immediately overwrote it and turned it into a pile of ... crap. However, I later reworked it, and in staged readings watched the actors and audience thoroughly enjoy the humor in it.

Hearing your work read aloud can be pretty good inspiration. Involving yourself with a group of writers or actors can help you accomplish this, although supportive friends and family might be helpful as well, even if they don't know how to critique.

If you haven't already, start collecting items: music, articles, videos, photos, objects, pictures, graphics, ideas, and research that inspire you to write the current story you are working on. Having these items at hand can motivate you to write and get you started faster versus the starting lag time most writers experience. Gather together everything you can into one convenient place. You may want to create a story box to hold the material.

CAPTURING IDEAS—GETTING YOUR HANDS AROUND THEM

The first thing is to get all of your ideas written down so that you have material to shape into a story you can develop. Don't waste time getting it perfect—it's more important to collect the ideas. Stage 1 is basically writing down your ideas and thoughts in any format—a mind dump. Subsequent stages help you show what you wanted to say in the story in unique ways that develop your characters, dialogue, situations, and events. Write your mind dump in an outline, notes, dialogue, scenes, whatever form comes out of your mind. Use whatever method is most freeing to your creativity to capture those ideas. If you work on a story in many ways or are collecting research material, make a note on where your ideas are stored and in what format so they can all be compiled at some point, or keep them together in a story box or drawer or shelf.

METHODS OF BRAINSTORMING

What if you don't have ideas for a story? Or what if you have one or two ideas, or even a few, but not enough for a whole story? There are many ways to generate ideas. Part of the 7-Stage process is the continuous development of ideas. The following are some ways to get started.

Clustering

In *Writing the Natural Way*, Gabriele Rico wrote about the concept of clustering: creating ideas by word associations. I often do this in groups on a large black or white board or poster paper. It's interesting to see word associations coming from each individual's perspective, everyone's minds working together in concert to come up with ideas. Usually, at the end of the exercise, someone will come up with a surprising story idea.

The exercise below will help you understand how to cluster for ideas.

Clustering for Ideas Exercise

In the center of your space, draw a circle large enough in which to write a single word. Start with one word—anything, usually the first thing that comes to your mind. Or if there is a particular subject you want to write about, start with a word that represents that subject.

Around that center circle add a second level of circles with the first words that come to mind relating to your central word. The words do not have to be connected and are often surprising, funny, or not related at all. One word can go in many different directions. When you've completed that list of words, look at the second ring of words, and around each one write the first words you think of that relate to the secondary word.

Continue this process through three to four levels of words. Now look over the words you've come up with and see how they relate. Often the relationship of the words will begin to form an idea for a story.

Create a story idea using these words.

Spider Web Exercise

This method is very similar to clustering but through a slightly different lens. Think of a concept or philosophy of life that is important to you; write that in the circle. On one of the attached legs write a word or concept the circled word makes you think about. Extend that word with secondary concepts. Follow with ideas to express those concepts until you gather enough thoughts to form a story line.

Example: A woman with empty-nest syndrome falls in love with a soldier who is the son of an enemy of her father, and she must choose whether to honor her father or commit her love to the soldier. Their fathers were once best friends.

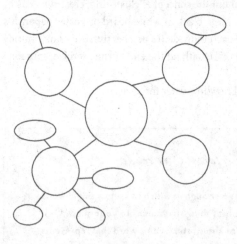

(4.1) *Clustering for Ideas*

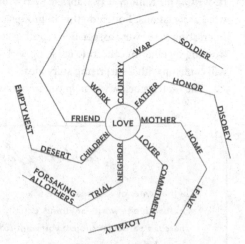

(4.2) *Spider Web Ideas*

Stream-of-Consciousness Writing

This method is to write your thoughts at one sitting without stopping. The point is to see what comes out of your subconscious that could inform you about your story. Do not edit, do not censor yourself, do not strive for clarity or force yourself to follow one thought until you have completed the writing exercise.

Write 5 to 15 Minutes Without Stopping Exercise

Use the stream-of-consciousness technique to allow your thoughts to flow freely to generate an idea. Try writing your idea down crudely. For a set period of time, write without lifting your pen off the paper, or type without stopping. Turn off your internal editor and allow your subconscious the freedom to release the raw passion to write as the words flow.

The Journalist's Technique

Journalists develop their stories by finding the answers to key questions, otherwise known as the "five Ws" (who, what, when, where, and why) and how. Using these same questions will help you do some investigative reporting on your own story. I've added a couple more Ws that I find pertinent to develop story ideas. Answer the questions in the following exercise.

The Journalism Technique Exercise

Who?	Who is your protagonist and antagonist?
Who else?	Who else is important to the story?
What?	What is happening in the story?
When?	When does the story take place?
Where?	Where is the setting for your story?
Why?	Why is this happening?
How?	How did your character get involved?
So what?	So what is the reason an audience would care?

Working Title

Sometimes an idea for the title is what starts you off. While writing this book I came up with a great idea for a title for a novel (I'll keep this idea to myself). Now I just have to come up with a story to go with it. However, you don't need to know the final title—titles are frequently changed as you get to know your story better and what it is really about, and then changed again by editors or the publisher's marketing department or by the producers. In fact, it may be that poetry, short stories, and plays are the few formats that generally keep the author's title. Still, it is often helpful to have a handle for your story from the beginning. Think about the main character or the point you are trying to make. Although both the story and what it is about tend to change as you develop your characters and the plot, if there is a title by which you refer to your story, it gives it more of an official place in your project planning.

Exploring Ideas:

1. What is your working title?

CREATING OBSTACLES

Ideas for crafting obstacles are everywhere. Life is full of challenges. You have undoubtedly faced many obstacles in your own life and know of intriguing challenges others have faced. Protagonists can have conflicts with antagonists who put obstacles or challenges in their way. The protagonist can also face obstacles from other entities:

- **Institutions**—big businesses, banks, government entities, faux charitable organizations, pharmaceutical companies, major corporations that are for-profit only
- **Society**—organizations, the local community or neighborhood, a networking group such as a golf club, a bridge club, family, or a church. Or negative organizations like a drug cartel, an illegal dog- or rooster-fighting ring, or a group in a Ponzi scheme. The obstacle can be the way people think or feel or treat others, issues that face societies, or the way that society addresses issues.
- **Nature**—hurricanes and tornadoes, floods, avalanches, fires, wild animals, deserts and jungles, treacherous mountains, weather, illness
- **Another**—other people with their own motives, or life forms or things that take on personas
- **Self**—what we do to ourselves either wittingly or unwittingly, vices, how we feel about ourselves or treat our lives or whether we take care of ourselves
- **Medical**—issues that the protagonist faces or someone close to him or her faces, i.e., debilitating diseases, handicaps, mental health issues, or malpractice issues

- **Alien**—forces from outside of our world, a meteor strike, aliens attacking, cosmic forces
- **Fantasy**—forces outside the protagonist's control because the writer thought them up just for this story

These are all arenas from which challenges can be created or obstacles crafted. The entire story can be built around the protagonist's conflict from one of these areas and then obstacles crafted from the protagonist's goal to overcome this conflict. For some stories, it might be suitable to choose from more than one category—as long as the development is organic and makes sense to the reader. Remember you want your audience to be willing to "suspend disbelief"; therefore whatever you write has to be believable in the world of your character.

There are many other psychological, cultural, sociological, physiological, and religious ideals and laws that offer ideas for the development of challenges in your story. Let's look at some of these. As you read through them, jot down ideas that occur to you for your story.

Maslow's Hierarchy of Needs

In 1943 Abraham Maslow wrote an article discussing the hierarchy of man's needs based on his clinical experiences. Originally there were five stages, but William G. Huitt wrote about the diagram evolving to eight stages. In the next column is a modified version of Maslow's Hierarchy of Needs, with some explanation of each stage. As you look at the diagram, where would you place your story and your protagonist on this pyramid? What would be an obstacle your character might face at that level or in attempting to reach a higher level?

(4.3) *Modified Table of Maslow's Hierarchy of Needs*

Stages to Resolve Grief

Facing death, overcoming grief from a significant loss (even if the loss is not from death) might be used in stories. Below are highlights of three different perspectives on the grieving process from an editorial "Beware the 5 Stages of 'Grief.'" Would any of these evolve into obstacles for your protagonist?

- *Four Stages* [Dr. John Bowlby]
  1. Phase of numbing—feeling of disbelief or unreality
  2. Phase of yearning and searching for the lost figure—longing for the deceased
  3. Phase of disorganization and despair—despair, sadness, even a sense of hopelessness
  4. Phase of greater or less degree of organization—assimilating the death and learning to live

- *Five Stages* [Dr. Elisabeth Kubler-Ross]
  1. Denial and isolation
  2. Anger
  3. Bargaining

4. Depression

5. Acceptance

- *Grief Work* [Dr. J. William Worden]

   T = To accept the reality of the loss

   E = Experience the pain of the loss

   A = Adjust to the new environment without the lost object

   R = Reinvest in the new reality

Ethical and Moral Obstacles

The following are concepts of ethical behavior to think about when you are writing. Can you incorporate these in a positive way into your writing? Can you show the negative side of being influenced by a lack of ethical ideas and behavior? Think about these concepts when you are developing ideas and clustering on the next pages. Think about using these concepts as you develop your characters, what they stand for, their goals and the obstacles in their way. Some of the most popular stories written are about characters with ethical dilemmas. Use these concepts as you develop your premise, theme, purpose, and story-line point.

Creating Obstacles From the Ten Commandments

Many cultures and societies have laws that parallel the Ten Commandments. Any of these can be adapted to make strong challenges for your protagonist.

1. No other gods
2. No idols
3. Do not misuse God's name
4. Remember the Sabbath
5. Honor parents
6. Do not murder
7. Do not commit adultery
8. Do not steal
9. Do not give false testimony
10. Do not covet

Character Counts Obstacles

A few weeks before I went to USC, I decided to go through the "Character Counts!" (http://character counts.org/) training at the Josephson Institute. It was a week long course, mostly for educators and others who work with students, to train us to how to teach ethics to kids. The reason I went through the course was that I wanted to learn more about ethics for creating my characters and how to develop ethical conflicts in their stories. Based on Josephson's research, below are the "Six Pillars of Character" the program teaches. (http://charactercounts.org/sixpillars.html)

- Trustworthiness
- Respect
- Responsibility
- Fairness
- Caring
- Citizenship

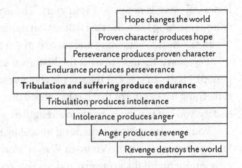

(4.4) *Obstacles Created From the Protagonist's Upward or Downward Spiral*

Ethical Behaviors Obstacles

Another list of ethical behaviors that your characters could be struggling with or against could include the following:

- Don't go through life doing wrong
- Live an honorable life
- Be truthful with complete sincerity
- Do not slander other people
- Do not harm other people
- Do not talk to others with disdain
- Despise evil and those who commit evil
- Fear God
- Keep your oaths, even when it is against your own best interest
- When lending money to others, don't charge interest
- Do not accept a bribe against an innocent person

The Protagonist's Upward/Downward Spiral for Testing Character

One additional model of obstacles places the protagonist in a crucible and shows what he can withstand before he either spirals downward or obtains a higher level in character. Both impact the world around the protagonist.

The Big Moment

By now you should have a number of ideas for crafting obstacles that your characters can face and strive to overcome. The biggest obstacle of all will be the climax or the climactic moment.

Building up to that big moment when your story reaches the climax is the payoff for your readers. Along with the climax, there should be other moments when your readers think, "This was worth the price of admission." These are critical story moments.

Exploring Ideas:

1. What do you visualize being the biggest moment of the story?
2. What other memorable moments might be in your story?

HISTORICAL TIMELINE— BUILDING A BACKGROUND

The historical events in the story can also be called a background or a backdrop for your story. Historical details can help formulate ideas and have an impact on your characters, even if the historical event is not part of your story. The events can happen before or after or during the story, or be something from the past that sets in motion a current event in your story. This is another way to add richness to your story and place it in a context that will set the tone for your reader.

Give some thought to what the historical context for your story might be: Is it a date or a time period? Maybe an event in the story is about something cultural or societal? By linking your story to something happening or that has happened that impacts people's lives, feelings, attitudes, culture, or society, you can use those events to strengthen your ideas and have material that will feed the story.

You can also portray something topical by relating it through a story in a different timeframe. Such as a story about the Vietnam War or World War II or a war between aliens in a futuristic society might highlight a concern and make a statement about the war in Afghanistan or Iraq or as of yet undetermined wars. *The Crucible*, by Arthur Miller, a play about the Salem Witch Trials, was inspired by the McCarthy era and the House of Un-American Activities, which conducted a witch hunt for anyone who might have at some point in their lives showed any interest in or sympathy or whiff of communist leanings. Miller himself had been targeted in the investigation.

A backdrop can also be an issue or a political or social statement such as abortion or corruption in politics, or perhaps your statement on the environment and global warming. Maybe you want to explore the degradation of society or the unique ways one society can contribute to the overall good. Perhaps your issue is how technology is dehumanizing people or how it is integrating people through the ability of instant communication.

The following table on pages 74–75 is an exercise to help you think about what events might influence your story and using historical events to build story ideas. In Stage 2 we will look at how those events can be integrated into the structure of your story. There is a book called *The Timetables of History*, by Bernard Grun, which I find invaluable for looking up by year the important events and discoveries in history, politics, literature, art, music, science, religion, and daily life, along with other topics.

Pick either the years or the categories that might impact your story and that pertain to the main character's interests and then chart them in a similar way as the example on page 74–75.

Exploring Ideas:

1. What background or backdrop might enhance your story?
2. Would it be organic to the plot?

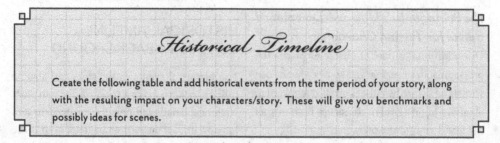

Historical Timeline

Create the following table and add historical events from the time period of your story, along with the resulting impact on your characters/story. These will give you benchmarks and possibly ideas for scenes.

CATEGORY OF WORLD EVENTS	SIGNIFICANT EVENTS	IMPACT
MUSIC	1969—Woodstock New York	His parents met and he was conceived. His mother never saw his father again.
HISTORY	September 11, 2001, 9/11—Terrorist attacks on the United States	Protagonist escapes towers, but wife is trapped and dies when the towers come down.
ART	2007—books found that show extent of Nazi art theft	His grandfather was a German soldier with a locked trunk in his attic.

By the way, I sometimes do this on an Excel spreadsheet and have hundreds of events, although I suggest starting with just a few. Don't get carried away by research until you need it.

Exploring Ideas:

Now that you've worked on developing some ideas, take a few minutes to answer the following questions.

1. Why do you find the work interesting from a writing perspective? (Think about your characters, the setting, concepts such as magical realism, etc.)
2. What words would you use to describe setting, description, narration, exposition, or include in dialogue? Find terms and adjectives to describe the quality you want in the language and dialogue. Are the words intellectual, dark, earthy, exotic, silly?
3. Whose story is this? Who is the main character or protagonist whose wants and needs cause the events of the story?
4. Often the theme is carried by the protagonist—she is unaware of some truth at the outset of the tale, but the rigors of the story force her into a new awareness, often at the moment of greatest stress. Can the theme be distilled down to the simplest possible statement or stated in a word? For example, what is the story about: trust, greed, responsibility, self-acceptance, generosity? Is there a word that comes to your mind to describe your story?

GENRE, FORMAT, AND FORM

Different formats and different genres have different rules and techniques. The sooner you understand which one you are writing in, the less work you will have to do later to adapt.

However, while you are in Stage 1 you are still forming ideas, and you can still refine or change either of these.

Genre

Deciding on the genre can be a little more difficult unless you know you are writing horror or sci-fi or fantasy or a historical work. Much of the time we start with wanting to write a story the whole world will read, and then we are all over the map with our ideas. As you go through the "Tools" at the end of this chapter and in each stage, you should clarify and refine your work to a more specific market. Writing to a specific market, whether that is a market of one or of millions, helps you focus. What genre do you like to read or prefer to watch? That will have already given you insights into the conventions of telling a story in that genre. However, it may not be the genre that is your best voice. Is your voice comedic or dramatic or cynical? This, too, will help you define your genre. You may find that you have a voice or a style or type of story that creates a whole new genre. That's okay, too. What are its conventions this story will initiate?

Format

I worked with C.B. Shiepe, the author of *Cliff Falls,* through that story's development. He had started before he met me with an idea for a TV series; then I was his editor through a made-for-TV-movie, a screenplay, and finally a novel. *Cliff Falls* lends itself to several formats. What surprised him was that he found the novel form the most satisfying because the length of that format allowed him time to go more in-depth into his characters.

Some stories are more cinematic, some more stage oriented, and some more descriptive. Some are better told succinctly in short stories or short films or ten-minute plays. The format you choose will help you formulate ideas.

What's the Best Storytelling Form?

There are so many forms of storytelling, from songwriting to novels to plays to screenplays. There's poetry and short stories and short short stories and teleplays. There's audio forms and video forms and monologues and ghost stories around the campfire and telling family-and-friend stories at reunions and fish stories and swapping lies over a beer. And then there are all the ways to tell stories on the Internet: websites, podcasts, blogs, videos, and technology not yet developed.

Some people, who never put a word on paper, are just storytellers at heart. I have read stories by mediocre to awful writers—in the grammatical sense—who had an incredible voice that held your attention in spite of their poor grammar and punctuation. That should tell you something about how important voice is. Voice is the way you tell a story, your unique way of expressing yourself both verbally and in writing. A good storytelling voice engages the reader or listener. And some writers are better at storytelling in one format versus another.

I'm often asked what my favorite format for writing is. I usually respond that it is whatever form I am writing in. I write in all forms, even some poetry, although I am by no means a poet. I often visualize and sometimes write my stories in more than one format. Many years ago I wrote a short story called "The Hero" about soldiers in Vietnam. In graduate school I rewrote it as a play, and when my friend Kevin Sizemore, an actor and producer read it, he said, "We are going to film this." I then rewrote it in a more contemporary setting occurring in Afghanistan as a short film. It was produced as a thirty-seven-minute film, and the director Shawn Fornari later did a fifteen-minute cut with his version of the story. Eventually I wrote a full-length version of the screenplay.

Some stories are best told in a particular format and do not lend themselves well to another form; other stories are so strong or so visual they can be adapted to tell in any format, but each format must rely on the strength of that media to best tell the story. In a novel you may choose to disclose an underlying thought, but in a screenplay you have to show that underlying thought through the character's behavior, images, and by using metaphors. The viewing audience can't hear what your character is thinking unless you use a narrator—a choice that should be created carefully—so the writer has to figure out how to show what cannot be explained. Sometimes you can tell the underlying thought in dialogue, but you must not insult the reader's intelligence in doing so—and if you have shown it, you don't need to tell it. On the other hand, the reading audience can't see anything but words, and sometimes illustrations or pictures, so the writer has to draw verbal images.

This book is about the written form of writing, including the written play and screenplay. All good stories, no matter how they are told, have structure and essential storytelling elements, which is what we are going to focus on—how to tell, or better yet, show—a good story. You should know something about the main storytelling formats before you choose which is the best format for your story.

The Novel

Novels have to show their story through words. Novels can be any length, can cover any genre, can be wordy or lean. A novelist paints a picture by tapping into all of your emotions and senses through words. A novel gives details, takes us into the mind and heart of a character and a scene in the way only words can describe. A good novelist knows which details reveal and which obfuscate the picture being created. Dialogue has to be sharp and interesting and include who is speaking because it isn't usually obvious. Even when the dialogue is distinctive and goes back and forth between only two people, it's easy to get lost trying to figure out who is speaking without some tags of *he said, she said*, or *Mary responded*.

A novel can be told from many points of view (POV) and go into the thoughts and emotions of its characters, giving insights and explaining events. The only images a novel creates are the ones it stimulates inside the reader's imagination. The novelist elaborates details. The setting and background for a novel can be as extravagant or as simple as your story demands. There isn't a budget concern for words other than what it costs to print them.

Characteristics of a Novel:

- Written in continuous paragraphs with chapter breaks
- Lots of exposition with description, narrative, and dialogue
- Italics sometimes indicate a character's thought or a letter or journal writing
- Formatted into chapters and sometimes into "parts" or "books"
- Less white space on the page
- Manuscripts are generally double-spaced and use Courier, Times Roman, or another plain font

The Short Story

A short story is told in a few pages and is usually more than five hundred words up to around twenty-thousand words. Less than five hundred words is considered a short short, and there are even fifty-word short stories. While a short story has similar characteristics to a novel, it does not contain as many characters and usually focuses on one or two. The setting is usually one or a very few places. The more time devoted to creating settings and characters, the longer the short story becomes. The end of the short story is usually something poignant or at least pointed, something that sums up the whole of what the story was about and what the key takeaway is. Sometimes the ending is a clever moral to the story. Short stories usually focus on one major theme and develop it through the setting and eyes and experiences of the main character. Again, there are no story budget considerations in a short story, so the story can cover what might be too expensive to film.

Characteristics of a Short Story:

- Written much like a novel
- Short stories are usually published in magazines, literary journals, anthologies, and short story collections in books
- Double spaced and use Courier, Times Roman, or another plain font

A Word of Caution

Don't overwrite your short story. If you are writing short stories, short plays, or short films, you will find the story map to be helpful as well as the 7 Stages. However, if you answer all the questions and do all the exercises, your short work will no longer be short. You will want to be selective in which questions you answer. Focus on the Story Map and make sure the elements are in place.

The Vignette

The original meaning of a vignette was something akin to a decorative border or ornament that seems to be unending; it also means a photograph or illustration that doesn't have a border, but rather fades out, according to Merriam-Webster's online dictionary. A vignette in literary terms is not a story, as it is not complete in and of itself and does not contain a plot. A vignette can be a sketch from the story or a moment in a story, such as something poignant about a character that describes the character or something from the character's life, but does not contain the plot of what is happening to the character. A vignette might be a meaningful moment from a story that would be interesting to read but does not give away the story. A tag, in which the loose ends of the story is tied up, or something meaningful has been stated, might be a vignette. A vignette says something in a way that gives us pause or helps us understand the characters or perhaps even the story.

Slice-of-Life

A slice-of-life is also not a complete story, but more of a sketch or reliving of a moment that rings true about life. Its focus is on a moment in a drama or a life and not the events prior or after. It can be a true moment out of life. Slice-of-life writing has a point or a purpose or a reason for telling something about an event and generally ends with something salient that the writer believes may be applied to life in general or may illustrate the writer's perspective on life.

The Play

A play is about dialogue, about characters interacting with each other (sometimes with the audience) verbally on a stage under the proscenium arch. In formatting plays, the dialogue runs across the page from margin to margin with the characters' names in a column down the center of the page over the dialogue. The action or description is in a wider column also down the center. (Plays that are published for reading are formatted differently to save space and pages.) Both screenplays and plays are written in present tense.

The playwright, unlike the screenwriter, is given far more visibility, and, in fact, it is considered wrong to change even a word of a play without the playwright's permission, although a director's vision of a play's setting can be changed. For example, I once saw one of Shakespeare's plays reset to the Civil War era and another one to ancient Greece. Reframing popular plays into a more contemporary or avant-garde setting is common and gives the story a new context. While playwrights' rights are respected, playwrights usually make less money unless they are very successful.

Like novels and short stories, plays can be any length, from very short to very long. There are famous plays that last for four hours. Although plays have a setting, the key to a good play is great dialogue. While there is movement in a play, sometimes singing and dancing or even raucous action, there isn't nearly as much movement and action as there may be in a screenplay. The setting just does not allow for it. Waiting for scene changes is boring to the audience and diminishes the impact of the play. Plays used to be three acts, then two, with the intermission being set at the time for a major set change. Plays are often one act now, and there are no scene changes, or they occur through lighting or very brief interludes, such as lights going dark briefly then coming back up right away.

In a play there is something called the "fourth wall" through which viewers watch the action. If you break the fourth wall you remind your audience they are in an auditorium watching a play, although there are some plays in which the audience may be actively engaged. Watching a play is a bit like being a Peeping Tom (or a voyeur) engrossed in what your neighbor is saying and doing. There is nothing quite like watching good live performances.

Plays are somewhat akin to poetry. In fact, at one time plays were written in more of a poetic form—think Shakespeare—with beautiful lines and metaphorical images that told the story, often on bare stages without set designs. Plays also have a connection to debate and oratory—think Aristotle—regarding the power of the actor to engage and persuade the listener that all of this is real and happening. The metaphor and significant language continues to be crucial in plays.

Unless you are on Broadway, or certain high-budget stages, consideration of the expense to produce a play is even more important than in a screenplay. It is always a struggle to break even in the theatre, much less make money. Plays should have minimal sets or sets that are not expensive to create. There should be only a few characters, less than six, and some theaters want even fewer, unless you are writing a musical. When writing plays, consider that everything you write will cost money that may not be recoverable, so focus the story on the dialogue and not on the set and costumes. Also, be aware of the need to function in tighter spaces.

Characteristics of a Play:

- Strong dialogue
- Little exposition, but written in present tense
- Sets, if existent, constructed as inexpensively as possible
- Use of lighting and sound to create setting and enhance ambience
- More white space on the page
- Some screenplay software has formatting for plays that playwrights use; or tabs in your word-processing program can be used; I created my own play-writing form using macros
- Vivid costumes and lots of makeup so the artists' features and emotions can be seen
- All scenes must be in one setting or it must be easy to break down sets to account for space and time constraints
- Use Courier, Times Roman, or other plain font

There is some variation in play formatting. Below is a sample page from the manuscript for *Tea*, by playwright Velina Hasu Houston, which has received awards and is performed on stages all over the world.

ATSUKO

Maybe she wanted too much.

HIMIKO

I never asked for anything. Except soy sauce and good rice. And dreams ... for Mieko.

> HIMIKO glows with love for her child and seems to see her as a tot. She beckons to her.

HIMIKO

Mieko-chan! My little girl!

> HIMIKO exits as if chasing "Mieko."

ATSUKO

Teruko, I saw your daughter last week.
> (a compliment)

She looks Japanese. That's nice. Too bad she isn't friends with my girl. My girl's always with Setsuko-san's daughter. Have you seen her? Looks Indonesian, not Japanese at all. Shame, ne.

TERUKO

But Setsuko's daughter is the only one who cooks Japanese food. My daughter likes hamburger sandwich and yellow-haired boys.

ATSUKO

My daughter always goes to Setsuko-san's house. I've never been invited.

TERUKO

Setsuko likes her privacy.

ATSUKO

She invited you to tea.

TERUKO

Well, if you're not willing to be genuine with her, how can you share the honor of tea together?

ATSUKO

She invited Himiko, too!

(4.5) *An excerpt from Velina Hasu Houston's* Tea *[Published by Dramatists Play Service, Smith & Krause,*
Vintage Books, University of Massachusetts Press, Alexander Street Press, used by permission]

The Screenplay

A screenplay is all about images. Screenwriting uses dialogue to express only what must be spoken while painting between the lines clear, crisp images with as few written details as possible, all in present tense and all in a unique voice that reinforces the tone of the story. The setting, the clothes, the characters are all images that show the story. However, the screenplay has a much more difficult time revealing background information or insights or the characters' thoughts. Information has to be revealed through a look, through an image that conveys a meaning, i.e. a metaphor, or through what the characters say.

Movie goers often complain that the films adapted from books are not nearly as good as the book or that the movie was nothing like the book. A movie has to convey in 90–120 minutes (give or take) what a book can do in hundreds of pages, which translates to hours of reading. The screenwriter has to discern which moments in the book are the ones that reveal what the author was saying, after interpreting what the author was saying. The screenwriter can't resort to long, languorous passages that detail every thought, every twist and turn that the novel explored. There isn't time.

What the screenplay does is show what the story looks like by using images and metaphors and strong dialogue. It paints a picture for us. It shows us something about life. But again, the screenwriter gives us only the details that we need to understand the story. In the screenplay the screenwriter must leave room for collaboration and input from others. The screenwriter shouldn't tell the director how to direct the movie or the director of photography (DP or cinematographer) how to shoot the camera or the set designer or costume designer how to design. Instead, the screenwriter gives the essence of the details, through action shots telling only those details that are important to the story or to give the other collaborators cues on what he is thinking and seeing. There have to be enough details to make the story visual for readers before it ever gets to the screen, but not full of details that slow down the images or the action. Where a novel can spend pages or even chapters on a scene, a screenwriter must keep things brief and moving.

Screenplays are also about action (not to be confused with action movies). Even the shout-out to begin a scene is usually *action*. The images move, the people move, the scene changes frequently from inside to outside and back. The images are an important aspect of developing the story. Because the image in a screenplay is important and dialogue, while crucial, is secondary, the action shots run across the page from margin to margin, while the character name and dialogue run down a center column.

Once written, the screenplay becomes a collaborative effort, and often without the writer's additional input unless a scene rewrite is needed, which the original screenwriter may or may not be asked to do. I have heard screenplays called blueprints, which I find a bit insulting, but in the movie business the actors and the director are the key players. The screenwriter, unless a major name or an auteur (who is usually the writer and director and pretty much the sole creator of a film), takes a backseat and watches someone else turn the vision into what they see, not necessarily what the writer sees. Screenwriters are sometimes not even invited and sometimes not even allowed on the set so that they do not interfere with the process.

When writing your story as a screenplay, unless you are going to be directing, producing, or in some way instrumental in the filmmaking, you have to think about leaving room for the director to include her insights, the actor's interpretation, the cinematographer's vision, the set designer's, and the lighting and sound director's input. You also have to consider budget. If you are an unknown, you probably won't sell a screenplay that needs a hundred-million-dollar budget, so don't write one. Use common sense to create scenes that can be shot on a low budget, maybe even that you can shoot yourself with a small crew for the Internet. If the producer or studio decides to upgrade your film, that's great, but you haven't lost a deal because the cost to produce it was more than an interested producer could finance.

Samples of screenplays can be found on the Internet on a variety of websites. Make sure you note the difference between the screenplay, the shooting script, and the transcript. The first is a draft written by the screenwriter, the second has been changed to prepare the script for actually shooting the film and may not be as the screenwriter wrote it, and the third one is what someone typed for subtitles from the dialogue after the movie has been completed and is ready for distribution.

Characteristics of a Screenplay:

- Usually typed into screenwriting software such as Final Draft or Movie Magic or one of the other programs available (Celtx is a free online screenwriting program my students often use)
- Written in lines which are formatted narrower or wider according to their purpose
- More white space on the page than for a novel
- Little exposition and written in present tense
- Brief lines of sharp, interesting dialogue that feed the action and inform readers about the character
- Formatted into scenes; new scenes are created whenever the setting or time changes
- The images or shots are explained simply
- Use Courier as the font

Below is a sample page from the screenplay *We Were Soldiers*, written by Randall Wallace, which is based on a true story. This sample has numbers on either side that indicate the scene number. Scenes are usually numbered when the screenplay is ready to go into production, so do not add them to your draft.

152   EXT. NEAR THE CREEK BED — DAWN   152
        Moore and his men reach a position by the creek bed; and then

        Moore stops, and listens.

                            NADAL
                    What is it, Sir?

                            MOORE
                    It's dead quiet. Nothing's wrong
                    ... except that nothing's wrong.

                            OUELLETTE
                    Maybe they've had enough.

                            MOORE
                    They've walked through machine gun fire,
                    artillery, and napalm. They're not gonna
                    quit now.

        He takes his radio, and calls Dillon at the Command Post.

                            MOORE (cont'd)
                    Matt, have all companies send recon
                    patrols forward of their positions.

153   EXT. AMERICAN PERIMETER - NEAR TREE LINE — DAWN   153

        Scouting parties of Americans, three or four men in each
        party, begin to move forward carefully, through the tall
        grass and the trees ... Geoghegan leads one group. We follow
        Geoghegan's group, who have moved ahead forty yards when--

        HUNDREDS OF NORTH VIETNAMESE, their bodies camouflaged with
        grass and brush so that they blend right into the landscape,
        rise up from the earth and begin firing. Geoghegan and his
        men fall to the ground and start spraying fire from their
        M-16's; Geoghegan shouts into the radio--

                            GEOGHEGAN
                    We have enemy attack! In force!

        Geoghegan's men and the other recon platoons are fighting for
        their lives ...

        The Americans still dug in on the perimeter lay down a stream
        of fire, and artillery falls; all hell breaks loose.

154   EXT. AMERICAN PERIMETER - AT THE CREEKBED - DAWN   154

        North Vietnamese boil up the same way attacking the creekbed,
        trying to overrun the landing zone from that direction too.

(4.6) *Sample page from the book* We Were Soldiers: The Screenplay, *by Randall Wallace*

[Published by Wheelhouse Books, 2002, used by permission].

The Teleplay or Television Script

Television scripts are more formulaic and written around a few key characters and their careers or lifestyles or a specific scenario that is repeated week after week with different plots. The story has to work within a time slot for a thirty- or sixty-minute show but will actually be shorter to allow for commercials. The act lengths are written to take commercials breaks into consideration and to keep the audience interested so they will stay tuned through the interruption.

Television tends to feel more immediate, as though it is happening in front of you. Some television shows are more like plays in that they take place on a stage with basically one or two sets, sometimes three. Some are more like movies since they have indoor and outdoor shots and include more actors. Television shows are shot with differing numbers of cameras, depending on the basic set for the show. Each series has what it calls the story bible that outlines information about the characters, the series, the background, the direction the story will take, important plot points throughout the season or series.

There is also more collaboration in writing for television, and the writers are usually called executive producers or producers and are considered much more important to the television series than sometimes screenwriters are considered to screenplays. Writers interested in television are encouraged to write spec scripts for popular series to show that they understand the series and characters and can develop interesting plots within the show's parameters. A miniscule percentage of these spec scripts sell. Producers generally want to read specs for current shows, but not necessarily their own show. Mostly, spec scripts are used to show the writer's talent and sometimes get the writer a job on another or a new series or are used as a sample to get an agent.

There are many entrance barriers to selling television scripts, and it is very difficult to break into television writing unless you start in a much lower position—often that means at the level of an internship for little or no pay—and working your way up. Unless given to them by an agent, many executive producers and actors will not read an unsolicited script for fear of lawsuits if the show is already working on something similar. An unsold spec script cannot be submitted as anything but a sample of your work. Therefore, realize the time you spend on a spec television script may only be useful as a way of learning the business or getting noticed.

Characteristics of a Teleplay or Television Script:

- Formatting is similar to screenplays, but each series has an individual style
- Deadlines are very short, and writers must be able to work under pressure to turn stories around quickly for a weekly series
- Dialogue is key, especially in shows with one or two sets
- One writer may be responsible for the basic story; however many lines (dialogue) are polished around a writer's table
- Sometimes experts are brought in to punch up jokes
- You often have to know someone to break into television
- Because of the numerous channels now available, television is a bit more open to newcomers; however, many of these are reality shows with a minimal need for writers

STFBEye 3-13 Endings and Beginnings Yellow Shooting 01/24/05 17.

6   CONTINUED: (2)   6

                        SUE
                (**SIGNING**; SUBTITLES)
             Next time will be better.

Levi looks to Sue as if to say 'good job.'

7   INT. BULLPEN — MORNING (DAY 2)   7

Sue and Lucy walk into the Bullpen, it's first thing in the
morning. They are met by Myles who is crossing to his desk.
Bobby, Jack and Tara are also already there.

                     MYLES
             Morning, Thomas. I understand you're think-
             ing about taking a new job.

Sue is blown away that he knows. She looks at Lucy, who's
equally surprised as are Bobby, Tara and Jack, who all stop
in their tracks. Did they hear right?

                     LUCY
             He didn't hear it from me.
               (a thought hits her)
             Do you have our place bugged?

                     MYLES
             So, it's true.

Lucy gives him a look.

                     LUCY
             You're not denying you have our place bugged.

                     MYLES
             Relax — I heard it from Candy who works in
             transfers. She's got designs on me. Thinks I'd
             be quite a catch — can't say she's wrong.

                     LUCY
             I want a number. I'm calling her and if she
             denies telling you, the de-buggers will be
             at our apartment this afternoon.

Sue is a bit uncomfortable that it came out like this. She
looks at Jack and then back to Myles.

                     SUE
             (trying to downplay it)
             I was approached about an opportunity to be
             the counter terrorism senior investigative
             analyst -
               (a beat)
             In the New York field office.

                                  (CONTINUED)

(4.7) Sample page from TV shooting script "Sue Thomas F.B.Eye," Written by Dave Alan Johnson
and Gary R. Johnson, [Air Date May 22, 2005 on PAX TV, used by permission].

New Media

The Internet and digital media, as well as technological advances in filming, provide amazing new opportunities for writers in the written, verbal, and visual formats. No one has completely figured it out, and the field is wide open. Some people are even finding financial success with writing and producing on the Internet. If nothing else, it gives the writer the opportunity to post his work for others to access.

It was recently suggested to me that since new media is easy to use and post to, there is an abundance of crap. I assert there was already an abundance of crap. Work that is good has the opportunity of going viral—being spread across the Internet by an audience who likes the material. The same is true for bad material, if there is a group who likes it. But at least more of the publishing and the producing can actually be done by the writer with more control over the content, and the writer can search out her own audience with less reliance on traditional publishers and distributors. And this can all be done affordably.

One new form of filmmaking is 3-D movies. Although 3-D has been around for decades, with recent advances in digital and film technology, it is a more feasible process. Televisions that show 3-D are now available. I recently discussed with someone training in this field the need for a new formatting style because 3-D has more visual dimensions. The style needs to address the visual opportunities in a manner that writers and directors can be on the same "dimensional" page. By the time this book is published, a new style may already be adopted.

Characteristics of New Media:

- There are none; create your own
- Check out the various blog sites, Facebook, Twitter, podcasts, YouTube and Vimeo, etc. for ways to publish
- Find consumer audio and camera equipment that is simple to operate to create your own videos; most of this can be fairly inexpensive for Internet content
- Research domain hosts for starting your own website
- Be innovative

Exploring Ideas:

1. Write a page in each of the different formats using some of the ideas you have developed to familiarize yourself with these forms. Sometimes it turns out you will prefer a different format than you expected.
2. Which story format will you use?
3. Which genre will you use?

Learning Techniques From Successful Writers

The following exercises will help you examine the techniques successful authors use in writing screenplays and novels.

Learning to Write Screenplays Exercise

There are several sites on the Internet that contain full screenplays. For this exercise, use the actual draft of a screenplay and *not* the shooting script or the movie transcription.

Read the first five pages. Go through the pages and find the information requested below.

- Note how the screenplay starts.
- What is the hook, and how is it written?
- Find examples of how characters are introduced and described.
- Find examples of how the setting is described.
- Find examples of the dialogue.

TOOLS TO DEVELOP YOUR WRITING SKILLS

The following questions will help you strengthen your internal compass. They have been developed to focus and clarify goals and agendas, strengthen choices, and create tension in the process of structuring your story. Remember, you are reading this book to help you hone your skills as a writer and to develop your writing compass. The following pages contain the tools to help you increase your knowledge about your story with questions and concepts for you to think about and answer.

At the end of every stage you should return to these pages and answer these questions. The answers should reflect what you have learned about your story and where you are in the story's development. This will help you focus on exactly what the story is that you want to tell and help you create more story-specific ideas.

This is not a test. Your answers may not be fully formed yet. The goal is to stimulate your analytical process and train it to become more creative. If you don't know an answer, move on—give the analytical side of your brain a chance to analyze the problem and then come back to the question later.

As you answer these questions, give consideration to two levels of writing. One is the internal: the underlying thoughts and motives behind the character's actions and events. The other is how you show this in vivid details and action—as opposed to "telling" what you are thinking. We will discuss showing and telling, motivation or cause and effect, and conflict in more detail in Stage 2.

Do I Need to Do This Section?

Sitting down to write is sometimes very hard. Answering myriad questions that make you stop to analyze and evaluate can feel like schoolwork. However, this stage will progress your writing to a new level. Don't shortchange yourself or the story you want to tell.

If you commit to this process, three things will come from doing these exercises: You will find your internal compass, which will help you to better understand the story you want to write; you will form new ideas that develop and enrich your story; and you will learn to tell a stronger story with fewer flaws—or perhaps without any—and grow as a storyteller.

How Much Do I Need to Write?

Keep your answers to a comfortable length. I have students who write phrases and students who write paragraphs. How much you write is not as important as the context of what you say and whether you are learning something new about your story or resolving a story problem. If you are just phoning in your answers, then you will not get the full benefit of the question. However, this is free-form; don't worry about grammar or punctuation. Sometimes a brief answer is all it takes to start the creative process.

Developing Your Story's Ideals

The following concepts should be returned to at the end of each stage to help you first define your ideals for writing the story, then to help you refine those ideals. In each stage your answers will become stronger, more focused, and more succinct. Although this may feel repetitive, the purpose is to help you look at your story from different angles and perspectives, giving a broader view of the big picture you may not have considered before. And, again, answering these questions will help you find your *writer's compass*.

What Is Your Story Really About?

Have you identified what you are really writing about? Are you beginning to understand what you want to say about a certain subject or issue? You may still be working this out, and that's fine. Your concepts will become clearer to you as you answer more questions and develop your ideas and your characters.

Exploring Ideas:

1. What is the story you want to tell?
2. Where is it coming from inside you?
3. At this point, what do you know or believe that your story is about?
4. Who are the protagonist and antagonist you are going to give voice to?

Theme

A theme conveys a concept. It is the over arching message you want your story to convey to your audience. It can start as one word, but it should expand into a phrase of five to ten words to clarify the theme as it applies to your story. You do not have to state your theme in a complete sentence. For example, the theme for the concept of love could develop into "love is the greatest force on Earth," used in a story about how the impact of one person's love stopped a crisis or changed a community, or turned the heart of a murderer. There are unlimited ideas that could use this theme.

By the way, sometimes the writer's theme doesn't come across clearly, and the reader is left unsure what they are supposed to take away from the story. At other times the theme may be very broad, or there may be multiple themes, and each reader takes something different away from the story, even from what the writer originally intended. Good stories have much to offer a reader and can impact a wide audience. Literary criticism is a major discipline because of people seeking to better understand the meaning at each level of great stories. The key is that your story should be written well enough that each audience member can find meaning in reading or watching it.

Many verbs can be turned into a concept and developed into a story theme.

Exploring Ideas:

1. What one word is a concept that could be developed into a theme for your story?
2. As you understand the story at this point, what do you think the theme or themes might be?
3. Write a short phrase that represents that theme as succinctly as possible.

Universal or Spiritual Theme

I like the term *spiritual* because I often use strong religious concepts or values as a theme, but these are generally also *universal* values. This theme is another perspective on what you are trying to say, your view of life, humanity, the world, your philosophy. This theme is also expressed as a phrase of five to ten words that consider the over arching message you want to convey. Using the above theme, my universal theme might further define "love is the greatest force on Earth" to "love thy neighbor as thyself." Now I've tweaked my story to be even more focused as I explore who that neighbor is and how the force of love made a difference.

No, you do not need a theme plus a universal or spiritual theme. I define both in my stories because that helps me focus my ideas, but it also lends a secondary, or deeper, level of meaning to my story. And, again, it helps me see things from different perspectives.

Exploring Ideas:

1. Do you have a universal theme for your story?
2. What is the over arching universal theme of your story?
3. What do you want to say about life? Your philosophy? The world?
4. What is the larger concept about the human condition you want to convey or explore?

Premise

In storytelling many people use theme and premise interchangeably, but I see them as different. A theme is what you are trying to say, a premise is what you believe to be true or false and want to prove. When writing an argument or forming a debate or trying to prove a point, we generally form a premise, a logical argument. If this is true, and this is true, then this must be true. I have adapted the idea of constructing a premise for storytelling. Continuing the example from above: If love is the greatest force on Earth, and if I love my neighbor as myself, then I can influence my neighbor through love. You can think of the formula as:

concept + action = outcome

If this is true (concept), and I do this (action), then this will happen (outcome). Now you know more about what you must accomplish in your story for people to accept your premise as valid.

Another way of looking at this model for the premise is if this is true (or false), then this follows, and this is the outcome:

true + true = true

false + false = false

Your premise for this type of formula would be something like: *Egotism is self-obsession; self-obsession stems from inadequate love; therefore love overcomes self-obsession.* The premise of your story would be to prove that love overcomes being self-absorbed, and that could even be more refined by either others' love for the "self" or the "self's" love for others.

Exploring Ideas:

1. What is the premise of your story? Identify the basic truth you want to prove to your audience and begin working on the formula for a premise.

Story Background

We discussed the story background earlier. A background can be an integral part of the story or more of a backdrop or setting. It can involve actual events or allude to the influence of actual events.

Exploring Ideas:

1. What is the background for this story?
2. Does it enhance the story or overpower it?

Story Line Point

The above concepts are somewhat ethereal ideals, whereas the story line point is the actual point of this story, the focused event you want to talk about. In other words, what is the goal the characters are striving to obtain that makes the story line point? To continue with the above ideas, *Jeff must overcome his racial biases and learn to love his neighbor to change his community.*

Exploring Ideas:

1. What is the actual point of the story you are writing?
2. What specific agenda will the characters need to get the above concepts across?

What is the Story/Dramatic Question of This Work?

The story question is the overriding dilemma that the character must resolve. The question the reader wants answered is "How are they going to do it?" Generally I correlate the story question with the story itself so that it embodies what I am writing about, as I did in the story line point. Can Jeff stop the violence in his community by befriending his neighbor? The word *befriending* is ambiguous, and in a later stage I would refine this to something more story specific.

This will be one of your biggest scenes and will tell the reader whether the payoff was worth the time they spent reading or watching your story, and will determine whether they will want to read or watch the next one.

You will want to give the above concepts much thought and continue to refine them. You will want to consider all of your choices and options and change and refocus the answers as the story evolves and develops. Don't shortchange your reader by minimizing the importance of the dramatic question. Many dramatic questions begin with the idea of "What if ... ?" Below are examples of dramatic questions:

- In the play *Trifles*, by Susan Glaspell: "Will the clues be found to convict the wife?" Or "As a man, can the prosecutor read the clues to solve the murder?"
- In most romantic comedies it is some variation of "Will the couple find true love together?" Because some genres have a general dramatic question, the actual dramatic question for your story should be more specific.
- In *Pride and Prejudice*, by Jane Austen; "What if you needed to marry off five daughters in a class-based society?" Or "How does a woman provide for her future in a society with limited options for women?"

Let me just say that these are my interpretations, not necessarily the ones a literary critic would suggest. We all interpret stories in our own way and focus on different elements the author wrote.

Exploring Ideas:

1. What is the story question or dramatic question this story will ask and answer? Jot down some possible ideas for a dramatic question that encompasses your complete story. Include dynamic specifics.
2. From what you know about the story at this point, do you have any ideas for how the dramatic question will be answered?

Log Line

In twenty-five words or fewer, write an active sentence in your story's words that tells the over arching story. There is not a formula for a log line other than to write it in a dynamic way that will compel a reader to want to know more. The story should indicate the situation and the complication. You might use the following sentence order: a description of the protagonist, the protagonist's function, the protagonist's conflict and with whom (the antagonist). "As a racist, Jeff fuels his neighbor Asaad's hatred until Rocky, a powerful drug lord, moves into the community, and Jeff and Asaad must band together to save the community." This came out to thirty words, and is too wordy. Let's condense it. "A racist, Jeff, fuels his neighbor Asaad's hatred until a powerful drug cartel arrives, forcing Jeff and Asaad to band together to save their neighborhood." The more concise, the easier to read, and the stronger the log line.

The above examples I created as I wrote this section to show you how ideas progress. If I wrote this story and continued developing these examples, by the time the work gets to Stage 7, they may have evolved and changed, but they would be refined, focused, clear, and stronger, as would the story.

Samples of log lines might be:

- *Rain Man:* After his father's death, Charlie discovers an autistic brother he didn't know existed inherits everything; Charlie kidnaps his brother to get control of the money.
- *Beauty and the Beast:* The Beast holds a beautiful woman hostage, hoping she will fall in love with him to break the spell that made him a beast.

Exploring Ideas:

1. In twenty-five words or fewer, write a first draft of your story's log line.

One-Paragraph Synopsis

At the end of each stage you will be requested to write a brief synopsis for your story, which will increase both in length and in specificity. This serves the purpose of both helping you refine and understand your story, and preparing the best possible synopsis you can for use in submitting your completed story.

Exploring Ideas:

1. By now you probably have enough ideas to put together a one-paragraph synopsis of your story that shows the concept you plan to develop. You will want this paragraph to be a little more refined and more grammatically correct than those you've written up until now. Use dynamic and active, not passive, language. Also, make the paragraph as tight as possible; try not to ramble, but rather be succinct.

MAPPING THE STORY

Now that you have worked through Stage 1, you should have a pile of index cards or pages of ideas in a notebook or computer file. Read through your material and then use the story map on page 94 as an example to help create your own story map. Place the story elements you have ideas for on the map. Don't worry if you haven't figured everything out. This map will show you how far you've come in developing your story, what you don't know yet, and the elements that may be weak in your story. The analytical side of your brain will get busy working on solutions.

I suggest that you create a fresh map after each stage and detail it with what you have learned about your story. By starting fresh you won't hold on to old ideas when your new ones may be better and stronger. If the old ones turn out to be better, you can always go back and reclaim them.

Below is another example of a story map from the story of Linda, the widow whose neighborhood was destroyed by a flood (see page 47).

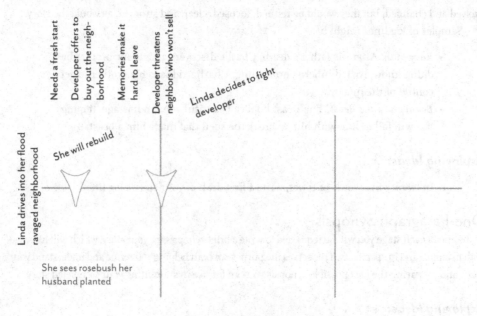

(4.8) *Example of Linda's Story Map*

As you can see, only the *Beginning* has details, and a second plot point has been added. The additional elements, such as the obstacles, climax, and falling action, have not been developed. However, there is the beginning of a story here that could be developed further. If you were mapping this story you might choose other ideas, or you might choose that these details represent different elements. It's your story; do it your way.

Exploring Ideas:

1. Do you have a complete story?
2. Can you feel the tension in the story?
3. Are the elements shown in a dynamic way that effectively expresses this story?
4. Where are the holes?
5. Which ideas are weak?

Putting the Process Into Practice Exercise

By now you should have some ideas for a story, either already in your quiver, or new ideas from doing the exercises on the previous pages. Using the process from before, do the following exercise. Remember, you probably don't have a complete story, so expect holes and gaps.

1. Place your ideas on the story map.
2. On index cards or pieces of paper, write any ideas that occurred to you as you diagrammed the map, one idea on each card. Add any details for obstacles, setting, dialogue, characterization, etc., as you think of them. Don't worry about whether they are good or bad or incomplete.
3. Organize and reorganize these cards or bits of paper into a flow, for a story with the tension increasing up to the climax and decreasing after it.
4. Using your organized cards/papers as a guide, type or handwrite these ideas into a few paragraphs (or more, if inspired to do so) for a rough story draft, adding any new thoughts that occur to you as you write.

The purpose of this exercise is to help you see how ideas beget ideas and to give you experience connecting the analytical side of your brain with the creative side. This should also help you understand the interaction of idea development, mapping, and writing the story in a way that is organic and not formulaic.

Creating the Picture Map

Visual imagery is a good approach to understanding your story. Take some time to put together a picture map of your story with the key elements you used in your story map above. In visualizing your story, you might want to lay out a chronological version first, unless you already have a definite story order you are thinking about. Remember, the tension should rise from the smallest challenge or obstacle to the largest one and not go up and down like a roller coaster. Don't stress on artistry. You want your picture to represent your story, not win prizes. Cutting and pasting pictures or using clip art works just as well. I sometimes use PowerPoint to draw stick figures. Use a large sheet of paper or even a bulletin board and push pins or your wall and tape. Constructed below is a picture using images to represent elements of Linda's story.

(4.9) *Example of Linda's Picture Map*

While you work on this map, your mind will focus on your ideas and how they fit together, what they look like, and the importance each idea has in the story, so this will not be idle or useless time. As you work on Stages 2 through 6, you can keep the same picture map and expand on it or develop a new one if your ideas have changed.

Exploring Ideas:

1. Does the picture reflect the story you want to write, or does it reflect a better idea that your story has evolved to?
2. Is your story focused?
3. What can you add to your picture map or take away?
4. Is the story shown in the strongest order, or is there a particular order you are seeing evolve?

Cranking Your Writing Up to a New Level

When I am writing, unless I am on a very tight deadline, I do the unthinkable: I retype my story from beginning to end. I do this at the end of every stage. The reason I retype is that computers make it easy to cut, copy, and paste, but when editing becomes rote and merely moving material around, it is difficult to make strong, notable progress. I assure you that this technique will move your writing to a new level, because you will be rewriting as you type.

Cranking Your Writing Up a Level Exercise

This is my process. You already know my fondness for 5x8 cards. Whenever I complete a stage, I break my story up into beats, the smallest unit of information that I can. In other words, if I can isolate a paragraph or even a sentence that would make sense, considering it is out of context, then I consider that a beat. If one sentence is dependent on another sentence or a group of sentences or possibly paragraphs to be one cohesive piece, then I consider that a beat. I then print out these beats separately onto 5x8 cards. Sometimes I have several hundred cards. I then read through the cards and move them around into a better order and remove anything that seems superfluous. From the new order I create a new story map.

Rather than on cards, I might print out on 8½ x 11 index-card stock. I number the beats and cut them apart and number the individual sections so that I can easily reconstruct. I usually see some holes, so I handwrite cards with any new ideas I develop to fill them. These are inserted into the stack of cards I printed.

Finally, once I feel pretty good about the organization, I begin retyping the story. A funny thing happens when I start retyping. Instead of typing in word for word, it's like my subconscious says, "You can do better than this," and I do. I rewrite lines as I'm retyping—not all of them; some of them are written exactly as I want them. Sometimes I rewrite lines I thought were perfect because now that I know the story better, they aren't quite adequate. Early in the book we discussed placeholders. Most of your initial writing is a placeholder until you figure out how to say it better. When I cull cards, my subconscious is telling me that I'm not losing anything—I can always add it back in. I'm not cutting anything that is going to disappear forever into the ether. A copy of it is right here in my hands. I also find redundancies this way and cull them.

I prefer to print the story out, read a section, and then retype that section. I have had students who use this method write out a log line for each scene or chapter and then retype each scene from memory, later going back to add back in any important details that were missed.

You will be amazed at how quickly your writing will improve. This is also a great technique if you are rewriting older material, and your strength as a writer has grown. This process helps bring the older writing up to the level of your newer work.

Yes, this is a time-consuming process, but it is well worth the effort. I suggest you do this at least once with a chapter or several scenes to see the effectiveness for yourself. Albeit a great deal of work, how much work is it to revise the same draft seven, ten, twenty-five, or thirty-six times?

chapter 5

STAGE 2—BUILDING
A STRONG STRUCTURE

The purpose of Stage 2 is to start forming your ideas into a structure, which will serve as the foundation for your story, plus increase the writing concepts that you will address. Stage 2 will help you regardless of whether you are starting with only a few ideas or a developed story. Stages 3 through 7 will sequentially build on this foundation.

At the end of Stage 2 there will be an opportunity to incorporate your new ideas into the story. However, while I encourage you to move forward at your own pace, don't allow too much time to lapse as you work through *The Writer's Compass.* You don't want to lose the momentum or continuity.

Let's start where we ended in Stage 1, prior to the "Tools to Develop Your Writing Skills."

WHO IS THE AUDIENCE FOR YOUR STORY?

We discussed the various formats of storytelling on pages 76–87. By now you have probably decided on the format you want to tell your story in. Although we all want to appeal to every person in the world, by defining a target audience or a specific genre, your style will have richer texture for this story's specific audience. You will also be able to write the story according to the accepted conventions of a particular genre. Defining your genre can be a difficult challenge since there are so many crossovers.

Some types of stories can be written in most genres: the hero story, the call to adventure, the love story, or love-lost story, the coming-of-age story, the underdog story, and others. Comedy and drama and romance can be found in many genres.

However, eventually you will need to specify the type of genre your story falls under when you pitch it to an agent or editor or producer, or even a reader. To market your story, you need a handle that these various reading constituents can recognize. It's a much more difficult sale if you generalize your story or, even worse, if you identify your story as one type, but then it fails to match the reader's expectations for that genre.

Exploring Ideas:

1. Who do you think your audience is?
2. What format are you writing in?
3. Why is this the best format for this story?
4. What type of story is it?
5. Is it dark, light, comedic, romantic, dramatic?
6. Is this a story of redemption? Succumbing to temptation and falling? A hero story? An overcoming-adversity story? A young-adult story? How would you define it?
7. Where does the work take place, and what is the environment? Give the setting, location, time period, season, and the physical and emotional environment.
8. What genre does this type of story fall into: action/adventure, mystery, horror, science fiction, fantasy, thriller, romance, comedy, chick lit, or something else (there are many categories)?
9. Why would anyone care? Ask yourself, and answer honestly, why would anyone care about this story and the characters: You may not know the answer until you've written more and contemplated the questions about your characters and about the story itself, but for now—why would anyone care?

CHARACTER OR PLOT-DRIVEN STORIES

At this point let's note that while this story could evolve from several different genres, it could also be plot driven, or it could be more of a character study. The plot is the construct of the story and its development from the beginning through the end. A plot-driven story is more action oriented and more about the sequence of events that lead to achieving the goal. A character-driven story is more about the characters—who they are and what they want. As the writer, are you more interested in developing the plot or the characters? If your answer is *characters*, that doesn't mean you can shortchange the plot, only that you are obsessed with writing about who the characters are and how they influence the plot, what they want and why, and who they become. In a plot-driven story the characters are more influenced by the plot.

Exploring Ideas:

1. Is your work plot driven or character driven?
2. Which is more effective for this story?

STYLE

Successful authors have their own way of telling a story with the language they use. A lack of description is a style. Using lots of metaphors or only a few is a style. Long or short sentences, ways of approaching a topic, vernacular or word choice, pacing, the attitude expressed by the selection of words, and the resulting message the story tells are all a parts of style. Point of view and the voice the character speaks in are a part of style. Many authors also use different styles for different types of stories, although some authors are known for a specific style that they always use in their stories. Is the story in first person or third or omniscient (we will discuss point of view in an upcoming section)? Is the writing formal, or does it have more of the grammar style of a backwoods village? Do you use fifty-cent or five-dollar words? Is the terminology highbrow, or does it have the flavor of a certain culture? Are the sentences long and descriptive or short and crisp? How do you punctuate? Style is the way you tell your story.

VOICE

Voice takes style another step and is the distinctive way all of the elements of style are put together to tell the story. We all have different intonations, various accents, and ways of emphasizing syllables, and we differ in the way we choose words. One of your challenges as a writer is to find your best writing voice and how to express yourself. Generally a well-read reader or an audience can pick out a particular writer's voice without being told who the writer is because there is a certain flavor, a certain way things are stated, a certain perspective on life that comes through the writing. Think of William Faulkner or Ernest Hemingway or J.R.R. Tolkien or James Joyce or Flannery O'Connor or Willa Cather, who all have distinctive voices in their writing.

One of the things I came to believe as a student at the University of Southern California was that today's writers tend to sound alike. We all attend the same conferences and workshops taught by the same people, read the same books of writing rules, and then critique each other based on the same criteria. The result is that editors get the same stories in the same style and voice, just different characters and settings. Don't be afraid to experiment, to develop your own way of being a storyteller. Again, reading will teach you what works and what doesn't. Don't just read the good stuff, read the bad and analyze why it didn't work for you. When you are at ease with family or friends, listen for the way you have of expressing ideas, your authentic voice.

As you share your writing with others, they may refer to your voice or tell you that your writing sounds like another writer's voice. You may not even know when you have found your own distinctive voice until others notice. When you find your voice, your writing will most likely improve since you will be writing in the style that best suits who you are, what you think, what you feel, how you express yourself, and what you believe about life and the world.

Since I like writing in many voices and styles, it was a long time before I found my authentic voice. My family are earthy people, farmers and rednecks and "Oakies" and pioneers and Cherokee Indians with a sprinkling of highly educated folk. For the most part we are a religious lot. For many years I wanted to escape that earthiness—to where I'm not sure—but I never really felt part of that whole heritage. One evening I had pages due for a playwriting class at USC. I worked full time and had other commitments, so I was struggling to get my pages written. I mentioned earlier the word-association game from which the word *guitar* gave me an idea for a play titled *Guit*. I decided this was the best idea I had going, so I worked up about twenty pages in the playwriting format. That night I took the rough pages to class knowing that my classmates were really going to beat me up with negative critiques, especially on the dialogue, which was just so "plain and uninteresting." When we read the pages I was stunned by the comments. They were all about how fast-paced and unexpected the story was and how unique and regional the dialogue. My professor told me this was some of the best work he'd seen from me. On the way home that night, as I thought about the feedback, it dawned on me: I'd found my best voice, and it was the voice that I'd been running from all my life—it was the voice of my heritage. What sounded plain and simple to me as the everyday language of my people was somewhat unique and distinctive to others.

Finding Your Authentic Voice Exercise

To find your voice, take one or two of the ideas you've developed and write them in different ways in one to two pages.

- Attempt writing using the voice and style of your favorite writers.
- Try writing from different personalities.
- Which one is the most comfortable?
- Which one sounds like a fit for your protagonist's voice for this story?

POINT OF VIEW (POV)

Stories can be told in a single or multiple POVs. Multiple POVs are when the story is focused on more than one character's thoughts, feelings, and motivations. The storyteller treats major characters as though they have one of the leading roles. Multiple POVs can be divided by paragraphs or by chapters or sections (sometimes divided off by asterisks). In one section, fictional character Adriana's thoughts and motivations are revealed during her interaction with Miguel, while his are not. In the next section Miguel reflects on the same events or after the fact on the previous events, and we see his thoughts and motivations, while we do not continue to see Adriana's. This interchange goes back and forth throughout the story. It can also be used to show what each character is doing when the other character is elsewhere.

The main character will generally have more POV sections than other characters. When using this method, it is better not to use a character's POV only one time or only a few times in comparison to the other characters' POV. When a character's POV is used early in the book, the reader expects to hear more internal dialogue from that character; if late in the book, then why is it needed at all? The reader takes this choice to be sloppy writing and usually figures the author couldn't think of a better way to show this character or her motivations.

Of course, if you are a noted writer you can do it your own way. *The Testament* by John Grisham, one of the many contemporary authors I read, does not follow the prescribed notions for POV or for introducing the main character. Since I don't want to give the story away, I suggest you read it to see how he uses more than one POV and his introduction of the main character. Both are against everything I was taught, but who can argue with *The Testament*'s or John Grisham's success?

Another way to use multiple POVs is more interactive: While they are interacting, I know what Suzy is thinking and her motivations at the same time I know Bill's thoughts and motivations. This can add to the tension, if done well, or become very confusing (and a bit distracting and hard to follow), if not done clearly.

Types of POVs

There are several POVs in which to tell a story.

- A *narrator* is an observer who may be one of the characters in the story or an outsider not involved in the story but who has knowledge of the events. The narrator tells what is happening in the story and some of the underlying motivations or feelings that the narrator knows or has learned.
- In a *first-person* story the main character is telling the story about what is happening in his or her life either as it happens or possibly an event that already happened, and uses *I* and *my* to refer to himself or herself. The character can also have flashbacks or project the future. However, the character can only know what he or she can see, hear, or surmise about the circumstances, or is told by another character who may or may not be truthful. A clever character can have an intuition or an interpretation, right or wrong, about what other characters are thinking based on their actions and the circumstances. This is a way of informing the reader what is on another character's mind or what the POV character perceives is happening when a character being discussed is not being seen by the POV character.
- The *third-person* story is related by the storyteller without any intrusion in the story. The point is to tell the story as though it is happening to people you are watching in your mind's eye as you are reading it. The characters are referred to in third person as *he* or *she*. The storyteller knows everything about the main character but has varying degrees of knowledge about what the characters are doing or thinking or what their motivations are, depending on whether the story is being told in one POV or multiple POVs. There are modified versions of this.
  - The *omniscient* storyteller tells the story in third person and knows everything about everything, so can inform the reader as the story unfolds. Because there is a tendency for author intrusion, this POV is used less. In this POV the author is all-knowing and therefore has the ability to reveal

information or to manipulate the story by what the author reveals rather than through showing the events.

- The *modified omniscient* POV is also told in third person, but the storyteller doesn't know everything and so cannot inform the reader of all of the other character's thoughts, feelings, and motivations. However, the storyteller knows more than just the protagonist's POV straight third person.
- *Second person* is seldom used. It is a very challenging way to write a story. The character is referred to as *you*. This takes two forms, which are closely connected.
  - In one form the character refers to himself as *you*, much like Bob Dole referred to himself as "Bob Dole." It is a way for the *I* character to attempt to see himself through the lens of an outsider.
  - The second form makes the reader a participant in the story, who is without the ability to interact. The storyteller tells the reader what he is thinking or seeing, or attributes to the reader thoughts or feelings the reader may not agree he has. Not only is this a difficult POV to write, it can be off-putting. In some ways, by using *you* to refer to *I*, you are drawing the reader in to say, "We both see things this way, even if you didn't realize it until now."

Sometimes more tension is created when the main character tells his own story in first person and has to guess the other character's thoughts and motives. Other times seeing the story from a slight distance in one of the third person forms allows the storyteller more room to share more information about all the characters, or at least some of the characters.

Exploring Ideas:

1. Who will tell this story?
2. What is the best POV in which to tell this story?
3. Is there more than one POV character?

SHOWING THE STORY VERSUS TELLING THE STORY

Sometimes when we form ideas, they come to us as images, other times they are thoughts that initially are not visual. Showing and not telling is sometimes one of the most frustrating concepts for a writer to understand. I'm embarrassed to say that the first novel I ever wrote made its way to an editor at a major publishing house, who very nicely spoke with me over the phone and gave me feedback. He told me that I needed to learn more about writing and the difference between telling and showing. It took me a long time to figure this out. After all, the very act of storytelling implies "telling a story." What the writer must learn to do is to turn as much of that telling as possible into showing. After this experience, I thought I had to show everything in a scene and tell nothing. However, I found that by showing everything I was slowing the pace. I also had the sense I was leaving out important information and insights by neglecting to tell some information that couldn't be shown.

In Oscar Wilde's *The Picture of Dorian Gray* is the story about a man becoming infatuated with a portrait of himself and trading his soul so that the painting of him would grow old rather than himself. He watches as the painting alters with each sin he commits.

> Yet it was watching him, with its beautiful marred face and its cruel smile. Its bright hair gleamed in the early sunlight. Its blue eyes met his own. A sense of infinite pity, not for himself, but for the painted image of himself, came over him. It had altered already, and would alter more. Its gold would wither into grey. Its red and white roses would die. For every sin that he committed, a stain would fleck and wreck its fairness. But he would not sin.

In this paragraph, Wilde is mostly telling us about the painting and that the painting is changing and that each sin changes it more. Because earlier in the story we have already seen Dorian Gray and the painting, we already have an image in our minds, so we accept that the painting is changing when he tells us about its "marred face" and "cruel smile." We can see the vivid colors graying. However, he doesn't show us the marred face: Do acne scars appear, are there wrinkles or scarring or aging spots? Is it a Mona Lisa smile? Or a twisted smile? What does a cruel smile look like? Although, because we have all seen a cruel smile, we can envision one without his describing it. He also tells us "It had altered already, and would alter more." This cements in our mind a change in the portrait. This showing of the portrait relies on the images created earlier in the story, but in actuality, it is more telling than showing.

Showing the story is using words that are active, visual, and engage the senses. Through description, showing puts visual images in the reader's mind, evokes sounds, smells, or the sensation of touch. Showing does just that—shows the story. Telling does not evoke images, or at the best, it provides weak images. Telling relates incidents, tells the action, explains the characters, relates information. It is expositional and narrative rather than visual. We can get away with telling when we have established or planted images already in the reader's mind or used metaphors to create those images.

One of the tricks in writing is learning to use images or metaphors that will show the story rather than tell it. A metaphor uses one thing as a comparison to something else to give it a broader or richer meaning. A simile is a type of metaphor that compares different things to create a new meaning. An analogy makes an argument in comparing things that seem to be different. Shakespeare was a master at using these.

Using metaphors helps make stories more visual. Visual stories draw the reader in so that they see it like a movie playing in their head, much like the way you see it when you are writing it.

Based on the first story map we created in "Creating the Story Map," chapter 3, which of the two following sentences in each pair gives you a visual image?

> **a)** Josh quits the job he hates and decides to travel the world as a surfer. Josh *slams the door in his boss's face, yelling, "You can't fire me—I quit!"*

> **b)** Josh is injured on a surfboard and nearly drowns. A *wave sweeps Josh off his board, he's stung by a jellyfish, and passes out.*

Each first sentence in the pair tells what happens. The second sentences suggest how the scene looked. I can add more visual details to further engage the senses, however; you don't want to give too many details, only the significant ones that stimulate the reader to fill in her own imagery. Too many details clutter what the reader is seeing. By limiting the details to the ones you want to emphasize, the reader will fill in visuals from her own experiences and knowledge, involving her more intimately in the story. Let's take those examples to another visual level, engaging the senses.

> **a)** Josh slammed the frosted glass door, freezing as shards shattered to the floor. He turned to see the surprise etched on his former boss's face. Straightening his shoulders, Josh shouted, "You can't fire me—I quit!"

> **b)** The board bouncing beneath his feet, the waves intensifying in strength, Josh saw the sea-green swell rising above, the light shining through it with an effervescent spray of brine raining over him. Then he was down, sucking in the salt, choking, praying the board didn't slam on top of him. He pulled his arms against the weight of the water, searching for up, his nose filled with salty water and the smell of fish and seaweed. A sharp prick to his side forced open his eyes. Through the assault of the stinging seawater and swirling sand, he saw an opaque mass, a translucent jellyfish pumping its body in the other direction. Thrill turned to terror. He'd been stung.

The details you choose should be important to what you specifically want the reader to visualize. Don't lose the reader in too many details. You also want to engage as many senses—hearing, seeing, touch, smell, and taste—as you can. But remember, less is usually more. A stronger noun or verb is far better than using multiple adjectives or adverbs. Use -ly words sparingly, as they dilute the strength of your writing.

Let's look at the story about Marlin from pages 48–50. The first version was more telling than showing, although there were some elements of showing in his *checking his watch, slipping onto his rear on the ice, sneezing and blowing his nose, standing on a corner at the stoplight, the dog peeing on his pant leg, dodging cars while crossing the street, and skirting around the children, shoppers, more dogs, and parents with baby strollers.* The second version was more visual with an image in nearly every sentence. Throughout both, I relied on the reader to fill in the details from the imagery I wrote—details that came from experiences with watches, cats and yarn, a thread unraveling from a sweater, colds and cold, snowy weather, cars, dogs, parks, burglars with ski masks, and neighborhood pharmacies. But the only senses I engaged were the sense of the cold weather and a little bit of touch. I didn't use color in my visuals, nor did I use smell, taste, or hearing. I just wrote a raw example and didn't fill in all the details. If I wanted to elaborate on this story or turn it into something more, I would add those senses in every stage, but specifically concentrating on them in Stage 6, where we will focus on the discussion of these details for your story while we are focusing on the language.

Showing also demonstrates the character of a person, the feelings of the character, or the action in a scene rather than telling it. The following is an example from Willa Cather's *My Antonia.*

> Antonia loved to help grandmother in the kitchen and to learn about cooking and housekeeping. She would stand beside her, watching her every movement. We were willing to believe that Mrs. Shimerda was a good housewife in her own country, but she managed poorly under new conditions: the conditions were bad enough, certainly!
>
> I remember how horrified we were at the sour, ashy-gray bread she gave her family to eat. She mixed her dough, we discovered, in an old tin peck-measure that Krajiek had used about the barn. When she took the paste out to bake it, she left smears of dough sticking to the sides of the measure, put the measure on the shelf behind the stove, and let this residue ferment. The next time she made bread, she scraped this sour stuff down into the fresh dough to serve as yeast.

The first paragraph explains Antonia's grandmother and puts who she is in context: probably a good housewife where she came from, but in these difficult surroundings, she's not doing as well. Without this "telling" explanation, we might not correctly interpret the next paragraph, which shows her character. She serves her family a bread that may be less than appetizing, made in a tin vat that may not be sanitary, and she is careful to leave dough in the vat to continue the yeast she needs to make bread. Cather could have chosen to tell us that "She is a woman who makes do with what she has and continues the best she can." Instead she showed us who Mrs. Shimerda was in the second paragraph. Cather could have left it at the first paragraph, but we would not have the visual imagery or the deeper insight, and the writing would not have been as rich. This is what differentiates better writers.

Another character description shows the character Krajiek through a metaphor.

> ... They hated Krajiek, but they clung to him because he was the only human being with whom they could talk or from whom they could get information. He slept with the old man and the two boys in the dugout barn, along with the oxen. They kept him in their hole and fed him for the same reason that the prairie dogs and the brown owls housed the rattlesnakes—because they did not know how to get rid of him.

Again, Cather could have simply said, "They kept Krajiek around because they did not know how to get rid of him." But what she actually wrote is so much better. She uses a slight twist in this metaphor of a rattlesnake. Several paragraphs earlier Cather had set up the metaphor with the prairie dogs and the owls and with the rattlesnake being their natural enemy. Usually we associate the metaphor of a rattlesnake with never knowing when it will strike, aware at any moment it can bring harm, however Cather adds another level to the metaphor in that even though you anticipate being bitten, you take care of and tolerate the rattlesnake because you can't rid yourself of it.

The word *action* often implies action-packed scenes of fighting or raucous events. Action is movement in the story. In *The Hound of the Baskervilles*, by Sir Arthur Conan Doyle, the action in the following paragraph is that Sherlock Holmes is following along behind, keeping an eye out for what might happen.

> He quickened his pace until we had decreased the distance which divided us by about half. Then, still keeping a hundred yards behind, we followed into Oxford Street and so down Regent Street. Once our friends stopped and stared into a shop window, upon which Holmes did the same. An instant afterwards he gave a little cry of satisfaction, and, following the direction of his eager eyes, I saw that a hansom cab with a man inside which had halted on the other side of the street was now proceeding slowly onward again.

Doyle could have written, "Holmes followed, keeping just out of sight, satisfied to see a hansom cab following along as well." Instead he helped us to visualize Holmes following along the streets of London which we've probably developed an image of from other stories we've read or from movies, being secretive, and giving "a cry of satisfaction" when he recognizes a clue. This is showing the action of the story.

F. Scott Fitzgerald, in *This Side of Paradise*, wrote about two characters coming together, using touch and sound to draw the reader in and show the characters' behavior toward each other.

> Silence for a moment. Isabelle was quite stirred; she wound her handkerchief into a tight ball, and by the faint light that streamed over her, dropped it deliberately on the floor. Their hands touched for an instant, but neither spoke. Silences were becoming more frequent and more delicious. Outside another stray couple had come up and were experimenting on the piano in the next room. After the usual preliminary of "chopsticks," one of them started "Babes in the Woods" and a light tenor carried the words into the den:
>> "Give me your hand
>> I'll understand
>> We're off to slumberland."
> Isabelle hummed it softly and trembled as she felt Amory's hand close over hers.

We see her anticipation, her coyness, we sense the nervousness, and then the song creates a naturalness that draws them together.

It is not possible to show everything without the story becoming overly detailed and ponderous. There is a balance between showing and telling. Part of creating your style is finding out what you will show and how you will tell.

DOES YOUR STORY HAVE A CONCEIT?

I always have a hard time explaining this concept because it is a little ambiguous and can mean different things in different forms. Merriam-Webster's dictionary says that a conceit is an organizing theme or concept. A conceit is over arching and infiltrates the way you tell the story from a unique perspective. A conceit shows the story through how it portrays the world and events, characters, and dialogue in a type of metaphor that applies to the larger context of the story rather than to an individual idea. There are very few stories that haven't been told—it's how you tell your story and the way you draw and advance your story that make it more interesting than the thousands of times it was told before.

An obvious example of a conceit would be the novel *Animal Farm*, by George Orwell. The conceit in the story is in using a farm and giving the animals a persona. The animals take over the farm and create their own society. Orwell was actually making a political statement about Russia during the Bolshevik Revolution of 1917. The conceit in this story is a metaphor that replaces what the author was actually saying by relating the story through a different reality.

The movie *Memento* uses the conceit of telling the story backward with a character who has tattoos all over his body that reveal information instead of images. Because the protagonist has no memory, he is just as confused as the viewer, and simultaneously they learn why he lost his memory. By revealing the story backward, the audience vicariously lives through what this type of memory loss would be like.

Stories like *Superman* use the conceit of a hero with superpowers; he is someone who everyone in the story world of Metropolis knows for saving kittens and stopping trains and criminals. When not rescuing, he is a meek man on the street whom nobody recognizes. The story of James Bond has a womanizing government agent who lives in a world of gadgets and fast cars with a license to kill as its conceit. The character MacGyver's conceit is that he is a smart guy who understands physics and can seal acid leaks with chocolate candy bars and use everyday items like duct tape and matches to save the day. In these character conceits, the reality of the altered superpower story world is more impacted than the shadowy world of espionage or physics.

A movie like *What Dreams May Come* uses a concept—Where do you go when you die and what happens if you kill yourself?—as a conceit. The conceit plays out in how it lavishly portrays Heaven and despondently portrays Hell. *Blade Runner* is a unique futuristic movie and a forerunner of its style. The way it portrays that world in its look and characterizations gives a unique perspective on what is humanity. Remember the ethereal feather in *Forrest Gump* or the line "Life is like a box of chocolates; you never know what you're gonna get." The conceit of using the feather and Forest's dialogue with his unique perspective on life and the fact that he is intellectually challenged, plus placing him as an integral part of historical events, are all part of a conceit. This conceit serves to show that through the disadvantaged, one may see the world in a different way. Albeit as meaningless as a floating feather to many of us, that view can be extremely profound, and those persons have a significant impact if we watch and listen.

A conceit is just a storytelling tool, and you do not need one to tell a good story. However, if you are considering using a conceit or realize that your story would be enhanced by using one, the following questions will help you. Avoid clichéd been-there-done-that, seen-it-before approaches, or anything that feels contrived or like a device. That type of writing serves the moment instead of the whole story.

Exploring Ideas:

1. Think of conceits in terms of an over arching metaphor. What metaphor could you use to tell your story?

2. What might the conceit for this story look like or entail?
3. How can you tell your story in a way that is interesting and different from the way we have seen this plot before? Can you tell your story in a unique way with several unique moments that will intrigue and delight the reader?
4. What can you sustain throughout the story that you can reflect in dialogue, action, events, or moments of the story?
5. What are some of the images and ideas you have for your story? Explore various conceits for those ideas and give examples of how they might play out in your story.

HOW TO "HOOK" THE READER

Once we understand who our audience is, how do we hook them? The hook is the first sentence through the first paragraph, or possibly page. One of the too common ways that writers attempt to hook readers is through shock or something violent. Sometimes the writer uses something outrageous, thinking the reader will want to know why and how that could have possibly happened, and often the reader does want to know. However, shock and violence are overused in storytelling, and readers are quickly numbing to its lure.

Below are some hooks for published novels. These first sentences add an element of surprise and intrigue that causes the reader to wonder what the story could be about.

> "Marley was dead: to begin with. There is no doubt whatever about that."—*A Christmas Carol: A Ghost Story of Christmas*, Charles Dickens
>
> Call me Ishmael.—*Moby-Dick*, Herman Melville
>
> Once an angry man dragged his father along the ground through his own orchard. "Stop!" cried the groaning old man at last, "Stop! I did not drag my father beyond this tree."—*The Making of Americans*, Gertrude Stein
>
> They shoot the white girl first.—*Paradise*, Toni Morrison
>
> Once upon a time, there was a woman who discovered she had turned into the wrong person.—*Back When We Were Grownups*, Anne Tyler

"Call me Ishmael" is considered one of the all-time great first lines. While only three simple words, they are said by the main character who is speaking directly to the reader. This comes across as intimate and draws the reader in. The name Ishmael also evokes a strong image of a man like the Ishmael from the Bible, who was Abraham's first son and not the one God promised Abraham. Ishmael's mother was a servant, and she was run off the property. Ishmael was abandoned, disinherited, and in the end the father of several great tribes in the Middle East. The name Ishmael is familiar to Christians, Jews, Muslims, and peoples of other world religions. The name implies this story will be a roller-coaster ride for the reader about a disenfranchised man.

Another way to hook a reader is to show from the start that this is going to be a story that will be of interest to him. Which is another reason you need to define who your audience is. This will become more important as your story develops. If you know your audience, then you should know or learn what interests them. What kind of story would pique their curiosity? Sometimes writers say, "I'm writing for me." This is valid. And there may be others who like what you like and will be interested in what you write. Just don't shortchange *yourself* as the reader.

Finding ways to interest your readers can come from current events. What do people care about? What are they thinking about as you write your book? How can you incorporate something from today into your story hook? What are the concerns or fears of this particular audience? Is there a new science discovery or a major catastrophic event or a political scandal or war that will be on people's minds? Your story may not have anything to do with that event (you don't want to date your book by being too specific to a reader of a certain era), but it may have impacted your protagonist and how she is thinking, just as it has your reader. The story may have evolved from that moment or be what is in the back of the minds of the characters in your story world. You don't even have to mention the event, but you might allude to it in a way that your reader will get the comparison.

> **a)** The waters were receding. They were allowing us to return home. I drove past piles of jagged water-logged boards and uprooted trees, the occasional couch or household debris sitting on the lawn as though left there for a garage sale. I wondered what I would find in my own yard.

> **b)** Like an airplane dropping its atomic load on an unsuspecting city, this day marked a change in the world.

The first opening connects the reader to one of the devastating hurricanes or floods of recent years that have had a nationwide, even worldwide, impact. However, the story doesn't have to be about that event. This could have been from a neighborhood water pipe bursting or something that creates a catalyst for your protagonist to make a decision to change her life. The second example refers to the incomprehensible devastation one event had on the world, and the reader will expect this story to be about something of that magnitude.

Writing the Hook

Placing a dynamic version of the story's dramatic question or of your theme in your hook, which we discussed on pages 89 and 92, is another way of informing your reader what your story is about and eliciting interest.

a) "How do I stop grieving for my son?" Eric asked from the stillness of his canoe. The tail of the bass began batting the fiberglass bottom as it fought against the air for water. "... when I know in the end I will always blame myself?" He struggled for a moment to trap the fish between his hands, then gently placed it in the calm blue water and set it free, watching as the trail of ripples drifted farther away.

b) Edward always thought that money was the greatest power on Earth, until he lost all of his. Now he's wondering whether he should have put more stock in love.

The first is a dramatic question: How does a parent deal with guilt and stop feeling responsible for the death of a child? The second is from the theme: Love is the greatest power on Earth.

You might consider what would be the most interesting thought your character would have about the events of your story. In other words, the hook is a detail plucked from the story. Or it could be the character's summary of the story.

Today is sunny and warm, quite unexpected after the freezing night, but, then, life tends to be that way. One moment you think the cold darkness will never end, and the next moment feels as though things can never go wrong again. Of course, that's an illusion. Flowers that are bright and beautiful and perfectly arranged often come from a funeral.

The narrator is telling us something about how they view life with the implication that what this story is about will tell us how they arrived at that view, and it appears there might be a death involved or a loss of some sort.

Another approach, and this one you will also use throughout your story, is to show the reader something unexpected, albeit something that has to be true (or organic) to your story. Use words and images or ideas that seem fresh and unique that tell what the soul of this story is in a way that the reader will relate to. What will the reader relate to? Again, you have to know your audience.

I never thought I'd be sitting on a stool, drinking sake, eating eel, drenched from the pouring rain, abandoned by my lover, and spotted with blood beneath my raincoat—and still feel calm. Maybe it's the sake.

Is this a horror story? A murder mystery? Thriller? Action-adventure? The cover and title will help define the genre. What the reader will take away is that the story is told in first person through the narrator's eyes, with unexpected twists and a sense of humor. If you, the reader, want to know how all those things go together, you will read on.

"It was a dark and stormy night ..." is a cliché hook. (In fact, there is a book with that title based on bad opening lines.) However, this line or other similar lines have worked because people know that unusual things happen on dark and stormy nights. With the right details, the reader becomes curious as to what happened on your dark and stormy night.

Teaser

As a hook, teasers—or opening gambits—are more common in television and in movies, although they are sometimes used in novels as well. Writers often want to use the biggest moment of the story as an opening to hook the reader, but that moment belongs to the climax. By using a teaser, the writer can create a short climactic scene of another event to portray an exciting moment and show what type of story this will be. This often works well for suspense, thrillers, police dramas, political thrillers, and action-adventure. The teaser should introduce the protagonist or antagonist with some background to the setting and the characters, and should be associated with the main event of the story in some way. There should be threads connecting to the actual story so that the teaser will feel organic and will tie in and not feel as though it was placed there just to trick the reader into thinking they are going to read one story, when the material is really about another story.

> A dark, starless sky barely reveals shadows as Krissy, holding a gun, chases a dark figure into an alley. She yells, "Stop! FBI!" But the figure manages to hop onto and over the cyclone fence and is making his way to freedom. Krissy fires. A figure she hadn't noticed on the other side of the fence falls over and the man she's chasing hesitates as they both stare at the figure. Then he darts away. By now her partner, Bill, has arrived. Krissy sends him after the suspect as she climbs over the fence and rushes to the fallen figure only to find the victim deceased. Examining the body, she quickly discovers it's already cold, and has been dead for some time. When Bill returns she explains what happened. They call for a coroner.

The actual story could be about Krissy, an FBI agent, hunting for the man who has eluded her, or it could be a story about Krissy figuring out who the dead victim is and what happened and why. The tag at the end of the story could be about Krissy and Bill catching the man who escaped her in the opening. If the teaser had been to show the reader something about the antagonist, it could have shown the murder and the body being dumped, or it could have shown the man who escaped, where he goes, and something about what he is plotting to do next.

There will still be falling action after the teaser—the story cannot maintain that high level of tension. The next scenes of the story would be about Krissy and Bill, to set up the protagonist and the backdrop of the story and their challenge. Then the rising action begins again toward the climactic moment of the actual story. We will discuss the tag, rising action, falling action, and climactic moment later in this section.

Mnemonic Device as a Hook

A mnemonic device is used to plant a word or a thought in someone's mind, often through an image or a metaphor that represents an idea. Every time that device is mentioned, the reader's subconscious remembers the idea that was planted. For example, green was once a mnemonic device for money or for jealousy and has now become synonymous with "protecting the environment." If it's green, it's environmentally proactive. "Green" has become a mnemonic device throughout the United States and in many other countries. By using green, depending on the context in an opening line, you can plant the idea of money, jealousy, or the environment in the minds of your readers. If your readers are interested in the impact of "green," you may entice them with the hook for your story. An example would be the line below.

> Now that I'm not green anymore, I don't know who I am. Who am I when I'm not me?

This might be a story about a person who is no longer involved in the environmental movement, or no longer jealous or wealthy or, unlike Kermit the Frog, simply no longer green. For the reader that does not care about self-reflection or the environment or money, and doesn't understand the concept of jealousy, this opening probably will not be a hook, unless the title and book cover make it clear that the green has to do with science fiction or fantasy or horror, and that is what interests the reader.

However, in creating a mnemonic device you do not have to rely on something already symbolic; you can create your own symbols. For example, if you want a scarf to be a metaphor throughout your story, you may give your character a particular scarf of a particular color or many scarves.

> As the icy sleet beat against my face, I pulled my blue wool scarf, the one Casey gave me the last time we were together, tighter around my chin and mouth. It still smelled of the champagne I refused to wash out. Sorrow, like the ice, pelted my senses and melted into inconsolable loss.

In this example, we've hopefully hooked the reader into wanting to know who Casey is, who the narrator is, and whether each is a man or a woman, and what happened after the champagne? We've also told the reader that the narrator is suffering a great loss, and that wherever the story is set, it is currently freezing cold. Now when we mention the blue scarf, the reader will remember sorrow, cold, and spilled champagne.

When you use the blue scarf, it becomes a metaphor for sorrow. Sorrow is something we can all identify with. By using a universal approach such as sorrow to connect your character's thoughts to your readers' thoughts, you will continue to stimulate your reader's involvement in your story. However, if it sounds too sad, readers who do not like sad stories will put the book back on the shelf or click on the next selection and move on. The way the ice against the face is used also elicits an image of sorrow and could be a second mnemonic device. You can also use your mnemonic device to signify later that everything has changed.

> I picked up the blue silk scarf, a nice pale blue, and ran the material through my fingers. Yes, this will do. A new scarf for a new beginning. I paid in cash. I left the store, dumping the old winter-worn scarf in the trash and winding the new scarf around my shoulders. Outside the gray clouds were replaced by blue sky, and the sun beat warmly on my face.

From this example we sense that she is putting the past behind her, and better days have arrived.

As we've seen from the examples, there are no formulas for writing hooks, and not everyone will be hooked by the same type of hook. However, it is important that the hook be the most enticing sentence/paragraph of the story and reflect what the reader can expect. As you know your story better, and as you develop it further, you will be better able to craft a stronger hook.

TIME CLAMP

In creating the story map, on page 45 we talked about a sense of urgency. Another way to think about developing urgency is by creating a time clamp. Give your characters deadlines to meet the goals that have been set, and lock them in a setting that keeps them from getting to the situation where they can complete their goal.

> Yvette works for an insurance company retrieving lost property of significant value. Her current assignment (goal) is to find the stolen $1 million in gold coins that disappeared in a plane crash in the mountains near Homer, Alaska. In the resolution to one of her obstacles, she winds up in Rio de Janeiro, South America, and manages to retrieve a map to the crash from the mastermind of the heist as he lays dying. If she doesn't get back to Alaska before the first big freeze of winter, the plane wreck will be covered in snow, and it may be another decade before there is enough of a thaw to retrieve the gold. Unfortunately, when she followed the mastermind to Rio, where he was shot and subsequently died, she was the first one the authorities suspected, and now she is being held by the police, who are not accepting her credentials or listening to her story.

Yvette is trapped in South America when she needs to be in Alaska before the first major snowstorm.

Another way to increase the tension in a time clamp is by condensing the time frame of the story to the shortest possible time. Think about the time span of the most important events and condense them as tightly as possible into the least amount of time to create a stronger sense of urgency. While it is doubtful that the events in a season of the show 24 could actually occur that quickly, by giving the story only twenty-four hours, albeit the twenty-four hours unfolds one hour per week in real time, there is an automatic increase in tension. Although this is a type of countdown, as we discussed earlier on page 45, the method holds true for longer periods of time when there is not a continuous threat. Begin your story when the really important activity starts, and end it quickly once things are resolved. Think about the briefest time period with the most heightened activity in which the events of your story can occur. Whatever is outside of that time frame is backstory, which you can tell in flashback, if necessary.

Exploring Ideas:

1. What is the time frame of this work? Does it occur in six days, six weeks, six years, six decades?
2. Do you have a *time clamp*, and is your protagonist *locked in a place*, which will cause the tension to increase?
3. What creates the sense of urgency?
4. What happens when time runs out?

DEUS EX MACHINA

Deus ex machina once referred to a mechanism that lowered the gods onto the stage to save a character(s) from some force that couldn't be overcome. Today it refers to the situation that occurs when writers have written themselves into a corner and do not know how to extricate the characters, so they create something or someone that appears as if by magic to save the day, which is not organic to the story. It's a false construct designed to save the characters and not very satisfying for the reader—unless you are writing a comedy or a farce. Providing an easy out is a good way to destroy the tension in a story.

There is a difference between creating a scene with obstacles in which we know the protagonist will eventually overcome or survive and creating a scene where we have slowly eliminated every possibility of escape. In the latter, each moment puts the protagonist in greater jeopardy and with no possibility of escape—doomed. We need to cleverly extricate the protagonist. not by a miracle, but by much earlier planting an opportunity for escape in a nonchalant, subtle, perhaps insignificant manner—but then there it is if the protagonist is clever enough to see it and use it to the surprise and delight of the reader. The method of suddenly coming up with luck and good fortune only works when the protagonist has already been through so much that the reader is hoping luck will finally be on the protagonist's side. And the reader usually doesn't accept good luck more than once or twice in a story, unless it is a fairy tale or a story with magical realism.

The following exercise will help you work through the problem of finding a way out of your dilemma.

"Saving the Day" Exercise

Your characters are three friends, two men and one woman, who are on the run. You decide whether they are the good guys or the bad guys or a combination of both. They left in the middle of the night and escaped into the mountains. They make it into a wooded area and set up a campsite.

- What are they running from?
- What did they take with them?
- What is their relationship to each other?

An argument breaks out, and one of them stalks off to be alone to think.

- What are they arguing about?
- What are the concerns of the remaining two characters?

Eventually, fearing the character may be in harm's way, the other two go after the missing character. After some searching, they discover the character has stumbled off a cliff in the dark and is lying unconscious on a ledge.

- How did they find the character?
- What are they going to do next?
- What is the logical outcome?

Write this scene in detail before answering the following questions.

- Now that you have written the scene, look at the details of what you wrote. Were you logical in what happened? How were you illogical?
- What did the characters have with them that they could use?
- Did what they have with them make sense in the context of the story?
- What tools did you give them to use that they didn't have with them?
- What, if anything, appears out of nowhere or as if by magic or luck?
- How did you make use of the environment to help them?
- What clever way did you give them what they needed to help themselves?

Taking It With You

As you write your story you will find your characters need certain things at certain times to help them on their journey. Rather than contrive something at the moment, think through what your story is about and set up the character having what they need when they need it. On page 59, I described "Creating the Picture Map" and gave Ray, who falls into the crevasse while crossing the mountain in search of the flower that could cure his wife, rock-climbing tools. I did this by giving him a backpack with supplies. He took what he needed with him. Whether I tell the reader what he's taking depends on the story and how he's going to use the items. If it is unlikely he'd take rock-climbing equipment, then he needs to have a reason for carrying those items. I could have foreshadowed this by noting the journey he's going to take is rough, mountainous terrain and that Ray is always prepared; then when he gets to the mountain and needs the equipment, it makes sense he's got it with him. If he's not expecting to be mountain climbing, or if he's not a guy who plans ahead, then he's probably not going to have the equipment he needs. In which case, the writer has to create a plausible way for Ray to get out of that crevasse with just what he's brought with him or what he can fashion from his environment.

The exception to this would be, as noted above, fairy tales and magical realism, or comedy and farce. Things can happen in comedy and farce for the sake of being funny that are unexpected and not logical.

"Taking It With You" Exercise

Rewrite the story you wrote in "Saving the Day" and either give your characters the tools they need in advance or create a clever way for them to come by what they need. Everything they use the reader must ultimately believe logical to have with them or must be available in the environment. The reader doesn't have to know what they took, just believe it makes sense once the item appears.

LOOKING AT CAUSE AND EFFECT

Although we have touched on cause and effect, also known as stimulus and response, while we are focusing on the structure in Stage 2, we want to really focus on what happens and what the outcome is and whether it is organic or appropriate. I have written stories with a throwaway scene or line, not realizing that I was putting my characters in a situation that either demanded far more of a reaction or far less impact. For example, on page 46, the paragraph about Mary's husband needing brain surgery looked rather different originally. Here's my original version:

> Mary's husband Leonard needs open-heart surgery (stimulus, cause). Her twin brother Fred is the most noted surgeon in his field, but since Fred's wife died he's had a drinking problem. Although he's on the wagon now, will he stay on the wagon long enough to perform the surgery and save Leonard's life (cause)? The tension is mounting as Fred disappears for days until moments before the surgery. Was he drinking? If Leonard dies, what happens to Mary and Fred's relationship (response, effect).

One of my writing friends asked, "Why didn't Mary just go to another doctor?"

Logically, my original example didn't work. My response is out of proportion to my stimulus. There are at least two problems with my original example. One is that heart surgery is common enough, and surgeons who do heart surgery are plentiful enough, that I was making a mountain out of a molehill, so to speak. The other is that just because I say someone is "the most noted surgeon," I haven't shown anyone a reason to believe that to be the case. In the example I finally used on page 46, I changed it to brain surgery because it is more believable that there are only a few doctors capable of doing this type of surgery when it requires training on newly developed technology.

One of the problems often found in the early stages of writing is that the cause and effect, or the stimulus and response do not match. One tiny event creates a massive overreaction, however, a major catastrophe has little to no impact on the story world, but is more of a secondary event. While it is true that a small event can snowball into something major, the writer needs to show that tiny event having a growing outcome to get the reader to buy into the avalanche. In March 2010, Eyjafjallajökull volcano in Iceland erupted. Although not a major eruption (stimulus, cause) as far as the power of volcanoes go (there are pictures of people standing near the flowing lava), the outcome of the ash plume of the volcano (stimulus, cause) shut down European air travel, stranding thousands of travelers for several days (response, effect). A volcano that killed no one in its path, as far as I'm aware, impacted many thousands of people's lives.

When creating events and obstacles in your story, consider what caused the event or what the stimulus was and then what the effect or the response of that will be on the story, and make sure that either it is equitable or that you show how it grows out of control organically.

> Eddy was robbed while walking down the street late one evening on his way home from work. The robber, who wore a black sweatshirt with a hood, didn't get much: a cheap watch, $30 in cash, and a credit card that Eddy was over his limit on. Neither did he harm Eddy—the thief wasn't even carrying a weapon. However, because he was much larger than Eddy, Eddy decided not to risk being hurt or killed and handed everything over. A police car approached, scaring the thief, who took off running. The cops caught him a few blocks later, and eventually everything was returned to Eddy. Unnerved, the next day Eddy bought a gun, determined that he wasn't going to risk being mugged again and this time allow something worse to happen. About a week later Eddy is approached on the street by a guy in a gray sweatshirt wearing a hood. Eddy pulls out his gun and shoots him dead.

Was the cause and effect balanced? Although upsetting, Eddy was unharmed and actually got everything back. While he may be mad and far more protective of himself, possibly even buying a gun, his reaction was over the top. I'm sure you've watched movies or read stories and thought one of the characters was out of character and overreacting to whatever happened and was therefore unbelievable.

There is a trial, and we learn that this wasn't the first time Eddy has been mugged. In fact, it's the fourth time, and because he's small he was regularly beaten up at school, not to mention being a punching bag at home.

We begin to understand Eddy's reaction and now see maybe it was more balanced, in terms of earlier causes and effect (backstory), than it originally appeared.

We also learn that the man Eddy shot was a mentally disabled man who had left his home to go for a walk and was now lost and just trying to get help to find his way home.

We now have a different take on Eddy's behavior and the outcome of his actions.

Exploring ideas:

Briefly list the main actions of your story, what caused them, and their results.

1. What caused the over arching event, and what are the results? Are they reasonable?
2. What is the cause and effect of the details, action, and conflict? Do they mesh with the character's personality? All of these together create the impact.
3. Do the events lead logically to the results or the conclusion?
4. Is the response to the stimulus and the outcome believable?
5. Does the cause match the effect?
6. In other words, is there reasonable motivation for the events that transpire? Do they reasonably balance with the characters' actions, reactions, and personality?

FLASHBACKS

When I was learning to write there was a trend not to include flashbacks. I don't know where that silly idea came from or how widespread it was, but in my writing group at the time they were frowned upon. A flashback is a useful way to convey information from the past without having to make the past a chronological part of the story. A flashback gives you the opportunity to show what happened and put the reader in a dynamic moment. In order to convey something from the past without a flashback, you have to "tell" it in dialogue or exposition. In a play most flashbacks have to be "told" or use lighting to create a moment out of sequence and context with the rest of the story.

Using a flashback is just another tool in your arsenal, another facet of how to tell the story you want to tell and a way to take advantage of something exciting or meaningful that happened to your characters and helped to shape them. Again, the movie *Memento* is one of those stories that uses flashbacks effectively.

Flashbacks do not have to be told chronologically, unless by telling them in order it better serves your story and creates tension through its own rising action. Some stories are almost entirely flashbacks: They start in the present and quickly revert to the past to tell the whole story; then the tag brings you back to the present for the eventual outcome of what happened to the characters. A flashback can be a reveal or a revelation or an epiphany or a mystery in itself that is leading the reader through the events that created the current events and challenges of the story.

There is a caveat about flashbacks in that the writer risks taking the audience out of being in the moment and if done poorly or too often, the shift in time and setting can remind readers they are reading a story or watching a movie or a play. Like every other tool in writing, the purpose of a flashback should be to move the story forward or inform the reader about the story or characters. The more dynamic, the better the story is served.

Flashbacks That Leapfrog

Another technique in flashbacks is for the characters to leapfrog each other. This has the element of surprise, and we can see the events from the protagonist's and antagonist's per-spective. We start with the protagonist's POV as the story moves forward; then, when we get to a critical juncture, we back up to see how the antagonist led the events to this obstacle. From there you can move forward from the event and do the process again, leading up to the next event. The order depends on which POV will keep the tension rising, and the technique should not be overdone.

FORESHADOWING

Forewarning, or foreshadowing, are subtle moments you plant that give the reader or audience a sense that something is coming. If it is too obvious, you will have a "Duh!" moment.

I read far too often lines like:

> If only Bob knew what awaited him around the corner.

> Jeffrey didn't know this was the last time he'd see his family.

> If Jane knew that when she woke up in the morning, everything would be different, she would have slept in—only Jane didn't know.

Although the point is to make the reader sense something unexpected is coming, not only is this author intrusion—the author telling us what the author knows that neither the character nor we know—but it's lazy writing and a cheap way to foreshadow something is going to happen and create an anticipation for tension.

When written well, foreshadowing can be very effective. Later the reader will say, "I should have seen that coming."

These are rewritten from the character's perspective.

> a) The day was perfect. The sun shone down and warmed Bob's face; a smile played on his lips. Another few minutes, and he'd be there. He was almost to the corner when he heard

a dog barking, its yelps growing louder and more urgent the closer he got. The noise was ruining his walk. At the corner he stopped, that prickly sensation of alert he sometimes got started at the base of his neck and ran down his spine.

b) Goodbyes were always difficult and Jeffrey hated them. He always wondered "what if I never see her again," and then he'd go through the day in a kind of dread until he realized how silly he was being. Today wasn't going to be like that. He'd be back, she'd be there, and life was good. His silliness wasn't going to ruin the day for him.

c) Jane never woke up early. She loved sleeping late, so when her eyes popped open at the crack of dawn, she was more than a little surprised. Tossing and turning, pulling the pillow over her head and wrapping herself in the blankets, it soon became evident she wasn't going back to sleep. She might as well get up and start the day, hoping it would go better than her morning's sleep.

The reader realizes that the character is being a bit naïve or sensing something that is now going to start playing out.

Using foreshadowing effectively creates surprises for your audience. There are moments that you plant as throwaway comments in your story that later add up to reveal something unexpected. Think of pieces to a puzzle that don't become the picture until the last piece has clicked into place. By using details for one event that actually are foreshadowing for another event, you can keep the reader from catching on.

Martha loved her morning coffee. She took great pains to make the perfect cup and then added a dollop of flavored creamer. **She hesitated before opening the refrigerator, her mind still on the bed and Mark's lovemaking. They'd been through so much, and this felt like old times, good times. In the door she discovered the amaretto-flavored creamer that her husband had brought home from the store last night, another way he was showing her he wanted to make up. She smiled. Most men brought home flowers when they were apologizing. She opened the container and sniffed, ummm,** almonds. **He used to be thoughtful like this. She used to not be such a witch. Why do things change in a marriage she wondered. Why can't people always stay in love the way they are when they meet? Maybe she and Mark were the lucky ones, if they had found their way back to each other. Martha promised herself today would be a day without nagging, a good day, a loving day as** she poured the exact amount of creamer she liked in a spoon and then **drizzled the creamer into her cup,** watching the color of her coffee turn from dark chocolate to milk chocolate brown. She sniffed deeply to inhale the aroma. **He would be out of the shower soon; she'd make him a great breakfast,** her way of repaying him.

Later we find that one of them has killed the other. The detail in gray serves the purpose of focusing on the coffee; however the reader may see it coming that he is poisoning her with cyanide. On the other hand, her last words in gray may be the tipoff that she is going to "repay" him by doing him in. By taking out the details in gray and focusing on the emotional side of the events, there is less emphasis on what later proves to be very meaningful, using just enough details to plant that the creamer was laced with cyanide or that the breakfast supposedly made in love was really what killed Mark. If, by the tone of the story, the reader already suspects that one is going to kill the other, then I might want to use the gray details about the coffee that give the impression Mark is going to kill her or her final detail in gray to steer the reader into believing she is going to kill Mark.

Exploring Ideas:

1. Is there a forewarning or foreshadowing in your story?
2. How will you use it—as a single moment in the story or will it be throughout the action?
3. Which details give clues that later will prove significant?
4. Are there details that give away too much?

SURPRISES, TWISTS, AND UNEXPECTED OR WRONG TURNS

Along with foreshadowing, the events in the story should offer the unexpected. Characters should do surprising things. There should be wrong or unexpected turns in the outcome or direction of the events. There should be lots of twists and surprises to keep the story from being predictable and to delight the reader.

I know readers who read more than one fiction book a week. In fact, my sister Janet and her husband, Joel, read so much that they have a hard time finding books and new writers that they haven't read in the genres they enjoy. She sees right through foreshadowing and figures out the twists coming and almost always knows what's going to happen next by the way something was phrased. Too many writers use the same patterns with the same outcomes in setting up the surprises.

The best way to keep someone like her interested is in the unexpected. Are there wrong turns your story can take that don't make the characters or the writer appear stupid? Anyone can make a mistake; if you can show your character just made a wrong choice and put him on the wrong path, you can add surprise to your story. You don't want to protect your protagonist, you want to put him out on a limb and then up the ante for him to fail. Maybe even let him fall and break his leg before the big race.

Another example of creating surprises or twists would be your protagonist thinking he is clever in spotting the person chasing him and then being the first to attack, when in reality the other character was cleverer in that she wanted to be seen to setup an unexpected trap. Later your protagonist realizes that his own cleverness did him in and caused him to lose this challenge or obstacle.

Sometimes the story or scene set up is the problem. By the time you go through the stage leading up to the character's or the event's twist, it has already become fairly obvious where you are going with the story. One effective technique is jumping ahead to the twist or the surprise and starting that scene at the moment of the reveal. The reveal is when we learn the unexpected or what caused the unexpected, when we learn surprising information that alters the course of the story or the reader's understanding of it. If the scene jumps ahead to the moment of the surprise or twist, it is more unexpected to the reader. The writer then goes back, using the technique of a flashback but writing it as though it is presently occurring, to reveal the steps leading up to the surprise. The reader still gets to be surprised and is even more intrigued by what happened leading up to the twist. If not done well, this can be a bit jolting, and the reader can feel as though they have whiplash. In *The Gatecrasher,* British writer Madeleine Wickham does a great job with this technique. She jumps the scene forward to the reveal that would normally occur at the end of the scene, surprising the reader with an unexpected twist. However, just about the time the reader says, "Wait, what happened? What did I miss? I wanted to read that." Wickham fluidly takes you back to the beginning of the scene and shows you how it unfolds. Since movies are fluid, you often see this technique used.

Exploring Ideas:

1. What wrong turns could your story take that would make sense within the context of the world of the story?
2. Every time something goes his way, how can you change directions so that events go against the protagonist or in an unexpected direction?

BACKSTORY

Many ideas that you write for your story won't wind up being used, for many reasons: Maybe the story takes a different turn, or the ideas you write don't fit into the time frame of your story. Often writers find they have written several pages that tell the character's history but actually slow the story down. Frequently the first several pages are lopped off the beginning of the story to get to a dynamic hook sooner. These often become backstory, things that are true about your character that don't quite fit into the story but may be alluded to in a way they are understood to have occurred. Sometimes you introduce a bit of the backstory through flashbacks. At other times, it may be a vague reference to something from one of the character's pasts with just enough detail to imply what the character has been through, without giving all the details.

- *The protagonist was a war hero, but was living a quiet unassuming life until burglars break into his home and tie him up as they ransack his house.*

Knowing that he is a war hero tells us something about the kind of man he is. We don't have to know what he did; most people have a vivid imagination and have heard enough stories about war heroes they can put together a quick scenario of an idea.

- *When the burglars come upon his congressional medal of honor, one wants to back off and one doesn't care and in fact seems to resent him even more. The man sits tied up in a chair realizing that he has to think about today and use his wits to stay alive to get out of this. He can't rely on something he did twenty years ago to save him, which may in fact make things worse for him.*

Who he is today is shaped by the past, but the details of past events are not necessarily important to the story. Whether what he did to become a war hero comes out or not using a flashback depends on the story you write. It also can be a fact about his life that while true, doesn't need to be elucidated.

Another example would be the victim of a crime in the past, such as rape, incest, being shot, being hit by a car, being abused. There are so many stories about these types of crimes against a person, the writer doesn't need to fill in all the ugly details. The reader can do that. But a passing comment or a quick reflection can indicate this happened and that it is a part of this character's history and what makes the character tick.

USING HISTORICAL EVENTS TO DEVELOP YOUR STORY

We looked at ideas for historical events in Stage 1, but here we want to expand on how to integrate the historical time frame or background and backdrop you may have selected. To give the story credibility, think about the time frame and what memorable events were happening in history during that period. Unless your story is about a period or event in history, the purpose is not to saturate your writing with an historical context, rather to give it a backdrop or background and to see how you can enrich the story by integrating details about an event or time frame into your story.

Exploring Ideas:

1. What is the historical context or time frame, event, or subject you could overlay to study?
2. Was there a war?
3. What inventions and discoveries were made?
4. What did we learn about the earth or science or physics that we didn't know before?
5. What did we still believe about the earth or people or the universe then that we now know wasn't true?
6. Who was important in politics, in the royal court, in society, in business?

7. List the date of these events (see the exercise you did in Stage 1), followed by the event.
8. Write how these historical events influenced the events of the story.
9. What was the result or the impact on your story and/or characters?
10. Is the end result or effect a feasible or organic outcome of the impact (cause or stimulus)?

DATE OR TIME FRAME	EVENT	IMPACT ON STORY	EFFECT/RESULT

Example of a Table for the Backdrop

SUBPLOT OR "B" STORY

Stories often have a secondary plot winding through them involving the secondary or minor characters during the course of the story. These plots may involve the protagonist or antagonist directly or indirectly. This story follows the same elements as the main story, only is less intense and does not need as many obstacles. With too much intensity, the secondary story overtakes the primary story. The connection between the plot and the subplot may be revealed throughout the story or not until the tag (a place in the story when loose ends are tied up).

> • *Georgia is attempting to win the "Miss World" beauty pageant. Her best friend is Teresa, who is always at Georgia's side, encouraging her. Teresa wants to be an actress, but she can't get that first break. Georgia's rival, Janeen, has a father in the entertainment industry. Janeen promises Teresa a role in her father's next film if she will sabotage Linda.*

The way Teresa's story plays out creates a subplot, as long as Georgia's story is fully developed as the main story, with Georgia struggling through obstacles to win the "Miss World" pageant. Teresa's story is just one of the obstacles Georgia will have to deal with, or Teresa will have to fight against. Teresa's struggle with whether to betray her friend for her big break would be a recurring thread, but not the main action. However, if the story becomes about whether Teresa will betray Georgia, then that becomes the main plot. Subplots would be mapped on an additional story map in the same way the main plot is mapped. Any interactive or connecting points should be shown on the main story map. The story of Georgia and Teresa is mapped at the end of this stage on page 128.

In some stories there are also "C" subplots. Another type of story with many subplots would be like the Oscar-winning movie *Crash* or the movie *Love Actually*, in which there are several subplots that seem to be unrelated or only partially related, but eventually they all form threads that come together and make sense for the theme of the story. Stories like these may have a plot that seems to be the main thread, or each plot can appear to stand separately until the writer brings them together either in the climax or the *End*.

Exploring Ideas:

1. Is there an appropriate subplot or more than one that works with this story without overcomplicating it?
2. What are some of the details of this subplot?
3. Who is involved in the subplot?
4. What purpose does the subplot serve to further this story or to develop the characters?

STORY TRUTHS

What are the truths of your story world? If you are creating a story with an over arching fundamental belief or theme, then there must be some truths about your world that may not hold true for the everyday world of most people. You will want to clarify these truths in some way for your reader. For example, people who live in a world of lawlessness generally still have an "inviolable code" of their own, a standard they live by or certain rules they don't break—think *The Godfather*. Or if your characters are in an Amish world, as in the movie *Witness*, there is another set of rules—such as "shunning" for a period of time until the penitent can be accepted back into the community—and the avoidance of violence or the rejection of modern conveniences. Perhaps your world is a science-fiction, fantasy, magical-realism, or horror story or is set somewhere in a galaxy far, far away—what might be the rules there?

Exploring Ideas:

1. Are you creating a world or relying on real-world concepts?
2. What are the truths about the world of this story?
3. What would the rules be for this world?

STORY ISSUES

There are two kinds of story issues. The issue of making the story events work out to an organic conclusion, and the issue the writer has with writing the story. Often the issues are apparent. About the story on page 114—*Getting Yvette to Alaska before the big freeze when she is being held in a police station in South America*—the writer may not have experience or knowledge of Alaska weather or travel in South America or police procedures there. By identifying the issues you may have in writing your story, you put the analytical side of your brain to work figuring out solutions and where to find answers.

Exploring Ideas:

1. What are the issues or events of this story? How do these issues or events become the challenges or obstacles?
2. What are the issues or challenges to the writer in writing this story?
3. How will you overcome those issues or challenges?

TOOLS FOR STAGE 2

Exploring Ideas:

1. Did you use the right conceit to enhance this story?
2. Is the conceit over arching, and does it permeate the dialogue, action, events, moments of the story?

Georgia's Story Map

On page 128 you'll find another story map to use as an example. This is an overview of Georgia, who is trying to win a beauty pageant for the "Miss World" title, and the subplot of her friend Teresa, who wants to be an actress. Teresa is tempted by Georgia's competition, Janeen, to betray Georgia (from page 125). In this story the climactic moment could either be the confrontation between Georgia and Teresa, or it could be Georgia's losing, depending on how the story is written. Let's also note a specific example of telling here. The tag is *Georgia finds freedom starting a new life*. In an advanced version of the map, I would want to show this. How will we see that Georgia finds freedom starting a new life? Perhaps *Georgia happily places a cake in the display case in her new bakery*. The idea that she might prefer to start a new life, maybe open a bakery in another city, would be planted or foreshadowed somewhere earlier in the story.

Georgia's Picture Map

Let's look at another way to create a picture map. Although we are following the chronology of the elements, the images are more to remind us of important key scenes, and in this case both plots are in a single image. The size of the images could be adjusted to show importance or to show main plot or subplot. See page 129 for an example of Georgia's picture map.

Tools for Development

After completing your maps, return to the section on "Tools," page 88, and answer the questions there again, being more specific wherever you can. Although this may feel repetitive, you will most likely be surprised by the increased clarity and continued development of new ideas.

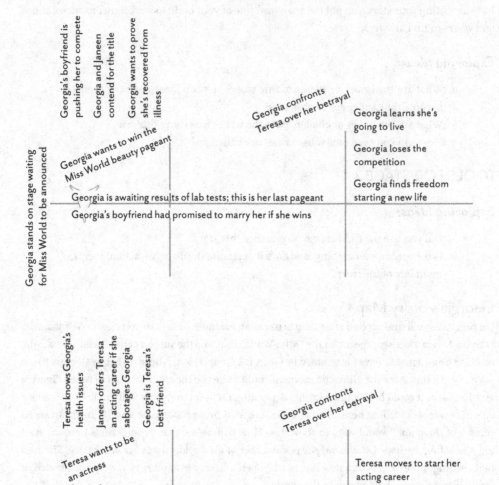

Georgia's boyfriend is pushing her to compete

Georgia and Janeen contend for the title

Georgia wants to prove she's recovered from illness

Georgia confronts Teresa over her betrayal

Georgia learns she's going to live

Georgia wants to win the Miss World beauty pageant

Georgia loses the competition

Georgia stands on stage waiting for Miss World to be announced

Georgia finds freedom starting a new life

Georgia is awaiting results of lab tests; this is her last pageant

Georgia's boyfriend had promised to marry her if she wins

Teresa knows Georgia's health issues

Janeen offers Teresa an acting career if she sabotages Georgia

Georgia is Teresa's best friend

Georgia confronts Teresa over her betrayal

Teresa wants to be an actress

Teresa moves to start her acting career

Teresa needs to succeed in her career to feel loved

Teresa is afraid she will run out of youth before she becomes a star

(5.1) *Georgia and Teresa's Story Map With Main and Subplot*

(5.2) *Georgia's Picture Map*

chapter 6

STAGE 3—CREATING VIBRANT CHARACTERS

In Stage 3 we want to focus on your characters. The more developed your characters, the more ideas you will generate for creating challenges, or obstacles, and action. Fully developed characters pique the reader's interest. When the reader identifies or sympathizes with a character, they are anxious to find out what will happen next and the final outcome to this character.

Some students tell me this is their favorite stage because their characters become real. The following questions and exercises are most important for developing the protagonist and antagonist, but you will also want to consider using them for your major secondary characters. This will more fully develop their personalities, especially if you are writing a novel. I always find this section on characterization is one of the most important and productive stages. In this stage the story comes more fully to life, and you will figure out many story details as you figure out character details. I generally use this process to develop most of my major characters.

A wonderful adventure awaits you as you explore your story world through this character! As you write about your character and answer the questions, become the character and see the world through this character's eyes. Let this character tell you who he or she is. As noted before, it is through answering the questions that you develop perspective on your story, which will help you create a story that it multi-dimensional and in turn will help you form your internal compass.

DO YOU REALLY KNOW YOUR CHARACTERS?

In this stage we focus on crafting characters who become so real you will know them better than you know anyone else, maybe even better than you know yourself. Although there will be many questions and details for you to figure out, each of these bits and pieces will help you put together a character that seems to your readers to actually live and breathe. You probably won't use all of these details in your story, especially in a screenplay or play. But the way the backstory and details inform you about the character will show not only in the character you create but in the decisions you make about how the character behaves, how the character reacts, and what the character would and—just as importantly—would not do. This in turn determines how your story evolves. The answers also give you stronger details for showing your character through imagery and metaphors.

Knowing the traits of your character's personality will help you increase the tension, sense of urgency, and interest in your story because now you can put your character in untenable situations and give them the motivation to behave in ways they might not otherwise—or at the very least struggle with themselves over what they are going to do.

In his book *The Purpose Driven Life*, Rick Warren says, "Most people struggle with three basic issues in life. The first is identity 'Who am I?' The second is importance: 'Do I matter?' The third is impact: 'What is my place in life?'" These questions also serve as a good foundation for understanding your character.

There are a number of "personality type" guides that can help you to understand more about the attributes of certain personalities. If you aren't sure you have good insight into people, you might want to familiarize yourself with some of these guides to help you develop consistency in your characters and to understand how they might react to certain events and what it would take to change their reactions or behavior.

Exploring Ideas:

1. Who is the character? Answer for the character in terms you would answer this question about yourself.
2. How does this character matter in this particular story?
3. What is this character's place in this story world?
4. What are the character's personality traits?
5. Does the protagonist have the fortitude to forge onward through the plot of this story?
6. Is the character strong enough, and what she wants compelling enough, that the character will struggle against all obstacles to achieve her goal?
7. Does the character's personality compel or hinder her reactions to obstacles?

Who is the Protagonist?

Have you ever read or written a story and not been sure whom the story is about? Or written a story with a secondary character that everybody likes better than the main character? The character with the most action and the most screen time or pages should be the character that carries the work. The protagonist needs to have the most compelling story, face the biggest obstacles, and be the one we most care about succeeding. He generally has the biggest character arc—that is, he is the character who changes the most. We discuss character arc in more detail in a few pages.

Although your protagonist should be your strongest presence, that's not to say that you can't have strong and quirky supporting characters. In the movie *True Lies* many people thought that Harry Tasker's (Arnold Schwarzenegger) sidekick Albert Gibson (Tom Arnold) had such a strong comedic presence in the movie that he detracted from the protagonist as the lead. He did bring a strong presence, but I think the character added more interest and expanded the fun in the story.

In my first novel-length manuscript the protagonist was a character I was interested in studying. However, a secondary character had the more interesting personality, backstory, and goals. I later realized that my protagonist would have better served as either a narrator or as a catalyst for some of the events. A chapter I submitted to a competition about the secondary character, who should have been the protagonist, even received an award. What I finally realized is that my main character was a facet of me through which I was trying to resolve some issues. Perhaps good for my own personal growth, but not so great for the story.

Exploring Ideas:

1. Which character is the most interesting?
2. Which character would readers be more interested in following and becoming attached to?
3. In what way is the protagonist transformed by the events of this story?

Who is the Enemy?

Who or what is the enemy (antagonist) that is trying to thwart the protagonist and creating the obstacles? Is it a person, a thing, a concept, or even the protagonist herself? Ask yourself, "Who is *your* enemy?" Who are *you* trying to defeat in the telling of this story? What goblin or monster from your life has raised its ugly head and has tried to defeat you as you contemplated this idea? How can you turn this goblin into your protagonist's enemy? By answering these questions you give yourself an enemy to defeat, to fight against through your protagonist. Watch the gloves come off as you put your own enemy into the shoes of your protagonist's enemy. But be careful, don't make the story about you—make the antagonist a natural enemy to the protagonist you create.

Exploring Ideas:

1. What is the protagonist afraid of?
2. Who is the antagonist for this story? Is it a person, a persona, or a thing?
3. What determines that this is the antagonist?
4. What is this antagonist afraid of?
5. What's at stake for the protagonist?

What Do You Know About Your Antagonist?

Pretty much everything that applies to your protagonist will also apply to your antagonist. When developing your antagonist, remember that even the "mafia" or drug cartels or serial murderers generally have a code of honor they won't betray. In other words, people who are evil or ruthless generally still have a moral code or code of ethics that they follow closely, believing it is what keeps them from crossing the line into total amorality. The more evil your character, the stronger keeping this possibly "bizarre code" must be maintained.

This "code of ethics" or "code of honor," no matter how outlandish it seems compared to the evil of the antagonist, *may* contain the qualities that makes the antagonist likeable or an acceptable human being—albeit clearly a transgression against the norm of ethics and morality for normal society.

- *Rafael is head of a drug cartel in South America. He is ruthless in his dealings with any man or authority who crosses his path. Retaliation is swift and vicious and always sends a message. Rafael's message: "I cut out the tongue of any man who betrays me, and I cut off the hands of any man who steals from me, and I cut off the feet of any man who leaves me." His victims' deaths always serve as an example. However, Rafael's one code is that all women, even the women and children of the betrayer, must be protected, and in fact, in more than one case he has provided support for the families of his victims. The only exception to this would be for the woman who betrays him, in which case he cuts out her heart.*

Rafael's code may be bizarre, but if we show him protecting and providing for the family of a victim, then we show an antagonist with more dimensions than just an evil one. And we leave his behavior open to surprises when he shows mercy.

There are many layers of being an antagonist. An antagonist can be a person with good intentions who is attempting to keep the main character or the antihero of the story from choices that are harmful. Or it can be the other person in a romance who doesn't want the relationship. Or the antagonist can be someone just trying to thwart the protagonist to get his or her own way. Or it can be someone who has evil intentions.

Exploring Ideas:

1. What type of antagonist is this character?
2. What are the antagonist's intentions?
3. What is your antagonist's "moral code"?
4. What is inviolable in this code?
5. What is your antagonist's one good characteristic?

Balance of Power

The balance of power in a story is a tricky thing. Conflict is created in the story when what the character wants or needs is threatened. Tension is created when the characters have opposing wants and needs during their interactions. If your protagonist and your antagonist have an equal percentage of power, then when they fight it out, the audience knows either one could win, which creates its own tension. However, think about the underdog stories in which the protagonist has no power and has to rise to the occasion. Or the community that beats back the evil forces of power over it. On the other hand, an antagonist with no power isn't much of a threat unless your story is the antagonist's rise to power. Think about your protagonist and antagonist and what percentage of power each of them have and how it changes as the story progresses.

Exploring Ideas:

1. Who has what percentage of the power, and how is the power being used?
2. What upsets the balance of power?
3. What is each character's motivation, and is it clear?

Names

In Stage 5, page 171, I will use examples with characters named Blake and Cutter. Originally I used Chuck instead of Cutter. For some reason, Chuck didn't sound to me like the name of a skilled knife fighter—not that it can't be, I just didn't see it. I started thinking about another name and came up with Cutter. When selecting names for your characters, you want to consider whether the name sounds like the person you envision or whether the reader will see another connotation in that name. The name Ted can evoke Ted Kennedy or Ted Bundy or neither, depending on the story you are writing. If it is about violence, you will probably put Bundy in your reader's mind; if writing about politics, Kennedy may come to their minds. These associations can either serve the story or put the reader's understanding of your character on the wrong track. You may also want to nickname your characters with something descriptive. In the case of Cutter, he is an expert knife fighter, and so Cutter as a nickname gives the reader a clue early on that his name has something to do with who he is. You can, but you don't have to reveal that his skill with knives is what gives him the nickname. Later, when he actually starts to use his knives, it will become clear. A character might also be called by his last name. Cutter would be an appropriate last name, but in this case it might have seemed too coincidental.

CHARACTER AND PERSONALITY PROFILE

Let's spend some time on the details and bits and pieces that will make your characters unique and memorable, vivid and a little different. This, too, is an old technique of going through a list of attributes for your characters and making choices.

My friend Audrey went through this process while she was writing a story with the working title of *The Sausagemaker's Daughters*. She created the following character profile on a large sheet of paper in a table, with her main characters across the top and their characteristics down a column under each character's name so that she could cross-compare to be sure the characters were different. Her completion of the novel was interrupted by several life events. Later, when she went back to finish, her charts and diagrams had been packed away during a home renovation, and she was unable to locate them. She had a hard time remembering some of the physical characteristics of her characters that she had so carefully charted out. My point is her technique for using a table to chart the characteristics of each character so that they could be compared was a great idea; but I suggest an easily identifiable story box would be a good place to keep your charts and diagrams, just in case.

Develop a strong profile for your main characters, but especially your protagonist and antagonist if using a persona as you work through these details.

Exploring Ideas:

This is where you will spend time developing who your character is and getting to know the character you want to create. As you work on this process, listen for your character to tell you who he wants to become. Shake things up by going against the stereotype and creating characters who are the opposite of what we expect them to be—but not illogically. Answer as many of these details for your main characters as you can.

1. CHARACTER'S PHYSIOLOGY

SEX	AGE	HEIGHT	WEIGHT
HAIR	EYES	FACIAL FEATURES	BIRTHMARKS
SKIN COLOR	SKIN TYPE	TATTOOS	DEFECTS
PHYSIQUE	POSTURE/CARRIAGE	GAIT	LEVEL OF FITNESS
MANNERISMS/TICS	PHYSICAL CHALLENGES	GROOMING	
EXAMPLE OF SPEECH PATTERN	HEALTH & PHYSICAL CONDITION	ACCIDENTS & ILLNESSES	GENERAL APPEARANCE

2. CHARACTER'S HEREDITY

NATIONAL/CULTURAL IDENTITY	PLACE OF BIRTH	RACE/ETHNICITY
DIET/TASTES/FOODS	CIRCUMSTANCES OF BIRTH	BIRTH ORDER
RELATIONSHIP W/PARENTS	SIBLINGS & ATTITUDE TOWARD EACH OTHER	HOLIDAYS CELEBRATED

3. CHARACTER'S SOCIOLOGY

SOCIAL CLASS	SOCIAL STATUS	EDUCATION
MARITAL STATUS	MILITARY SERVICE	IQ
GEOGRAPHIC LOCATION/RESIDENCE	RELIGION/RELIGIOUS PREFERENCES	WHAT IS THE CHARACTER'S OCCUPATION/CAREER?
WHY DID PROTAGONIST CHOOSE THIS CAREER?	IS THIS THE ONLY WAY THE PROTAGONIST EARNS MONEY?	RELATIONSHIPS WITH CO-WORKERS
POLITICS/POLITICAL AFFILIATION/BELIEFS	COMMUNITY INVOLVEMENT	

4. CHARACTER'S PERSONALITY

DESCRIBE THE CHARACTER'S HOME LIFE	LOVE AFFAIRS/ RELATIONSHIPS	SEX LIFE/MORALS/SEXUALITY
SPECIAL TALENTS/ SPECIAL SKILLS	MUSICAL/VOCAL/ARTISTIC/ LITERARY CAPABILITIES	ARTISTIC/LITERARY/ MUSICAL TASTES
READING MATERIAL/ MEMBERSHIPS/ SUBSCRIPTIONS	TRAVEL ISSUES/CONCERNS	SPECIAL INTERESTS/ AMUSEMENTS/ HOBBIES
WHAT DOES THE CHARACTER SPEND MONEY ON?	FEELINGS ABOUT ANIMALS/PETS	FEELINGS ABOUT FLORA
WHAT DID YOUR PROTAGONIST EAT FOR BREAKFAST?	WHAT IS THE PROTAGONIST'S FAVORITE THING TO WEAR? A HAT? CASHMERE SWEATER?	

5. CHARACTER'S PSYCHOLOGY

WORK ETHIC	VALUES	BAD HABITS/ADDICTIONS
AMBITIONS	FRUSTRATIONS	TEMPERAMENT/ PERSONALITY TYPE
WANTS/NEEDS	PERSONAL STRENGTH	FATAL FLAW
OBSTACLES TO OBTAINING WANTS/NEEDS	A DARK SECRET	A CONTROLLING PASSION
A FEAR	A REGRET	ATTITUDE TOWARD OTHERS
ATTITUDE TOWARD SELF	OTHERS' ATTITUDE TOWARD CHARACTER	ATTITUDE ABOUT LIFE
COMPLEXES/PREJUDICES	A DREAM/FANTASY	FAVORITE COLOR

6. CHARACTER'S DEVELOPMENT

What does this character carry in a wallet or purse? (i.e., pictures, IDs, credit cards, clippings, mementoes, money)
What are this character's goals?
To what extent does this character change?
What obstacle(s) prevent this character from reaching the goal(s)?
What is the outcome for this character?
PRIME motivating incident (What event created the need for action or change for this character?)
PRIME motivating force (What is driving the character to take the action or make the change?)
What things does this character want others to know about himself?
What things does this character least want others to know?
How does this character complement other characters?
How does this character conflict with other characters?
What is this character's relevance to the story?
If this is a secondary character, what is the relationship to the main character?
If an adversary, what is the relationship to the main character?
How does this character complement the main character's personality type?
How does this character conflict with the main character's personality type?
What is your character's life symbol?
What lifestyle has the character built to protect her self-identity? Most of us build lifestyles to protect our worlds and our perceptions of what the world around us should be like. Has your character built an environment to protect him from negative influences, enemies, or stimulus that would force them to change?

Avoiding Straw Characters

A straw character is a character you create to serve a purpose that the protagonist could serve better. In a writing group, one of our cowriters was working on a novel that she'd started with a character who was sort of a hippie, speak-your-mind type of guy and the protagonist's boyfriend. His sole role in the story was to introduce the rebellious nature of the main character through his demeanor, speech, and actions at a party. Only, we were seeing him and not the protagonist. Since this was the first and only time the family would meet him, it occurred to me that this one-scene character was actually standing between us and the protagonist. It would be much more interesting to see the protagonist interacting with her family and their reactions to her rebellious nature than to see it played out in a character that was going to be gone in a few pages. We were investing ourselves in a character whose sole purpose was to introduce the protagonist. The writer cut the character, and the resulting scene was more about the protagonist and her interactions with her family, and much stronger. If the boyfriend was going to be an ongoing character, then he might have been an interesting character to include. But readers get frustrated investing their emotions in a temporary character.

Exploring Ideas:

1. Do you have any straw characters that stand between your reader and the protagonist?

What Do the Characters Really Want?

We already know that the protagonist and antagonist should want something, to give the story momentum. Each additional character must have a purpose in the story, either in that they convey information (or feelings) that informs the audience or in that the character creates actions that aids or thwarts the protagonist or antagonist. Characters who need or want something, especially if it is in direct conflict with the protagonist or antagonist, add tension to the story.

Exploring Ideas:

1. What's at stake for this character?
2. How serious is the outcome for the character?
3. Is this the most important issue in the character's life at this time? Will the outcome determine the course of the character's life to be the best or the worst it can be?
4. Is what's at stake organic to who the characters are and what really matters for this story?
5. Does what's at stake become more intense when you consider the setting, the people, the circumstances, the obstacles?
6. In what way is each character transformed by the events of the story?

What Would Your Character Say to an Interviewer?

This is an old technique. By picking your favorite interviewer and pretending that person is asking your character questions or by your being the interviewer and playing hardball, you will learn things you may not have realized before about your characters.

Interview Exercise

Let your characters tell you who they are. Do a Charlie Rose or Barbara Walters interview to get an in-depth overview of your character. Choose a time limit of five to fifteen minutes and write using stream of consciousness (writing whatever comes off the top of your head without stopping to edit or read back).

Character Arc

In most stories the protagonist has an arc. Much like in the rising action of the story, the character changes, grows, and evolves through the action, although a character can spiral down as well. The arc of your character is the change they make in who they become and what they believe from the start of the story to its conclusion. Everything that happens to the protagonist, every choice she makes, will impact that arc. In a plot-driven story the character may have less of an arc; in a character-driven story the character will have a strong arc. Other characters, including the antagonist, can also have an arc. The protagonist's change should evolve from the events of the story and what happens to the character, and be influenced by other characters' responses to the protagonist's behavior. If the character doesn't change over the course of the story, the character may not be facing enough of a struggle.

There are some stories in which the protagonist does not change or have much of an arc. A comic character who is created to be comical (e.g., an absentminded professor or a comic-book character) may not have an arc of transformation. The story is about the character being funny and not necessarily about transforming the character. A comedic character is not the same as a character in a comedy situation. In a television series, movie sequels, or book series, there is generally less of a character arc for the protagonist in each episode, or the show risks losing the character the audience wants to watch. Instead of an arc, these characters may have self-realizations or gain insights into life and people. The protagonist may learn something and grow in a certain facet of their life or personality in each episode. It may be that the protagonist impacts another character's arc. It is over the course of the series that the protagonist or other main characters may have a significant character arc.

For readers to become involved with your character, the audience must empathetically struggle with the character, hoping the character will survive and achieve her goal or overcome the dilemma (or, in the antagonist's case, will be thwarted from what he wants). Your character must be compelled to achieve something so vitally important that she will stop at nothing except for what the character believes is immoral or that which goes against her principles. Even then she must question her choice and struggle with her conscience and her values in an overwhelming desire to achieve the goal, or make a concious decision to give up reaching that goal.

Answer the questions below regarding character arc. Once you have determined the changes that illustrate your ideals for the story, decide which one will have the greatest impact on the character.

Exploring Ideas:

1. How is the character (in particular the protagonist) going to grow and change? How are you going to develop this character's arc?
2. Think about your ideals and decide what changes your character has to make to best illustrate these concepts.
3. What significant threatening events create the moment of change for this character?
4. At what point in the story does the most significant event occur? Is it at the beginning, and all other events build on it? Or do all the other events lead to the one significant realization of the need for change? Is it in the middle and pivots the character(s)' direction?
5. What is the turning point for this character?
6. Or how does this character impact the protagonist's turning point?
7. What is the self-image of each of the characters? Do the characters see themselves honestly?
8. Is the character arrogant, proud of what she has accomplished, modest, or ashamed of who she is?
9. Does she not like something about herself and want to change?
10. Does she not realize she needs to change until some compelling event makes her see things differently?
11. Does she have a compelling need for something?
12. Does the character have a lifestyle she loves and some event threatens that, or is the character forced into a lifestyle she hates and wants to be different, thereby compelling her to take action?
13. Does the character change in a significant way?
14. What is the psychological or emotional impact on the character by the end of the story?
15. If the character is not changed, how can the events work to better explore the weaknesses or problems of this character?
16. Is there an unrealized need the character has as opposed to what the character is trying to obtain?
17. Does the story cause the character to become aware of a need to change?

DEFINING THE GOAL

Goal setting is interwoven with the nature of the characters you create. James Bond, MacGyver, and Superman's over arching goal may be to stop the train from going over the end of a washed-out bridge, but their approaches will be entirely different.

We talked on page 43 about the "Golden Apple" goal setting. Most characters want to acquire something, get relief from something that is negatively impacting their life, want to get revenge for some wrong (whether perceived or actual), or are compelled to achieve something great, usually to make up for something wrong they have done. What the main protagonist wants should elicit the reader's concern over whether he will get it. The audience should identify with and care about the protagonist's goal. At the very least, the protagonist's reason for desiring the goal should elicit empathy so that your reader will care about the protagonist reaching that goal.

There are at least three structural types of goals. In one, the story opens with the goal already firmly entrenched within the protagonist, but an event starts your story and makes seeking the goal at this time mandatory or impossible. In the second, the story opens in the everyday world, and something happens to set your protagonist on a quest. In the third, the protagonist's goal keeps changing as the story evolves and the events in the story create a need for a larger goal. Changing goals should always evolve to a larger goal, and if the protagonist retreats and chooses a smaller goal, the result should cause an even larger goal to become necessary. In all cases, there are obstacles or challenges, often set in motion by the antagonist, that thwart the protagonist's efforts to reach this goal. As the character meets these challenges and struggles to overcome the obstacles, there are often internal issues that the protagonist must also deal with.

- *If Sir Gregory's goal was to save the king, but finds the king has been murdered, then his goal might become to punish the evil duke who murdered him or to save the queen or the princess or prince or perhaps the country as the duke keeps moving toward his goal of acquiring the kingdom. In order to defeat the duke, Sir Gregory may have first determined to get to the castle in time to save the king (first goal). When he fails, he then has to figure out how to locate the king's family (second goal). He may have to cross the moat and break through the gate and then defeat the dragon and finally fight his way through the duke's army (third goal). Finally he confronts the duke in a climactic combat to rid the kingdom of its enemy (over arching goal).*

Each of these goals will require his being prepared to meet the challenge. This means he will have some sort of plan for how to succeed, especially since he failed the first challenge.

There should always be at least one over arching goal, with small goals that move the protagonist forward. The goal may change as the story develops, and your characters face new challenges that spin them in a new direction. Continuously evaluate the obstacles and challenges your character is facing and rethink how the goals should be changed or tweaked to meet new circumstances.

Exploring Ideas:

1. What is the protagonist trying to accomplish?
2. What is the protagonist trying to avoid?
3. What is the important thing or object or ideal that the protagonist wants?
4. What or who will keep the protagonist from getting what they want?
5. What is the *internal goal*? What inner conflict is the protagonist trying to resolve or inner desire is burning to be fulfilled within the protagonist? The protagonist may not be able to articulate this conflict or desire, but it will temper all of his actions and reactions.
6. It is imperative to have a strong *external goal* that creates action for the protagonist to strive for, as an internal goal may not create action. What is the external goal?
7. What is at stake if the protagonist does not reach the goal?
8. Who is the antagonist?
9. How will the antagonist keep the protagonist from reaching his external goal?
10. How will this impact the protagonist's internal goal?
11. What will the protagonist do to overcome that antagonist?
12. What event or turning point created the need for action or change or is driving the protagonist to keep going?
13. What is the protagonist's most immediate goal to help him reach his ultimate goal? Define the one concrete goal the protagonist is trying to achieve that drives him through the entire story and the obstacles he has to overcome to reach it.
14. What are the protagonist's and antagonist's agenda/goal? What does each want, and what will they do to get it?
15. Do the characters want and need opposing things?
16. How is the protagonist thwarted from reaching the goal?
17. Rethink your goals and what's at stake: What does the protagonist want that he is willing to risk everything—life and limb—for? What does the protagonist want more than anything else on the face of the Earth?
18. What is the protagonist willing to risk to get it?
19. What obstacles prevent the protagonist from reaching that goal?
20. What will the character do next if the goal is reached?
21. What will the character do next if the goal isn't reached?

CREATING OBSTACLES

We discussed creating obstacles beginning on page 70. The obstacles you create should be unexpected and a challenge to the protagonist. The protagonist and antagonist should be working to outsmart each other at every turn to keep the tension high and the reader engaged. Be sure the obstacles are organic to the story and, as noted above, fit the type of protagonist you have created.

Exploring Ideas:

1. Briefly describe what the main protagonist and antagonist want in the story.
2. What drives each of the characters?
3. Are they looking for adventure?
4. Do they want security or some form of recognition?
5. Are they looking for fame or power, or searching for love?
6. What motivates them to action?
7. What are the issues for each character?
8. How will the issues become challenges for each character?
9. How will the issues or challenges of the protagonist impact this character?
10. How will the issues or challenges of each character impact the protagonist?
11. How will the issues or challenges of each character impact other characters?
12. What one word describes what the character is seeking?
13. What is the internal conflict in seeking this goal?

The Job Principle

You are probably already familiar with this concept or have possibly felt all the odds were against you in your own life. In the story of Job in the Old Testament, his life went from bad to worse. He lost his children, then everything he owned, which was a considerable amount. He lost his health and then his friends, who basically told him all his suffering was his own fault. Finally, God lectured Job that he was no one to question God and reminded Job just how small he was in the scheme of things. The "Job Principle" is when, other than death, things can't get any worse. However, in the end everything was returned to Job with far more than he lost. So even when you use the Job Principle on your characters, they can still recover and come out the winner.

In the following pages we are going to discuss how to make things worse for your character.

Don't Protect Your Characters, Make 'Em Work for It

Writers sometimes don't want to put their protagonist in too much jeopardy. It appears they are protecting their protagonist, when in reality it often has to do with the writer being afraid to take risks. "What if I write myself into a corner?" "What if I put my protagonist in jeopardy and don't know how to get her out?" That's what writing is all about—exploring what could happen and developing it, finding a way out of the corner, learning something about human nature or physics *or magic,* or what it takes for your protagonist to face the worst and overcome it—or not—to figure out solutions to your protagonist's dilemmas. Remember, putting your character in a crucible or giving the character a fear that stands in their way adds to issues your character will have to deal with. Indiana Jones's fear of snakes created scenes filled with tension.

Exploring Ideas:

1. In what way are you protecting your main character?
2. What worse jeopardy could you put your characters in either physically or emotionally?
3. What are each of the characters afraid of that makes them vulnerable to their counterpart?
4. What is the protagonist afraid of that the antagonist can use against her?
5. What is the antagonist afraid of that the protagonist can use?
6. What is a phobia each of the characters has?
7. What is the protagonist's biggest fear and how are you going to confront her with it? How will she react?
8. Write "And then it got worse!", and then determine what happens next that is worse.
9. List the choices you can make to create a more tension-filled work. What different conflicts and choices could the characters be faced with? Which ones most powerfully illustrate your ideals, create tension, and dramatize the story?

"And Then It Got Worse" Exercise

By continually upping the ante and making things worse for your protagonist, you increase tension in your story and attempt to surprise the reader. The television series *24* became masters at both making things continually worse and adding the element of surprise.

1. Write the biggest obstacle in your protagonist's path or the biggest challenge. List the crisis points, and follow this line of thought with "And then it got worse!" Define what happens next and continue with this until you have turned up the heat to boiling for your protagonist. Write at least five ways that things could get worse.
2. Energy is created by tension and engages the reader. What event in the work creates the most tension? What is the highest energy beat?
3. Is the climactic moment the same as the highest energy beat or the moment of greatest tension? (Theoretically it should be.)

Why Doesn't the Protagonist Give Up?

When you stop protecting your protagonist and start increasing the jeopardy, either physically or emotionally or both, the reader will begin to wonder, "Why doesn't he just give up and go home?" As bad and as perplexing as the obstacles are is how strong the protagonist's motivation should be to keep going. You have to craft your character in such a way that it is either not their nature to give up or the stakes are too high to give up.

As we noted earlier, developing stakes that are high is a matter of developing stakes that are of life-and-death importance to your main characters. *Mary has invested her entire life, or at least her life savings, into her pet grooming business. A bad month puts her into a downward spiral financially.* This can feel like a life-and-death issue to Mary if you developed her character in a way that we see how much this pet-grooming business means to her.

Exploring Ideas:

1. Why doesn't the character quit?
2. What compels the character to keep struggling no matter what happens, against all odds?
3. Ask yourself, "Why would the character do this in this story? Or is the character's behavior just because I want this event in the story? Is it just because it is convenient?"
4. What will happen to your protagonist if he gives up?
5. What will happen in the story world if your protagonist gives up?
6. Does the work establish the everyday world of the protagonist so that it is clearly understood what is at stake if he cannot resolve this dramatic dilemma?

What is the Protagonist's Crucible?

Leadership guru Warren G. Bennis commented in his nonfiction book *Geeks and Geezers*, "The crucible is an opportunity and a test, a defining moment that unleashes abilities, forces crucial choices ... teaches a person who he/she is. People are destroyed or emerge from the crucible aware of their gifts and goals, ready to seize opportunities and make their future."

The crucible is putting your main character in the most difficult moment of her life, and the result of the crucible is finding out what she will do, how the protagonist will respond, who this character really is. This may be the climactic moment of your story when it all comes together at once, or the crucible may be just before the climactic moment, with the climax being the result of the crucible. Or the crucible might be the hook, and the rest of the story is about the protagonist finding the answers.

Exploring Ideas:

1. Does the crucible fall to your protagonist or antagonist?
2. What is the crucible for this character?
3. Do any of your secondary characters have a crucible?
4. How do the other characters impact the protagonist's crucible?

How Joseph's Dreams Turned Into Nightmares

In order to create tension and elicit your reader's growing concern, your main characters should be faced with overwhelming obstacles that just seem to get worse until the story is resolved. We talked about "and then it gets worse" in the last few pages. We'll use the story of Joseph, which you may know from the account in the Old Testament or from the popular musical *Joseph and the Amazing Technicolor Dreamcoat*.

First, Joseph's wealthy father gives him a fabulous coat as a (life) symbol of his love, which only serves to incite Joseph's brothers' jealousy. Then we learn Joseph has a special talent for interpreting dreams—only, his dreams get him into trouble when he naively insults his entire family by prophesying his own greatness. Later, when his father sends Joseph to check on his brothers, we find their jealousy has developed into hostility. The brothers throw him in a well and plot to kill him (antagonists). Just before one brother can save Joseph, the others sell him into slavery.

As a slave Joseph winds up in a foreign country where he becomes a trusted servant in charge of a household—because in spite of his circumstances, he is a man with dignity and honor. But these qualities also make him highly desirable to the woman of the house, who attempts to seduce him (a new antagonist). Rather than betray his master, Joseph flees. Just when we think it can't get any worse, the scorned woman claims Joseph attacked her using the robe he left behind as evidence against him (subplot B).

Joseph's good name is now ruined. He is thrown into jail and left to rot. But Joseph remains true to himself, and so eventually the jailer grows to trust him, putting him in charge. After the great Pharaoh's baker and cup bearer incur Pharaoh's wrath and are jailed, they both have troubling dreams, and Joseph uses his special talent to interpret those dreams. They promise to tell Pharaoh of Joseph's abilities, and the reader believes at last Joseph will be freed (subplot C). But the baker is hanged and the cup bearer forgets about Joseph until Pharaoh has a dream no one can interpret. Then the cup bearer remembers the one man who can save the day.

Joseph is brought from prison to interpret Pharaoh's dream. When he does so, he is rewarded for his talent with position and riches. Then he proves his wisdom by preparing the country for the impending disaster while enriching Pharaoh's coffers. But now he faces the greatest challenge of all—confronting the brothers who betrayed him. This is the final and most important test of Joseph's character. He has wealth, power, and the support of the Pharaoh. He can do anything he wants to these men, but he chooses to test what sort of men they have become by accusing one of them of stealing from him. He holds the brother prisoner until the other brothers return, bringing his youngest brother, whom their father is terrified of losing. Joseph has his servants plant stolen property on the youngest brother and once again accuses them, at which time he sees whether his brothers will protect the youngest one (climatic moment). All ends well when one of the brothers offers to accept the blame, and Joseph finally reveals who he is (revelation) and forgives them. The outcome is that he gets what he wanted most of all, to be reunited with his beloved father and younger brother (resolution). Joseph's family moves to Egypt to be near him and avoid the famine (tag).

Characterization Mapping

Below is another way to look at the relationship of your characters and to see how much importance you have given to each one and whether they are being developed appropriately for your story.

Start at the top with who the characters are in the backstory or beginning of the story and move down toward the conclusion of the story. The circles are for the main and secondary characters, and their placement from the top to the bottom represents where they are located in the story. The size of the circle or ovals (triangles or trapezoids, if you prefer) should be comparable to the number of pages they are actually in the story, as well as their importance to the story. Moving from left to right is where you place the circle in relationship to being either the protagonist, to a supporter or friend, to an obstacle, to finally being the antagonist. The bottom circle on the right is dashed because the reader won't know whether these characters are still antagonists or have moved on the scale until after the climax.

This is just another tool to help you visually see the relationship of your characters. It will reveal if you might be shortchanging a character or if a particular character is getting more space in the story than is warranted, considering his importance to the story.

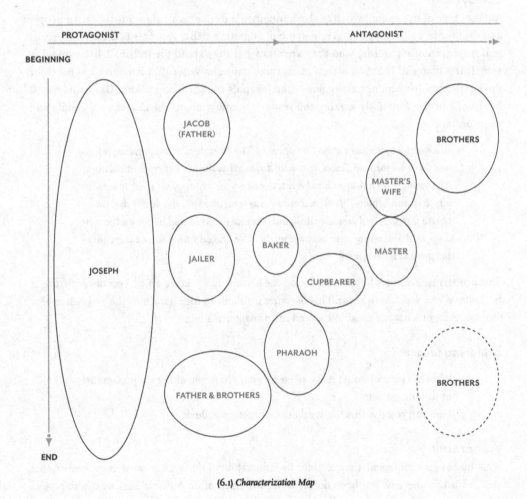

(6.1) *Characterization Map*

Character Map Exercise

Create a character map for your story. The shape you use doesn't have to be drawn exactly—it is just an approximation for how you perceive the characters' relationships in your story.

Life Symbol

Another type of metaphor, which is also a mnemonic device, is a "life symbol." Often people and events are defined by a concrete symbol, something that represents their interests or philosophy, in other words, who they are and what they stand for in life. A life symbol is something material that you attach to an important character that becomes a symbol for the character's life and her struggles—like Joseph's coat of many colors. Used this way it becomes a device for subtly jogging the reader's memory about the character's agenda and its importance.

- *In a novel-length manuscript I wrote called* The President's Trigger, *the protagonist was a washed-up Soviet hero, now displaced in the present geopolitical world. As a young man a dragon had been tattooed on the inside of his wrist to serve as a type of mind control. It turned out he was somewhat allergic to the dye, which caused flare-ups and over time disfigured the dragon, as he and his life had become disfigured and out of sync with the world. The dragon tattoo served throughout the story as a life symbol.*

Think in terms of a nun's habit or the locket the heroine never takes off that carries a picture of her beloved who was lost in a war. This becomes symbolic to the character's life and either what she stands for or what has most influenced the protagonist's life.

Exploring Ideas:

1. What life symbol would make sense for your character, either the protagonist or the antagonist?
2. How can you use this life symbol as a mnemonic device?

Vulnerability

What makes your protagonist vulnerable? By vulnerability I don't mean weakness—rather, that area in his life where he has been deeply wounded. Each of us does the best we can to protect that part of us. Characters with that kind of vulnerability bring out the audience's protective nature—we all identify.

In creating the character's vulnerability, avoid something contrived and, whenever possible, stay away from all the cliché wounds: she was raped, he was abused by his father, he never fit in with his family, she was adopted at birth and never got over being given away—unless you can present it with a twist. Create a vulnerability that is new to this character and organic to his life in that much of what he does and how he behaves evolved to protect that wound, but the character isn't just about being wounded. There are moments in the story that threaten to expose the wound and bring out the character's vulnerability. A short story might be about that moment when the character has to face his vulnerability.

In my short story "The Bus Boy," *Ollie is a recovering alcoholic who has already lost everything. He is slowly rebuilding his life but is still only one step away from ending up back on the streets. He is vulnerable to the aftermath of one bad choice or if someone else seeks to do him harm. Ollie has one small dream left, which is his goal in this story. But his vulnerability to losing everything again makes that dream seem out of reach and impossible.* When he makes a choice that will probably put him back on the streets, the reader is afraid for him. Readers tell me that they really cared about whether Ollie's dream came true and what happened to him. They empathized with him, and he became a character they can't forget. People identify with Ollie's vulnerability—a weakness that keeps many people from their dreams. They know what it feels like to be vulnerable and frightened and to have a dream that seems just out of reach, to make choices with unintended consequences. To read how the concept of vulnerability plays out, you can find the entire story on my website at http://thewriters compass.com.

I believe that one of humankind's base fears is being unimportant, ignored, and unnoticed as we go through life. When our characters have that moment of fearing no one cares, and that it is all for nothing, most readers will identify because it taps into our own deepest anxieties.

Exploring Ideas:

1. What is your protagonist's vulnerability?
2. Why this particular vulnerability?
3. How does this vulnerability manifest itself?

CHARACTER TIME LINE

Just like the history and story time lines, your characters have a time line for events and how those events impact the way they respond. Take some time to work out your characters' time line by completing the exercise below.

Character Time Line Exercise

The protagonist or antagonist must have a dramatic purpose that must embody the character's needs, with resulting behaviors that trigger actions. Chart events in each character's life to identify and arrange the chronology of major scenes. These events can be what occurred as background to the story, during the story, or what the writer projects will happen after the story.

1. List dates or the time frame of events that influence the protagonist.
2. List the cause or stimulus of each event.
3. List the effect or result caused by the event.
4. Is the outcome feasible?

DATE OR TIME FRAME	EVENT	CAUSE/STIMULUS	EFFECT/RESPONSE

TOOLS FOR STAGE 3

Following are a number of general questions to help you get a handle on who your characters are and what their relationship to the story and each other is. By the way, the tighter the universe in the story world, the tighter the circle of humanity, the more organic the connection, the more tension between connected/related people, the higher the stakes!

Exploring Ideas:

1. Who is the character?
2. What does this character want?
3. In one sentence, what is this character's goal or dramatic purpose that must embody her needs, stakes, and resulting behaviors *that trigger actions*?
4. What is the character's motivation?
5. What causes this character to behave this way?
6. Is the character likeable? Intriguing? Interesting? Fascinating?
7. Would individual readers want to spent time getting to know this character and his or her story?

8. Why would the audience care about this character?
9. Why now? Why do you want to look at this particular character in this particular situation now?
10. Is there a particular problem you want to explore?
11. What is the world of this character?
12. What routine does the character follow?
13. Whom and what does this character love?
14. Whom and what does this character hate?
15. Who are the character's friends?
16. Who are the character's associates at work or in their career?
17. How does the character come across (cynical, trusting, dominated, domineering, etc.)?
18. How would your character state their philosophy of life?
19. What do we learn of this character's history or backstory?
20. What is the protagonist's status in life?
21. What is the protagonist's career?
22. Who is she when out and about in the world?
23. How does the protagonist behave with family and friends?
24. What does the protagonist think about or do when all alone and no one else sees?
25. What is the protagonist's philosophy of life?
26. Can you map out the character's actions and see what is driving his or her actions?
27. What would the protagonist dream? (Perhaps the character's dream or ambition is to become someone important or to become the best at something, but in this story the most this character can hope for is to not embarrass herself by failing and losing or causing the group or team to lose.)
28. If the character could impact the world, what would she change to make an ideal world even beyond the world of the story?
29. What does your antagonist dream of?
30. What is this character's ambition?
31. How does this character envision the perfect life?
32. Can you change the sex, age, career, background of this character to put a twist in your story?
33. What is at stake for the secondary characters?
34. Is it compelling enough for this character to have a place in this story?
35. Does the character have a specific role to play and a challenge to offer that feeds the tension of the story?
36. What are the tightest relationships your characters can have to connect them more closely?
37. If you have a conceit for this story, how can you refine it with what you now know about your characters or the metaphors you have created?
38. Write a dynamic one-page synopsis of your story.

Marlin's Story Map

On page 48, we discussed Marlin's story, the hapless character who is trying to get to the pharmacy to get a prescription filled before it closes so that he is prepared to meet with his boss the next day. The map shows how the resolution of one obstacle leads to the next obstacle. Below is Marlin's story map.

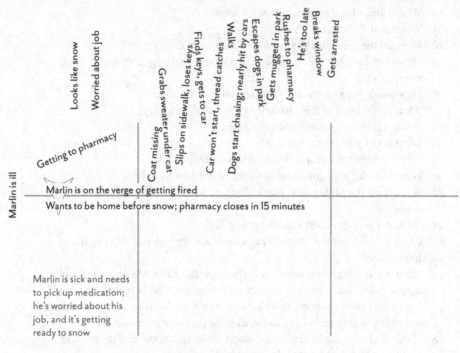

(6.2) *Marlin's Story Map, Resolution of One Obstacle Leads to the Next Obstacle*

Tools for Development

Return to pages 88 and review the questions. Write the answers according to what you have learned in this stage.

chapter 7

STAGE 4—STRUCTURING SCENES, SEQUENCES, AND TRANSITIONS

Let's start by clarifying the term *sequence*. A sequence in a screenplay means a series of scenes that form a unit or a cohesive group around a central idea or plot point. On page 34 we discussed a 6-Scene or 6-Sequence screenplay. There is also an 8-Sequence model taught by some universities such as the University of Southern California's School of Cinematic Arts.

A sequence in a novel refers to that writing without action that occurs between scenes in which the character expresses emotion, evaluates, sets goals, plans the next move, adds information, or the writer sets up for the next action scene. For our purpose, this is the definition we will give to the term *sequence*.

SHAPING THE STORY

Stage 4 is an in-depth look at each of the individual scenes, sequences, and transitions of your story. Think of Stage 4 as a process for getting the best writing into each of these. In particular, this stage will help you to advance the structure of your story and determine whether you have filled in the holes and have incomplete ideas. This stage will take your writing to a new level by giving you a deeper understanding of your story and helping you evaluate your story section by section. This does not mean that these will be your final ideas or scenes, as you may continue to add or change some ideas in Stages 5 and 6.

Stage 4 is probably the most work intensive of the 7 Stages. But when you complete this stage, you should have a very structurally sound and organic story. The work you do in Stage 4 will make unnecessary the need for additional revisions you might otherwise need to do. *If you stick with the process, you may experience frustration; however, that will probably be followed by amazing breakthroughs in both your story and in your writing.* As always, in this stage you will most likely continue adding new ideas.

Again, some of the questions may sound repetitious—they are. The purpose for repeating the questions is to ask them in a new way, to get you to think about them from different angles, to push you deeper in your thought processes and to give you perspective.

CHECKING FACTS

Stage 4 is the dividing point in the 7-Stage process. I constructed the first three stages to develop the story, Stage 4 will help you analyze the strength of the components of your story. And the last three stages help you to refine your story. Therefore, Stage 4 is a good point to check facts and do some of the research, now that you have enough of your story completed to know what you need to know. Since this is the final development stage, if a logical fact blows your plot apart, you can still make adjustments, and you haven't wasted time on refining the story. Look for any places that the facts could be obviously wrong to the reader. You might also find that research will help you fill in holes where you weren't quite sure what you needed to write. Save your notes until the end of working through this stage, then do the research and follow up by incorporating your new ideas and facts into the work you've done.

If you are relying on a true event as the background of your story, you will probably want to include several real facts about that event to give your story credibility. You can always create a story with the concept of "What if it didn't happen that way, but happened this way instead?" The reader will buy it if your changes have enough truth to be believable.

Even obscure facts should be truth based. There is always someone who will know that this is a mistake and careless on your part. If you use a specific day in a specific location, and you say it was raining cats and dogs, however the truth is that there was a dry heat wave, you will lose your credibility with the reader who knows the truth, as well as to any of that reader's friends. That being said, there are many facts that you can change to suit your story by not being too specific and by only adding in enough details to make it sound real. Using the name of a fake city instead of a real city works if you give enough details so that the reader can visualize where it would be and what it would look like. In my short story "The Bus Boy," mentioned earlier, I used the city of Long Beach, California, which is real, and wrote about a part of the city where I once lived. Although similar locations do exist in that area and some of the streets are real, most of the locations were fictional, created to serve the story. I used my own experiences and knowledge of a place to include enough details to make it sound and feel real.

If you are inserting a character into a real event, you will probably want to have a plausible reason for why that character is there. If it's a major event everyone knows about involving only a few people, your readers might wonder why they've never heard of this person before, so you will have to give the character a reason for being in the story but out of the limelight. You could write the story with details that sound similar to the real event, but change some of the details, such as the location or time frame, so that your readers will identify with the actual event but understand this is not that event.

If the event involves many people, then you can easily write a reason for this character's involvement. For example, a story about a serial killer could involve many police detectives and officers that no one has ever heard of. However, the story of a second murderer connected to the real killer would be less believable unless you had a viable reason for why he was never caught or known about. In which case, it might be easier or less convoluted to write about a fictional serial killer and his partner, using selected details from real events. Or you might write about a fictional victim that no one ever connected to the real killer and so has never been identified. Again, it might be easier to create the story and characters. You will want to be very careful writing about people and events that aren't real and connecting them to people who are real—you don't want to distort the truth or be insensitive to survivors and family members or sell a story that will get you sued for defamation of character.

And note that science fiction, fantasy, magical realism, and other genres like these still require fact checking. You don't want to base your facts on bad science. You want your readers to accept your story because it is based on enough facts to make it plausible. Readers will not accept ideas that go against what they know about the laws of physics or aerodynamics unless you create a plausible logic. Knowing the facts help you determine what is plausible.

I don't know if this will hold true for you, but writers I've talked to often say that they had a gut instinct and find during the research that their writing was in the ballpark of the actual facts. I think this has much to do with the process of what we learn throughout our lives being stored in the "digital repositories" in our brain. You put in a key word or phrase, and out pops the answer from some place you didn't know you had the information stored.

There is a quote that many people use: "Never let a few facts stand in the way of a good story." I always thought that Mark Twain said it, but I couldn't find it attributed to him. What he actually said was, "Get your facts first, and then you can distort them as much as you please." I'm advocating know your story first, then find the facts you need and then "distort" them as much as required to create a good yarn. I do have one caveat: If you are telling a true story—not a story based on legend, but a story about a real person or a real event—don't tell lies. Or, at least, make sure your audience knows the event is real, but the story is fiction.

On page 167 I will note a good place to begin your research. However, if needing to research stands in the way of your writing, then move ahead with your research. As you go through the scenes, sequences, and transitions, note any facts that need to be checked or any research you need to do.

ARE THE SCENES ACTIVE AND RELEVANT?

By now you should have a pretty good handle on your story. This is where you tear your story apart and say, "I can make this better." By breaking the story down and examining each component more closely, you will:

- Discover weaker areas that can be strengthened
- Find holes in the story
- Determine where the story needs building
- Decide where there is too much detail given to unimportant events
- Create new ideas for adding energy and excitement
- Expand segments that are relevant

- Eliminate segments that are not relevant
- Develop aspects of the story that should be mined to their fullest creative advantage

We'll start with some issues we want to address in this stage, and then we'll discuss the three main components of stories: scenes, sequences, and transitions.

Breaking Up the Story

Because there will probably be many scenes, sequences, and transitions in your story, you will want to use separate sheets of paper, index cards, or computer files for your answers. As mentioned before, my process is to break up my story into beats and print each separately onto 5x8 cards or index card stock, then to mark them for what I perceive are the scenes, sequences, and transitions. I then answer the questions for each separately. As I develop new ideas, I create new cards that can be slipped in to my pile of story cards. I am often surprised to learn what I thought was a sequence would really make a great scene, or a scene I wrote would be better as a sequence or only alluded to in a transition since there isn't enough information or opportunity to create tension. Sometimes transitions are actually sequences or can be shortened or even eliminated to be more effective.

Since your process is not necessarily the same as mine, use whatever method of dividing up the story seems best to you. Although this is work intensive, it should not feel overwhelming and cause you frustration (other than the frustration we all go through just before we reach a breakthrough in our development as writers), as that will defeat the benefit this stage can add to your work. In this stage you have the opportunity to see significant growth in your story.

THE OPENING

Writers often find that the first several pages, even chapters, of their writing contains unnecessary information for the reader. It is usually background information and useful to the writer as a method of brainstorming and development. While these ideas started the story, they may often be cut (any necessary details may be moved to a later point in the story as lines in dialogue, flashbacks, or exposition in other scenes).

Exploring Ideas:

1. What is the most dynamic beginning for this story?
2. Can you cut or condense the opening without losing anything that moves the story forward?

3. Can you cut the opening and increase the tension or tighten the sense of urgency?
4. What have your characters revealed to you that should be included in the plot that you have not yet written?

WHAT'S WORKING AND NOT WORKING?

By now your internal writer's compass should be nudging you toward your true north—follow it. If your instincts tell you something doesn't feel right, then something is probably wrong. One of the reasons for all of the questions is so that the analytical side of your brain can figure out problems and solutions. Once you've identified a problem, give the analytical side of your brain a chance to work on it. Move to a different aspect or section of the story, take a break, read a book, watch a movie, go hiking or bicycling, do something different that will stimulate your creativity.

Remember, a scene doesn't work when:

- It's too convoluted or complicated
- You've had to skip areas of explanation because they were boring to write, but their absence leaves the reader confused
- You forget the reader doesn't know information that is in your head, but not on the page
- You make illogical assumptions or ask the reader to believe something you haven't shown them to be true
- You think your audience is stupid and you don't respect their knowledge as informed readers

Remember that readers love a good yarn, and they are willing to follow you if you make the story:

- Interesting
- Move at a fast enough pace for the genre you are writing in, but not so fast that you leave out good storytelling moments
- Speak to their intelligence
- Filled with tension and energy so that the reader can't put it down

What Is My Story Missing?

The story map is a broader gauge to see where your story has missing elements. In the following pages we look more closely to find where there may be unanswered questions or holes in your scenes and sequences. As you answer the questions, don't skim—be aware of when something isn't working in your story or when something seems to be missing. I'm sure you have had the same experience when reading your work that I have when reading mine: You know something isn't quite right, but you skim through it and think you will come back to it later. Stage 4 *is* later—it's today! Don't ignore the niggling feeling you get as you read. This is your compass kicking in to tell you something needs to be fixed.

Exploring Ideas

1. Start by rewriting a sentence in twenty-five words or fewer that describes the story using active words. By now you should know and understand what you want to say, which may have changed from where you started.
2. What have your characters revealed to you that should be included in the plot?
3. How does the story begin?
4. What is the story's ending?
5. What scenes do you need to get there? Be sure to list the ones you know are missing.
6. What is missing that you might find answers for through research?
7. The way you present your story is important so that a literary manager, editor, agent, producer, director, actor will pick it up and say, "This is something new and exciting!" What should you change to accomplish this?

Storyline Timeline

Let's look at the time frame of your story and see what is going on and which major story events will happen.

1. List the date or time frame of these events, followed by the event.
2. Next, write how these influenced the events of the story and, finally, what happens as a result.
3. Ask yourself if the end result is a reasonable outcome.

TIME FRAME	EVENT	IMPACT ON STORY	END RESULT

When Do I Tell Versus Show?

As you break down the scenes you should note where you are showing and where you are telling. Not all scenes are shown; some scenes are only alluded to. This is where we sometimes need to tell rather than show. As noted before, showing some scenes slows the story down. Briefly telling what happened in a scene—versus showing a whole scene—may better serve the story and keep it moving forward. Placing too many active scenes together could possibly cause the reader to become lost if there isn't a sequence in which the character reveals her feelings or evaluates the information gathered from previous scenes.

HOW DO I BREAK DOWN THE STORY TO MAKE IT STRONGER?

In the following pages I will show you how to break the story down into components so that you can examine each part to see whether it keeps the story energized and informs the reader, builds character, or advances the story. Each question is designed to help you think through the component and to either enhance it, rearrange it, or possibly eliminate some segments that actually detract from the story. You will also see where the sequences should be scenes or whether scenes should be sequences, and where you have missed opportunities by alluding to a scene or where you have slowed a story down by overwriting.

What are the Beats to the Story?

There are many ways a beat is used in writing. A beat is the rhythm in each line of a poem. A beat can also be each line or sentence, sometimes a phrase or paragraph that builds a scene. These scenes then create the story. Basically, a beat is one idea or thought that builds upon another idea or thought. The beats of the story are the smallest components you can break the story into that still make sense. There is not a formula for how small or large a beat is.

For example, on a page of dialogue, each speaker's comments would be separate beats. If the speaker has more than one line/sentence or several thoughts in the speech, then each of those might be a beat. In narrative, a beat is an independent thought. There might be one thought across several paragraphs, depending on the amount of description used, or there might be a separate thought in each sentence. In a screenplay or a play, a beat might be a line of dialogue or a single moment in an action shot. In a novel or short story, a beat could be a sentence or a paragraph or more and includes the moment of energy, action, or thought, along with any description that goes with it. When that thought or action changes, the beat ends.

However, for our purposes, each beat should be a cohesive whole and can be as long or as short as you need to work with it. A beat should not be so short that it will take you longer to break down the beats and work with them than it did to write the story. Nor should this be a frustration to you because you are working with sections that are too small. You can also write a single sentence or phrase with the central idea, theme, or metaphor of each section as your own mnemonic device for what the scene or sequence contains, if that works better for you.

The Difference Between Scenes, Sequences, and Transitions

The scene is where the action takes place. A scene is faster paced and different from a sequence or transition. Sequences can be a sentence or several pages, and their purpose is to convey thoughts and emotions, plan the next event, or set goals. Basically a sequence provides information. A sequence is the part of the story where the character has time to reflect on events and show more in-depth emotions and thoughts, which lead to the next scene or sequence. A scene may also contain emotions, thoughts, and planning as part of the scene. Scenes with quick moment-to-moment action, and shorter sequences with less emotion, thoughts, and detail speed up the pace. Scenes that contain more thought, emotions, and physical details slow down the pacing, as do longer sequences.

A transition is a few words, a simple statement, or even a paragraph or more, which indicates a change in time, place, or point of view (POV) from the last scene or sequence. Scenes and sequences can be alternated or used in multiples, depending on how you want to pace your story. A transition slips in between scenes or sequences to make the change smoother.

Scenes

While a scene is about action, as noted above it may still contain thoughts and emotions, but those are not the purpose for the scene. The purpose of a scene is for something to happen in such a way that the reader can visualize it.

In a screenplay a scene is specifically set off by a shot header that states where the scene is and if it's day, night, morning, evening, afternoon, or continuous. The scene changes whenever there is a change of location, setting, or time of day, or sometimes characters, or when the characters move from inside to outside or vice versa.

In a play a scene is more often delineated by a change of time, although it can also be the setting change, and is shown by either the stage going dark, lighting changes, sometimes music. When the curtain comes down and goes up without an intermission, that can be a new scene. A change in lighting, or people leaving the stage for a moment and returning to a different spot on the stage, usually denotes a scene change as well.

In a novel or short story scenes contain the action of the story, although they can also contain exposition. A scene is what is happening in a particular place at a particular time between a set of characters. The scene generally has its own mini rising action and climactic moment on a much smaller scale. The scene changes when the time, location, place, or characters change, or shortly after that mini climactic moment.

Scenes should be shown in an active moment-by-moment detail to keep the reader involved and the action immediate. The scene should be full of tension created by conflict. Even when the scene is between lovers and friends, what they want from each other isn't necessarily the same thing. When it isn't, it creates tension, which gives energy to the story. Energy is that little thump of adrenaline that gets you excited, makes you scared, keeps you reading. Allow yourself to feel that energy and recognize when it's absent. You'll find the writing becomes more dynamic when you can recognize what isn't there that should be or what shouldn't be there that you've included.

Sequences

A sequence is when the character takes a breather and reflects on events with in-depth emotions and thoughts. The character evaluates what happened in the last scene, whether actually written or only alluded to. Long sequences may break up a scene into segments. For example, a flashback of a paragraph or more in a scene would break a scene into two parts.

In a sequence we also learn how the character or characters will respond to the events in the previous scene, what the new immediate goal is, and whether it has changed or if the characters are in a quandary. The sequence also refreshes the reader's memory about the overall goal and any important clues or details the reader may have missed or forgotten, if the events occurred very many pages back.

The sequence can also misdirect the reader by the character's believing one thing when in actuality something else is happening. The reader may or may not be aware the character is wrong. If the reader knows the character is wrong, this can build suspense in the reader's alarm for the character's naiveté, unless the reader believes the character shouldn't be that gullible or that stupid. If the reader doesn't know the character is misinformed, then the reader also goes down the wrong path, which can end up in both reader and character being surprised—as long as the wrong path is organic to the story and makes sense in the end.

Finally in the sequence the character makes a plan that leads to the next scene or possibly another sequence, depending on your story development. Too many sequences, or sequences that are too long, diffuse the energy in the story.

Transitions

A transition generally has the same meaning in all formats. We are transitioning from one scene to the next, from one setting to the next, or changing time frames or characters or from a scene to a sequence or vice versa.

The single purpose of the transition is to move the reader forward to a new time, place, setting, or point of view. It can be a word, phrase, sentence, or even a paragraph, but generally not longer. Try to vary the transition length and the way it is used, keeping in mind how it will enhance or introduce the scene or sequence. Ask yourself: "Does the transition move the reader from the last scene or sequence, or change the time, setting, place, or POV in a manner that continues the story and doesn't confuse the reader?"

Acts

Acts are a larger component of the story that contain scenes, sequences, and transitions, more along the lines of the breakdown in the structure chart. An act break occurs when a story has a major change in either direction or time or focus. Not all stories have act breaks. Novels sometimes call act breaks "Part #" or "Book #." In a play an intermission usually indicates an act change. Act changes in a screenplay are not so obvious, but in a TV script an act change can be set for commercial breaks.

Sequel Notes

As you work through the questions in this stage, look at whether this story could grow into a series. Is there potential for a sequel, a second book to follow the characters' lives or the events even further?

Is there enough material for a trilogy of screenplays? Could you create an episodic series for television or for the Internet? Although there have been plays written that follow a theme, it is more rare for plays to have sequels. You might also look at the story to see whether it might be told in other forms: a play as well as a screenplay, a screenplay as well as a novel, or vice versa. Make notes as you go through the story for how you might build a sequel or what you might use or change. As you look over these ideas, would any of them better serve the story you are currently writing?

TOOLS FOR STAGE 4

Answer the questions below as they apply to each of your scenes, sequences, and transitions. Yes, it is a lot of work, but how much work is it to go through your story twenty-five or thirty times without understanding what needs to be fixed?

Exploring Ideas:

1. Break your story into beats in any system that works for your writing process. Or, rather than beats, separate your story into scenes, sequences, and transitions. Mark which one each is at the top of the card or page. You will want a separate answer sheet for each scene and each sequence.
2. Keeping your story in order, match the scenes to correlate with the elements on the structure chart.
3. Which scenes in each element should be strengthened? Eliminated? Added? If you are using index cards, remove those you don't need (they aren't lost to you, just taken out of the group) or add new ones.
4. Are the scenes active and always relevant to the core dramatic dilemma?
5. Pull scenes out that seem to slow the story down too much and see if that picks up the pace and reads better. Is the story still clear and organic?
6. Which scenes overcomplicate the story?
7. What objects and mnemonic devices stand out that could be enhanced to benefit the process of storytelling?
8. Did you adequately resolve the main story question that kept the reader up all night to find out the answer?

Scene Development

Many of the questions for structuring the novel and structuring scenes are similar.

Exploring Ideas:

1. Give the setting, location, time frame, season, and the physical and emotional environment of this scene.
2. Write an active description of the scene in twenty-five words.

3. Where you place your emphasis tells the reader what the most important aspect of the scene is and clarifies the direction of your story. What is the most important thing you want to impart to the reader in this scene? Are you focusing on that?

4. Enhance scenes and pick up the pace by looking at the details to see whether they are appropriate for the pacing of this scene.

5. Is the scene boring? Rewrite mundane scenes into interesting scenes.

6. Does the scene say what you want to say clearly?

7. Does this scene keep the story active and relevant to the core dramatic dilemma?

8. Does this scene tell the story in the best possible way?

9. Are you using the right POV for this scene?

10. Is this scene an *essential key scene* needed to tell the story? In what way?

11. What is your purpose for writing this scene? Do you just like your own writing? Does it add to the story? Does it further the story or add texture? Does it add some new information about the character or event?

12. Who is in the scene? Any scene with more than two people becomes increasingly complicated to write as well as more difficult to control and create tension. Carefully consider who is in the scene. What is each person's role in this scene? Is that role necessary to the scene?

13. What is the protagonist's immediate goal in this scene to help reach the ultimate goal? Think about what the protagonist wants to achieve, what the other person in the scene wants to achieve, and how you can put them at odds with each other to create more tension in the scene.

14. What will each character do to get what he wants? When answering, consider the following:
    a. How will it be stated (light, comical, deadly serious)?
    b. Do the characters want or need opposing things?
    c. Who has what percentage of the power, and how is the power being used?

15. Why is the character doing this, and why in this place? Does it move him closer to the goal, away from the enemy, or perhaps it puts him at odds with what is at stake for him?

16. Why would a character do this in this story? Is it just because it is convenient? Why would she go there/turn this way/do that?

17. Does the reason feel organic or manufactured?

18. Whose POV is it told in? Although it is important to be consistent in how you handle POV, if you have more than one POV character in a scene, you will want to give some thought as to how effectively each character could interpret the scene.

19. Should a character be added or eliminated to make the scene more effective?

20. Once you identify the main conflict, answer the following:

    a. What is each character's motivation, and is it clear?

    b. What is the character afraid of?

    c. How is the character thwarted from reaching the goal in this scene?

    d. What is the highest energy beat? Energy is created by tension and engages the reader. What point of the scene creates the most tension? What is the climactic moment of the scene?

    e. What is the payoff moment?

    f. Why doesn't the character quit?

    g. What will the character do next?

21. What is the conflict or disaster in this scene?

22. What caused the overriding event in the scene, what is the result, and is it reasonable? Is the impact appropriate?

23. What will the repercussions of this scene be in later scenes, and is that the direction you want the story to go?

24. How will this scene be resolved?

25. Is this the most active way to show this scene?

26. How does the scene end? Will it make the reader turn the page to see what happens next? What should you change to make this a page-turner?

27. Is the buildup full of business rather than active plot points that affect the protagonist's dramatic journey?

28. What are the story questions that will be answered?

29. What did you leave unresolved that put your character in greater danger so that the audience wants to find out how it will be resolved?

30. What new story questions did you raise?

31. Is this scene in the best possible arrangement of the events to execute the story? Does the tension rise or fall?

32. Could this scene be alluded to in a transition and deleted to increase the pacing of the story? Would deleting the scene impact the story's clarity? Rather than a scene, does this really fit the description of a sequence?

33. Rewrite an active sentence in twenty-five words or fewer describing this scene.

After answering the above questions, what you have tried to accomplish in this scene should be much clearer and you should be able to rewrite a more focused description of the scene.

Sequence Development

Exploring Ideas:

1. What is the emotional state of the character after each scene? How did the previous scene leave the character, and how is the character responding?

2. What are the character's thoughts? Has the previous scene left the character disoriented or thinking irrationally? At what point does the character start thinking rationally?

3. What is your purpose for writing this sequence? Do you just like your own writing? Does it add to the story? Does it further the story or add texture? Does it add some new information about the character or event?

4. How does the character review what has happened to him? Is it in a manner appropriate to the type of story? (In a mystery, the character might review clues and form some opinions; in a romance, the character might idealize moments with the object of his affection or plan future encounters.)

5. How much time does the character spend analyzing? Is it appropriate for the pacing?

6. Does the character remind the reader of important events that will impact the story, and why they are important?

7. As the character analyzes the situation, does he reveal more about himself, the situation, other characters?

8. Does the character evaluate the goal?

9. What planning does the character do to move forward to accomplish his story goal or overcome the latest obstacle? What decision does the character make for a new short-term goal to take him closer to the story goal? Does the information cause the reader to anticipate more excitement to come?

10. What action does the character take to move forward and plunge into the next scene facing the next obstacle? Rather than leaving the character sitting and waiting, have you caused him to be proactive and move toward the next scene to keep the reader engaged?

11. Is there another character in this sequence, and what is that character's purpose?

12. Is there an opportunity to create a dynamic scene out of this sequence?

Transition Development

Exploring Ideas:

1. Does the transition move the reader from the last scene or sequence or change the time, setting, place, or POV in a manner that continues the story and doesn't confuse the reader?

2. Can the transition be eliminated or shortened?

3. Is there a missing scene alluded to in the transition? Should that scene be written?
4. Does the transition have potential to become a scene or sequence that would increase the story's creativity and development?

Mary's and Fred's Story Map

Below is an example of Mary's and Fred's story map from page 46. Mary's husband, Leonard, needs brain surgery, but the only doctor who will consider the operation is her brother, Fred, who has a drinking problem since his wife's death.

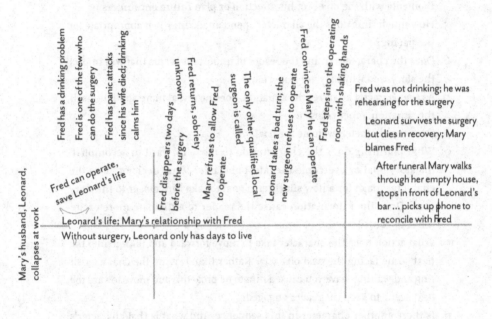

(7.1) *Mary's and Fred's Story Map*

Tools for Development

Now return to the Tools for Development on page 88 and go back through those questions. Update your answers to reflect the new information you've gained from the work you've done in Stage 4 and the changes you've made.

Whew!!!

That was a lot of work. However, I would be very much surprised if you did not find it well worth your efforts. Let's take a break and do the research you've noted before we move on to Stage 5.

RESEARCH

This is the point where you stop and follow up on the research notes you have compiled.

- Don't overdo the research.
- Don't overthink the research.

Research enough so that you can use appropriate terminology, equipment, technology, science, geography, and landmarks. However, add your own level of quirkiness to it all. As you research, new ideas will be created. Keep track of these ideas and include them as appropriate.

Although the Internet is an easy way to research, remember being on the Internet doesn't make it valid. A good way to research is to ask a librarian for help. Librarians are trained to know where to find information quickly. Newspapers and magazines are also a good source, especially if they lead you to an expert you can interview.

Keep track of your sources. List the name of the book or magazine, the author, publisher, and page number, or copy down the website precisely and be sure to note the date you found the source, as web material can change from one day to the next. If you need to return to the material later, having all these details will help you relocate it, or you may even need to cite references.

- Set up a logical method of doing your research and taking notes, whether on note cards, a computer file, an Access database or an Excel spreadsheet. Include the source information so that you can go back to it if you need to retrieve something.
- Incorporate any new details or changes into your story right away or make notes where they should go. Include these on your tracking sheet.
- Go through your new ideas and see which ones will enhance your story. Then add them in or set aside ideas that sounded good but don't really work.

Return to working on your story.

chapter 8

STAGE 5—INCREASING TENSION AND ADJUSTING PACING

In Stage 4 we looked at the scenes and sequences to find holes, to clarify scenes from sequences, and to eliminate what wasn't working. By now the story should have a strong structure and most of the elements of the story in place. In Stages 5 through 7 you will look at the final steps to refine the story you have created. Stage 5 focuses on increasing the tension you need to sustain the story and to ensure that the tension rises. It also is the place to adjust the pacing of the story so that it moves quickly enough to be a page-turner, but slow enough to let the reader savor and stay involved. Although you have entered the final stages, throughout this process you will probably continue to discover new ideas that you can incorporate into your story or that will give you answers to story questions you hadn't figured out yet.

I have found that these latest ideas:

- could possibly enrich the story, even this late in development
- may actually already be somewhere in the story
- could take you in the wrong direction because they are overworking the story

Decide which ideas do which, and sort them out accordingly.

Read through this stage first and then go back and apply the questions to your story.

BUILDING THE SCENE VERSUS THE ROLLER-COASTER APPROACH

One of the problems that frequently occurs in storytelling is building the energy and then letting it fall. Although there is a natural rise and fall to stories—not everything can be kept at a rising peak—there is a way to keep the energy rising, even when a sequence causes the energy to dip a little. The roller-coaster effect happens when there is a rising moment of energy or tension in a scene, followed by a declining moment of energy or tension in the next scene. *If the tension falls when it should be rising, something is probably out of order.*

All beats or scenes that show energy or action in the story should rise in a natural progression. If a high-energy scene is followed by a lower-energy scene, the story's overall energy will be diffused, and high-energy moments will lose their power. Sequences, which do not necessarily have energy beats (although they may have "aha moments"), can be interspersed to give the characters and reader time to reflect on the story; however, the next scene or energy beat should rise higher than the last one.

This does not mean that the story must be told in chronological or a linear order. As you progress through the questions, you should sense which scenes, flashbacks, and sequences have lower- or higher- energy beats, and you should be able to order them in a way that pushes the energy up toward the climactic moment. One way to tell that your scenes are out of order is if the scenes in themselves seem right and say what you want, but in the current order something seems wrong or out of place. When this occurs, try switching the order. This is something like when a sentence's phrases are out of order or the verb and noun are in the wrong place. Such a sentence doesn't read as well, and it might not even make sense, as it does when everything is positioned correctly.

You will also want to consider the order when creating sentences. If you list items, or when you talk about events, make sure the order develops in a rising or logical order. You've probably read dialogue in which the explanation of how something is said is given after the character spoke. The reader conjures an image or a voice for how things were said and then is told that it was said in an unexpected tone or with a different emphasis. The reader then has to stop and rethink the way they originally viewed the material. This is occasionally noticeable when you listen to audiobooks. Even though the actor/reader has probably read the material several times, I can sometimes tell that a line of dialogue was read according to the way the reader heard it, followed by a slight hesitation when the explanation for what was said is a little different than how the line came across. This also becomes frustrating if it happens very often to your reading audience. The danger is that every time a reader has to stop to refigure things, it diffuses the energy and tension, and you risk the reader putting your story down.

Exploring Ideas:

1. Are the events in the best possible order to execute the story ? Glance through the work you did in Stage 4 and see if any scenes might be out of order.

IS MORE LESS OR MORE?

Tension and pacing work together to build the story. One of the tricks of pacing is to know when to use more description and dialogue and when to use less. Of course, fewer details and less dialogue make for a faster-paced read, which is great for getting through a scene quickly, but not always useful in building tension. The exception is a screenplay or a play. Because details get in the way of stories in these forms, every detail must be precisely what is needed to keep the story visual—and no more—in order to keep the story moving forward. Those details must be told in present tense in the voice of the story. In screenplays and plays you set up the scene quickly and use quick shots of the expressions or hand movements of the people involved or the dialogue to slow down the action and to build tension between the characters.

Although too many details slow the pacing, they can also increase the tension in novels and short stories. In a fight scene you may want to show how fast all the movements are, but if you take the reader through too quickly, they may miss the importance of what is happening and diffuse the tension you are trying to create. In some cases you can create more tension by showing the dynamic action to the reader step-by-step.

a) Mark dashed across the room and swung, hitting Trevor in the jaw. Trevor fell backward onto his butt and then jumped up swinging.

b) Anger infused Mark's dash across the room. Once within arm's length, he let go and punched Trevor in the jaw. Trevor stumbled backward over an ottoman and landed on his butt. He immediately recovered, jumped to his feet, and swung back.

c) By now, Mark was furious. As he walked across the room he had one goal in mind—his fist connecting to Trevor's jawline. He took one step closer before he drew back his arm and then let his fist fly forward, dead-on. Trevor stumbled backward over an ill-placed ottoman and landed on his butt. In one fluid movement, he jumped to standing and pulled back for a swing at Mark.

d) Mark pretended to be listening, but he was focused on Trevor's hand on Cecily's arm. The gesture was friendlier than it should be from a womanizer to a woman who'd just become engaged. As he watched Trevor's hand slide up and down her arm, Mark's fury increased to rage. Mid sentence he handed his drink to the idiot in front of him, who kept yammering on about his latest golf game, and started toward Cecily. Halfway across the room he could see Trevor's index finger travel across Cecily's shoulder, up her neck, and press her chin up as his mouth moved in for a kiss. Cecily turned her lips away. Mark's focus changed from retrieving Cecily to his fist connecting to Trevor's jawline. He flew forward the last few steps and smashed his fist into the side of Trevor's head, driving him away from Cecily. Trevor tripped backward over the ottoman behind him and landed hard on his backside. In a second he was up, fists raised, ready to fight. Cecily stepped in between them. "Enough!"

These four examples tell the same event in different styles. The first one is rapid-fire; the second is more surprising in the suddenness. The third one we see coming—although the action slows down, there is a little more tension built in anticipation of waiting for what is coming. The fourth one gives more details, and we can see and more fully understand Mark's motivation and that Cecily is the reason for his anger. We see what Mark is thinking and something of Cecily's thoughts, by her turning her lips away and stepping in at the end, and we learn something about Trevor's character. The style you use depends on the way you are telling your story and the way you want to build the tension in your story.

Pacing can also be tweaked by how you put the words on the page, whether each action is a separate line or all in one paragraph:

Anger infused Mark's dash across the room.

Once within arm's length, he let go and punched Trevor in the jaw.

Trevor stumbled backward over an ottoman and landed on his butt.

He immediately recovered, jumped to his feet, and swung back.

Below is another example.

a) Blake pulled his knife from the holster in his boot and threw it. Cutter gasped and went down, the knife protruding from his belly.

b) Blake stepped back. Cutter's reach was longer, and one deep swipe from his knife could be deadly. Blake crouched down, maintaining his balance in order to bounce backward again if Cutter lunged. He reached into the knife holster in his boot. Cutter eased forward on his right foot. Blake moved from a crouch, leaned back on his left leg pulling the handle free, and threw the knife. The blade struck deep into Cutter's upper torso, centered between his ribs. Cutter sucked in, stared at the knife and then stumbled backward. He stopped when his back hit the building and then slid down the wall.

You can feel there is more tension in the second scene in the anticipation of what's coming: We know it's a knife fight, but we don't know the outcome as quickly. Even though the details slow the reading down a bit, it gives the reader a chance to take in the full scene and watch it unfold action by action, shot by shot.

Unless you are writing the hook, before coming to this point you will probably have written a scene or scenes that informed the reader of what led up to this moment. The reader would already know what the fight is about and who the protagonist is and may figure at this point in the story he's going to win and the bad guy lose. In the first example we may be prepared for this moment, but it's over quickly. In the second example it's drawn out to add more tension. The tension could be increased even more by adding more details about the fear or the weakness or expertise of one or the other, what the odds of one of the character's winning or losing are, giving the reader time to realize it may not be an outcome they expect. At the very least the reader will appreciate and gain respect for how hard the protagonist had to work to win.

Blake stepped back. Cutter's reach was longer, and one deep swipe from his knife could be deadly. The image of Blake's partner lying on the street, a knife stuck deeply in his chest, flashed through his mind. Cutter had been faster with his knife than either one of them could pull their guns, and at a distance far enough away so that he just vanished into the night as Blake tried uselessly to revive Ari, blood gurgling in his throat as he coughed, "Get him!"

Blake's eyes focused on Cutter's eyes, looking for that glimmer, that slight movement saying he was ready to throw. He crouched slightly, all the while maintaining his balance in order to bounce backward again if Cutter lunged. He reached into the knife holster in his boot. Cutter eased forward on his right foot; he was toying with him.

> Cutter smiled. "It won't be so easy for you—a slice here, a missing ear, a gouge
> there, one less eye, maybe a nice deep slice across a tendon or an artery."
>
> Cutter wasn't going to throw. He wanted to see fear in Blake's face, make him
> nervous, cut him bit by bit. One wrong movement would doom Blake. Cutter opened
> his mouth to speak again, and Blake took advantage of that momentary loss of focus.
> He moved from a crouch, leaned back on his left leg pulling the handle free, and threw
> the knife. The blade struck deep into Cutter's upper torso, centered between his ribs.
> Cutter sucked in, stared at the knife and then stumbled backward. He stopped when
> his back hit the building, slowly sliding down the wall.

A couple of cuts wounding one or both could be added to this scene, since we know Cutter has the longer reach. He could inflict pain on Blake and increase tension for the reader, who begins to wonder if maybe Cutter is going to win. As the character's anxiety or introspection of the moment increases, so does the tension—as long as it's not overdone. You know it's overdone when the energy diffuses instead of increasing.

After writing such a scene as this, you may decide to go back to when you first introduced Cutter and make a comment about how long his arms are, which is a plant (or foreshadowing) for later when you need to use that fact to add tension. In many books, especially action-adventure, the protagonist survives, so you need to do whatever you can to keep the reader guessing.

> Cutter was a bulky man, not heavy, but tall—his length was in his legs, with thighs
> and calves thick and round like an Olympic skater's. His arms were long, too, like
> the long limbs of a gorilla. In hand-to-hand combat, his opponent wouldn't stand a
> chance. Blake couldn't reach from Cutter's fists past the length of his arms to land
> a solid blow.

By planting ideas early on that give the protagonist more to have to fight against or overcome, you increase the tension. Even though the reader knows the protagonist will probably win, the question becomes how big of a fight will it be for him, or what are the odds against the character, and is this the time the protagonist will lose? By creating events in which the protagonist sometimes loses, the reader knows it's possible it could happen this time or that a lot of damage could be done.

If you want your action scenes to be short and snappy, you have to prepare the reader with lots of tension beforehand either in the hunt of one for the other or in whatever events come before. Then the first example between Blake and Cutter might be adequate. It would also be adequate if this was a scene between the protagonist and a minor character. You don't want every fight scene to be a major battle unless you can continue to raise the stakes. Each fight scene, just as each action scene, should rise to a higher level until the highest-energy beat, which is the climactic moment.

These concepts also apply to scenes that are not violent and do not contain physical fights, but rather are scenes of mental battles between opponents—even in lovers' quarrels.

Exploring Ideas:

1. Is the buildup full of exposition, narrative, and description rather than active plot points that affect the core dramatic journey?
2. Can you increase the tension by adding more details?
3. Did you add too many details and diffuse the tension?
4. Are the details logical for the scene and organic to the characters?
5. Did you set up characteristics in advance that will help the antagonist or weaken the protagonist?

USING DIALOGUE TO INCREASE TENSION

Dialogue can also increase or diffuse the tension in a scene. When two people are speaking, there should be moments when they are at cross purposes, i.e., one trying to get information, the other trying to avoid giving the information, or one character inferring something while the other character is misunderstanding what is being said, either intentionally or not.

Exploring Ideas:

1. Think about the balance-of-power idea we discussed in Stage 3 on page 133. How would shifting that balance increase the tension?

TYING UP LOOSE ENDS

While working on the tension and pacing, you want to start tying up loose ends. As you work through your story, look for the setups that you could pay off in the upcoming pages. Things with small payoffs should generally occur reasonably close to the setup. Events with larger payoffs can be spread out further. There should be continual payoffs throughout the story so that not everything is a question of what will happen and when. Rather, there are events that happen and are resolved, but during that resolution or before that resolution, the next larger event occurs that has to be resolved. These types of events may not reach the level of an obstacle for the protagonist, but can rather be smaller incidents along the way. Do not hold everything back for the "big payoff." One, because you'll frustrate the reader, and two, because it is more fun for the reader to be let in to the story, rather than to be kept outside and less involved.

In Georgia's story about the beauty pageant, I could keep the reader guessing about who is sabotaging her, but by letting the reader know about Teresa's goals and her being tempted by Janeen, Georgia's competition, the reader becomes more invested in what is happening between Georgia and Teresa. A payoff occurs every time the reader learns something the protagonist doesn't know. If I keep both guessing throughout the story, the reader becomes disenfranchised. Even in mysteries there should be some information the reader feels they are privy to that perhaps the characters do not have.

Exploring Ideas:

1. Throughout the story did you answer the minor story questions and tie up loose ends?
2. Did you continue adding new questions?
3. Did you reveal some secrets to let the reader in on what's really happening from time to time?

IS THIS THE RIGHT ENDING FOR THIS STORY?

As you work on the tension and the pacing, does the story end in a way that resolves everything that should be resolved, or does it leave the reader feeling alienated or confused or frustrated? Because I spend so much time commuting, I listen to lots of audiobooks—generally unabridged fiction because my preference is to savor all the words. In a recent novel, with an introduction touting the writer's sense of humor and cleverness, I found myself thoroughly enjoying those attributes of the author's storytelling, and his unique perspective. I thought to myself that I would be looking for more of his books. And then the book ended, and the story was left with an unsatisfactory resolution. Although in itself the ending implied something akin to "crime doesn't pay," I was very disappointed, and I felt that there were loose ends where I wanted to see more of an outcome for the characters. I may be the only reader who felt that way, but I reminded myself to mark this author off my list of must-reads.

The ending is critical. Readers will forgive much of a story's shortcomings if it has a great ending. I would say that the hook is critical for engaging your readers, and the ending is critical for keeping them.

Exploring Ideas:

1. Will the ending emote a strong response within the reader? If not, try rewriting for a stronger ending.
2. Does your ending resolve the story?
3. Does it answer your major story questions?
4. If you left unanswered questions, why was this the right choice for this story?

TOOLS FOR STAGE 5

Exploring Ideas:

1. Did you prove your premise?
2. Will the reader understand the theme of your story by the end?
3. Will the reader find the ending to your story satisfying or a turnoff?
4. Is this the ending you want your story to have? If so, does it really work? Be honest with yourself.

5. Is the ending memorable, and will it send the reader scurrying to the bookstore for your next work?
6. Did you adequately resolve the main story question that kept the reader up all night to find out the answer?
7. Write a dynamic two-page synopsis of the story.

Ray's Story Map

Below is an example of the story map from Ray's Picture Map on page 59. Ray is trying to get to the flower that could be the cure to his wife's cancer, while deciding whether he has made the right decision for the rest of his life.

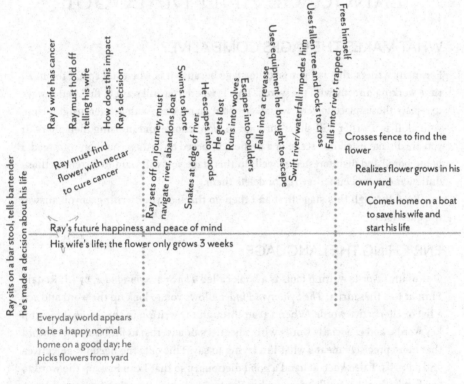

(8.1) *Ray's Story Map*

Tools for Development

Return to page 88 and once again answer the questions from the perspective of the new knowledge you've gained about your story.

chapter 9

STAGE 6—ENRICHING LANGUAGE AND DIALOGUE

WHAT MAKES THE PAGES COME ALIVE?

For many writers, this is their favorite stage because it is when you spend the most time working directly with the words. This is where you will want to find better ways to replace those "placeholders" we talked about on page 24, with greater insight. Here your skill as a writer will shine through in word choice and in using metaphors. If you are disinterested in a scene or a section, or bored by it, then count on your reader being bored and disinterested as well. In this stage you will want to ferret out those dull moments and either rewrite or delete them.

Read through this stage first and then go through your writing as you answer the questions.

ENRICHING THE LANGUAGE

One of my favorite writing tools is a book called *The Synonym Finder*, by J.I. Rodale. Similar to a thesaurus, *The Synonym Finder* allows you to look up the word and see a list of alternative words. When I read through my writing in this stage, I look up key words, and especially words with adjectives or adverbs, to find a stronger word that more precisely means what I'm trying to say. This cuts the need for adjectives and adverbs. I also keep at hand a good dictionary so that I can look up the word to verify whether it actually means what I'm trying to say. By using fewer and stronger words to say what you want, your writing becomes clearer, more specific, and more visual.

The Synonym Finder is also great for those of us who have favorite words that we overuse. In this stage you will want to look at how often you use the same word.

Exploring Ideas:

1. As you read through your pages, sharpen the language.
2. Did you repeat the same word in a sentence, paragraph, or page?
3. Are there better/stronger/more potent/more precise word choices that could be made?
4. How many times did you use the same nouns and verbs in a sentence, paragraph, page, or chapter?
5. How often did you use *–ly* words?

Metaphors

We've discussed metaphors throughout *The Writer's Compass*. Metaphors, details, and ambiguity are all related in that you will sometimes use metaphors to give the reader a powerful visual image and to make the writing feel less general and more specific. A strong metaphor adds color to writing and gives the reader a more vivid image of what you are saying. In this stage you want to think about the metaphors that are organic to your story and use them when it will give your scene or your character's identity more clarity. You may even have a character who speaks in metaphors. However, don't include so many metaphors or such complicated metaphors that the reader becomes lost or that the metaphor overpowers the story.

Ambiguity

As noted previously, the word choices you make should be specific. Don't beat around the bush—rather, say what you mean when writing. Consider the image you are trying to create in the reader's mind. The details you give are that extra brushstroke that makes the difference in what the reader sees.

Example 1:

- *A field of flowers.*
- *A field of daisies.*

Example 2:

- *A very long day.*
- *He put in a long day plowing, harnessed to the oxen before the first ray of sunlight, not stopping until after the sun melted below the horizon.*

Exploring Ideas:

1. Is the writing ambiguous without enough details to make the imagery clear?
2. Do the details liven up the story and engage the reader?
3. Did you engage all of the reader's senses through taste, smell, touch, hearing, and seeing?

4. Did you keep the story visual in the reader's mind's eye?
5. Where could you improve the imagery or give a metaphor that would enhance the story?
6. Where have you overtold the story?
7. Does the story get lost in the metaphors?
8. Are the metaphors appropriate for the story?
9. Are there details that you should remove?

Using Metaphors and Dialogue to Show Your Characters

An important way in which the reader sees the character and identifies or is intrigued is through how this character sees the world and the character's voice or how he expresses his view of the world. The voice comes through in the character's manner of dialogue, in the way the character dresses or responds to other people or new situations. In addition to that, giving the character a metaphor for his life helps us see the character more clearly.

In a romance, I used a metaphor in a line of dialogue that goes something like, *We could never make it together. You're hospital corners; I'm an unmade bed.* The character, a woman, is expressing herself as somewhat disheveled, somewhat scattered or laid-back, while the man she is talking to is more rigid, more analytical in his thinking and behavior, and is always dressed impeccably. This dialogue metaphor shows something of each of their personalities, at least as interpreted through the female character. *He had an arrogance about him, like a Rolls-Royce in a world of VW bugs.* Immediately we see that the narrator thinks this character feels he is several standards above everyone else. Notice in both of these I referred to the narrator with *interpreted* or *thinks*. What one character thinks about another character isn't necessarily true. Misinterpretation by one character of another creates tension, especially in romance, suspense, and mysteries.

I've seen the following description more than once: "She looked like a long, cool drink of water to a thirsty man." I'm not quite sure how this metaphor came about, but we essentially get it that this character is tall and very appealing.

Metaphors also show how the character interprets the world. *Los Angeles means one of two things to most people—sunshine or traffic jams. To me it meant something else—gray streets, gray buildings, gray faces.* This character sees the world, or at least Los Angeles, as dull and colorless, and maybe the issues for this world as neither black nor white, but very gray.

We've already mentioned Forrest Gump's box of chocolates, which is a metaphor for life; another Gump metaphor for life is "Mama always says there's an awful lot you could tell about a person by their shoes. Where they're going. Where they've been. I've worn lots of shoes." Metaphors like these create both universal truths for the audience to relate to and express a view of the world in new ways, but they also tell the audience what kind of story this is and something about the characters they are investing time to read about or watch.

Exploring Ideas:

1. How does this character view the world?
2. How does this view manifest itself in the character's dress, demeanor, speech, actions, mannerisms, tics, etc.?
3. What does the character's voice sound like?
4. What is his or her speech pattern? How does it differ from the other characters?
5. How does the character use words to express views?
6. What metaphor would show the character's view of the world?
7. What metaphor could be used to describe the character?
8. Did you show the character to the reader in descriptions, metaphors, and through other characters' dialogue?
9. Did you bore the reader by telling details that are unimportant to the story or character development? It is possible to give too many details and either slow the story down or clutter the imagery in the reader's mind. If there are too many metaphors the story can get bogged down and even lost.

Creating Effective Dialogue

As we noted before, dialogue is key in plays and screenplays, but good dialogue is also an important part of novels—it's just that novels aren't quite as dependent on the dialogue. Dialogue should give your characters personality while remaining organic to the story. The purpose of dialogue is to give information, show the reader something about your characters, or move the story forward. As we noted before, dialogue can increase or diffuse the tension in a scene. Writing effective dialogue is important to telling a good story and developing strong characters. When analyzing dialogue, look at how it is presented. Can you tell who is speaking just by the tone, word usage, or manner of speech?

Learning to Write Dialogue Exercise

There are so many subtle differences and varieties of style in the way we communicate. To understand good dialogue, go to places where people congregate and listen to how they speak. Make notes about word usage, cadence, and metaphors. Watch body language to see how the speaker shows what is being said.

- Does the person speak from an analytical or precise point of view?
- Is her language full of images or ambiguous?
- Does she use large words, does she speak in circles, is her language simple?

- Is the language colored with regional phrases?
- Does the speaker's voice sound sad and pessimistic, or is there an optimism or hint of surprise in how she talks?
- Does one speaker invade the other speaker's personal space?
- Does one speaker interrupt the other or even let the other person get a word in edgewise?

Talking Heads

This is generally a screenwriting or playwriting term, but it can occur in other formats. Talking heads happen when the imagery has been lost due to long passages of dialogue. All the reader can see are two heads communicating. Avoid talking heads by reminding the reader of the setting, emotions, tone, physical movements, weather, or by engaging any of the other senses.

Dialogue Tags

Make sure it is clear who is speaking. In novels and short stories dialogue tags are: *he said, she said, Mary asked, Peter answered.* A dialogue tag is only the words used to identify the speaker, but does not include any words that further express action or feelings that may be attached to the tag. Very early in learning how to write I was taught not to use details along with the tag, which isn't necessarily correct.

> - *"It's not my notebook! I didn't write those things about you," Joan said.* (Instead of adding "Joan said nervously" or "angrily" or "defensively," or "Joan said with a twitch in her eye.")

Avoid weakening the writing by using *-ly* words in your tags. Although there are times when the *-ly* word is a good choice, usually it is the easy choice. The *-ly* word or a descriptive word for how the character is speaking becomes a crutch, rather than strengthening the dialogue. If the dialogue is strong, the reader doesn't need to be told how it was said. Depending on how you are building tension and whether this is supposed to be a surprise statement, the reader should already know Joan's thoughts and that she is either being tripped up or wrongly accused, and therefore the tone of her response would be obvious.

However, this may be a part of the writing where the reader is learning about Joan and whether she might have written those things. Or the dialogue could be said in a tone other than what the reader may be expecting, which would require a tag to explain it.

> "My feelings for you haven't changed, but my logic says I should dump you." Bill exhaled in a long, slow sigh.

Versus:

> "My feelings for you haven't changed, but my logic says I should dump you," Bill said in exasperation.

In the first part of this example we used two sentences and didn't use "said," because it was implied in the next sentence, assuming this wasn't already clear by the content and order of speakers. In the second part of the example we tagged on what he was feeling in the same sentence. The way you write this is a matter determined by your style, voice, and pacing, rather than rules; either way works. However, using descriptors of how things are said should be saved for when the reader will misinterpret the intent of what is said. Instead use strong dialogue and add emotions or thoughts or physical actions to show the readers the character's intent.

If you want snappy dialogue, the best way to identify the speaker is to throw in "he said," "she said." *Said* is the most unobtrusive way to identify the speaker. In reading dialogue in novels, *said* quickly and easily denotes the speaker without interruption, and the reader's eye catches it without having to slow down very much, if at all.

However, in listening to an audiobook I quickly became annoyed by an author who used "[insert character's name] said" after every line of dialogue. It was much more noticeable in hearing than in reading, although using it every time might have been too much even for the reader.

If when you are editing or doing a read-through you have to stop to figure out who is speaking, then know your reader will get lost even more often. If you identified the speaker in the last line of dialogue, you don't need to identify the speaker for another couple of lines of dialogue—unless you have more than two speakers. Don't make the reader have to stop and count back to see who said what. The exception would be using vernacular in the dialogue that clearly identifies who the speaker is. Make it even simpler for the reader by putting all of the dialogue by one speaker in the same paragraph and then creating a new paragraph for a new speaker. If you have one speaker with a long section of dialogue, more of a monologue, you will probably want to break it up into paragraphs.

To keep your writing from becoming monotonous, alternate the way you write your tags. Remember, descriptions slow the reader down, so if you want to draw out a scene during the dialogue, you will want to use more description, revealing what the character is thinking and feeling and their physical movements, rather than how they are speaking. If you want to speed up the scene, you will use less description.

Effective Dialogue Tips

- The most effective dialogue is expressive, using words in a distinctive enough pattern that immediately identifies the speaker and the speaker's emotions without the use of a tag. Words that express the action or emotions can accompany the line of dialogue with or without the speaker's name.

- In dialogue, cut unnecessary words for sharper, clearer writing. Using complete sentences slows the pacing. E.g., *"If you come one step closer, I'll shoot," Mary said* [tag], *pointing the gun at John* [description of action]. Use instead: *"Don't come any closer." Mary trembled as she pointed the gun at John* [no tag, description of emotion and action].

- Dialogue tags should identify the speaker to keep the reader from becoming confused. Words like *said, asked, answered* blend into the writing and are so subliminal the reader doesn't even notice them.

- In fiction, most of the time, the tag should come after the speaker's name and not before, although it can come before, during, or after the quote. There is something jarring about *said Julie, responded Spencer*—use this method sparingly for variation, especially when you have several speakers and must use several tags.

- Using a description that expresses the speaker's emotion—*Jim yelled, Ralph barked, he murmured, she giggled*—are used when the words of the dialogue are not expressed in a manner that immediately makes clear their tone or intent, or when a statement is meant to be facetious.

- When using adverbs or *-ly* words, for example—*Lucy remarked angrily, Josh explained patiently, he sputtered nervously, she whispered coyly*—look to see if the adverb is redundant and if you can get by without it. Next, see if you can change the sentence to make the adverb's meaning clearer through the dialogue. It is okay to use adverbs for clarification or emphasis, but use them sparingly.

Dialogue in Screenplays and Plays

The same holds true with action shots describing the scene in screenplays. If you want the scene to move more quickly, you will want to use fewer action shots and descriptions between lines of dialogue. However, you don't want too much white space (see "Talking Heads" on page 180). Because dialogue is centered in a screenplay, there is more white space around it. Too much white space means you have too much dialogue and not enough shots and descriptions to ground the reader and keep the image of the scene in their mind's eye—remember, the screenplay emphasizes images.

In a play, dialogue is the most crucial element, and the dialogue goes across the typed page, so too much white space would be too many descriptions and not enough dialogue.

Dialogue tags are not used in plays and screenplays, since the character is identified as a header centered over the dialogue. However, sometimes parentheticals are used (see the example in the following section).

Parentheticals

Plays and screenplays use parentheticals to describe how something is said, and sometimes use a gesture or facial expression accompanying the dialogue. A parenthetical is a few words within parentheses on the line under the character's name and indented more than the dialogue, but less than the character's name. The purpose of the parenthetical is to show the character's intention for what they said.

Jake
(annoyed, fists clenched)

I love you!

This line of dialogue might be said in many ways, but you want the actor and director to understand how Jake feels at this moment. Ordinarily you wouldn't tell Jake to "clench his fists," as you would leave that up to the actor and director to determine the character's body movements and delivery. But in this case, the writer has a reason in that this is a moment that will pay off later; or maybe the writer is explaining previous behavior. Therefore, the writer knows the line needs to be delivered in a more precise manner and needs to give the actor and director guidance. If you have written your scene with an obvious delivery of annoyance, a parenthetical won't be needed.

Who's Speaking

In the 1998 movie *Six Days Seven Nights*, David Schwimmer has a line that never really came across to me as organic. On a talk show Schwimmer told about making the movie and talked about this particular line. He said that when they did readings, Harrison Ford always said the line, even though it was supposed to be Schwimmer's line. Finally, just before they shot the scene, Schwimmer insisted that it was his line, so Harrison Ford let him say it. Later, when Schwimmer related the story to a family member, her comment was that it would have been funnier if Harrison Ford had said it. Sometimes a line can be stronger if spoken through the lens of another character's perspective and voice.

Exploring Ideas:

1. Would the scene be stronger if another character said the line? Try reading lines of dialogue through another character's voice and see what impact that has on the tension in the scene and on the story as a whole.

On the Nose

This is also a term used more in screenwriting and plays but can apply to dialogue in novels and short stories. It means the exposition or dialogue says something too precisely, often insulting the reader's intelligence.

- Big John says, *"You're pointing a gun at me."* In a play or screenplay it can be seen that a gun is being pointed at Big John, and both the character and the audience probably already know why a gun is being pointed at him. He's stating the obvious, unless he's being facetious.
- In a play or screenplay Big John might say, *"What's with the gun?"* Maybe Big John is surprised by the gun and really doesn't know why a gun is pointed at him, or maybe he's trying to diffuse the situation by playing innocent.
- In a novel, because the reader can't "see" what's happening, Big John might say, *"You're pointing a gun at me?"* but again, this might be too on the nose.
- Better yet the description of the scene indicates that a gun is being pointed at Big John who might respond something like, *"Be careful with that thing—it could go off,"* which signifies that he sees the gun, wants to pretend he doesn't know why, and that he's trying to diffuse the situation.

Stating the obvious is one way to insult the reader's intelligence. Another way is telling the reader something you've already told them or something they would know through life experience. Sometimes when you relate a fact you're not sure the reader is familiar with, by not explaining it you are allowing the reader who does know in on the secret with you and creating another level of intimacy in the story. Just don't expect readers to understand or be interested if you continually write details only a select few would understand.

Exploring Ideas:

1. Do you subtly imply those things that would insult your reader's intelligence by telling them outright?
2. How many times do you mention details that only someone with special knowledge would get?

Singsong Voice

Sentences with the same structure begin to sound like rhyme and have a singsong voice. Not all sentences should have the same structure. Do not always use the subject and verb in the same order. You will begin to bore your reader. Vary the structure of your sentences. Use phrases and remember that commas are your friends. Liven up your sentences by using multisyllabic words.

As you can see from the above sentences, the reader quickly becomes bored when everything sounds the same and the emphasis or rhythm is not changed in the sentence order.

Exploring Ideas:

    1. Do you use varied sentence structure?

Active or Passive Voice

Do you use active or passive verbs? Active verbs sound more immediate and as though they are creating action. Passive verbs are words such as *has, had, was, gone, went, is,* etc. A passive sentence seems inactive or sounds like action will be happening or has happened, and we may have missed it. An active sentence creates the feeling that something is happening right now, and this makes for more tension in the story. Microsoft Word has incorporated passive writing recognition into its software. When that squiggly green line shows, look at the phrase or sentence and consider how you can rewrite it to improve your story. However, don't be a slave to someone else's sense of grammar if your style uses the language a little differently—as long as it works.

Exploring Ideas:

    1. Did you eliminate passive voice and replace it with active writing?

Is Your Point of View Consistent?

We discussed POV in Stage 2 on page 101. As you go through your story, ask yourself the questions below. Sometimes by rewriting a scene from another perspective, the writer gives his readers an unexpected glimpse into the story, which can increase the reader's feeling of intimacy with the characters and story.

Exploring Ideas:

    1. Is the POV consistent?
    2. Am I using the right POV to tell this story to its best advantage?
    3. Would the scene have more tension if I revealed details through another character's POV?
    4. How many POVs are there in the story?
    5. Do the POVs serve the story or diffuse the tension or confuse the reader?
    6. Do I show things that in this POV could not be known?
    7. Is the tense and subject-verb agreement consistent?

Author Intrusion

A sort of aside: Author intrusion was much more common and allowable before the 1900s. The author made commentaries on the characters or action of the story or told the reader what was going on in the story. In *The History of Tom Jones, a Foundling,* by Henry Fielding, for example, Fielding speaks directly to the reader to explain where we are in the story. "Before we return to Mr. Jones, we will take one more view of Sophia." In another place Fielding wrote, "The reader may remember that Mr. Allworthy gave Tom Jones a little horse, as a kind of smart-money for the punishment which he imagined he had suffered innocently." These types of author intrusion were common among novelists in the eighteenth and nineteenth centuries.

Today authors use more subtle tactics to speak to their readers and slip in information they want to convey that perhaps the character doesn't know. In other words, the author makes a comment that did not come from the character's point of view. A common tactic is something like: *Mark didn't know this would be the last time he would ever see Sabrina.* If this is told in Mark's POV, how could Mark tell us what he didn't know? Anything that the author writes that the character doesn't know, or when the author's personal agenda is slipped in and doesn't feel organic to the story, is author intrusion.

Years ago I watched the James Cameron movie *The Abyss*, which won an Oscar for best visual effects and was nominated in other categories. Later I watched the scenes that were cut from the film. Very clearly there was a much more political agenda to the original version of the movie, which in my opinion weakened it. Fortunately those scenes were cut. When the writer intrudes with his world view, rather than the character's world view, it is at the peril of the reader becoming disenchanted with the story.

Which Details Matter?

In plays, the details you include as you write the descriptions should be only the ones you need. If *Marlin picks up a beer stein in a pub*, then you've said what you need to say to create a semblance of a pub in either a minimalist or a full-blown setting, and a stein. And only use the stein if Marlin's going to drink from it or use it to throw at something or hit someone. You've heard the saying, "If you put a gun in a scene, you have to shoot it before the end of the play." In part that means that what you put in a scene has to have a purpose for being in the scene. The second part of that is if you show a gun—a weapon—you are creating tension and promising the audience that something is going to happen using that weapon. You have to make good on that promise because that item is creating tension that must be released. This also holds true in a screenplay. You should include in the details what the characters specifically need in the scene that will be used. Leave the rest of the details to the set designer to create the ambience that will make the story work on the stage or the screen in that particular setting.

Novels and short stories are different. If you don't tell the reader what's in the scene, the reader won't see it. Does that mean you have to create a picture like an artist? Of course not. You rely on the readers bringing their experiences to help them visualize the scene. If *Deborah enters a 1950s style café*, most people in America have an idea of what that might look like, and images will begin to form in their mind. If you add that it is *complete with black-and-white linoleum floors, red vinyl booths, a jukebox, and a life-size portrait of Jimmy Dean*, most American readers will add those images to enhance the picture they've created. However, you might be filling in details that are different from their experience, and you might actually change the image they were building or confuse it. If these details matter in your story, or you feel they give the reader a clearer picture by setting the ambience for the background of the story you are creating, then you should add them, but be judicious in the details you add so that you do not cloud or smear the reader's picture. There is another saying: "Don't take a knife to a gunfight." In other words, put what you need in the scene that is useful for the characters.

Every word in Hemingway's "Hills Like White Elephants" has meaning; there was nothing extra. Faulkner wrote long, wordy passages. Joyce wrote in a stream of consciousness. Your voice and style are the way you put details and information and characters together. In every example given in this book, you would have probably written it differently, added different details. No problem—you are creating your style, your voice, your way of telling a story.

What Did You Choose to Tell?

As discussed previously, the story can be told (rather than shown) when the overview is needed and giving details would slow down the story and not serve the story's purpose or move it forward. A scene of violence might be filled with tension, but the victim telling what happened might have even more tension. Showing what the victim is saying and doing as she tells the story of the violent event that occurred allows the reader to see how this violence impacts the character and the results in the character's life.

There was a time when sex scenes weren't shown, nor were overtly violent scenes, especially on television. Many of these shows are now favored television series, and such movies remain on the AFI Top 100 list, in spite of their so-called naive writing (by current standards). Today's movies are filled with horrific violence, and TV shows are filled with gore from crime scenes. Yet the successful stories and books from the past prove that it is often the subliminal inference or the scene that is alluded to that most affects the audience as they fill in the details with their own imagination. I'm not saying don't use violence or sex. I'm saying don't use it to shock the reader, especially if there is a stronger way to tell the story. Writers sometimes seem to think their purpose in showing a good story is to see who can outshock the reader or viewer and to make the story as graphically realistic as possible. There is a large segment of the reading and viewing audience that actually avoids movies and novels like these. You have to decide who you want to include or disenfranchise as part of your audience.

Exploring Ideas:

1. Did you show and not tell most scenes?
2. Are the scenes you chose to tell effective?
3. Is the story better served by telling particular scenes or events or showing them?

Is the Writing Convoluted?

If it is convoluted, it means the order is tangled or the story was developed in a way to prove your premise or theme, but not in a way to make sense. It can also mean that the obstacles are way out of proportion to the impact they created, or that the outcome is out of proportion to the events. Make sure that you have untangled sentences and that paragraphs and scenes are in an order that does makes sense. Also be sure that there is logic in what you write and that the writing and ideas are organic to the story and do not appear to come out of left field.

Exploring Ideas:

1. Are the scenes convoluted?
2. Are sentences twisted?
3. Are paragraphs out of order?
4. Are the story scenes and events, and the cause and effect, logical?

Non Sequiturs

A writer once told me that she was told the ending to her story was a non sequitur. I told her to go back and get clarification. A non sequitur means that the conclusion doesn't follow what went before. I really liked her ending and thought it was a great twist and that it did follow. What I finally realized was that the voice and style of her writing changed for the last two paragraphs, and it wasn't that the story ending was a non sequitur, it was that the style changed, which is a different problem.

Now That I Know My Story, What is the Best Hook?

Because the hook is so critical for getting a reader interested in your story, you generally have to understand what you are really writing about to write the best one. At this point you want to take some time to evaluate your hook. Starting on page 109 we discussed the importance of the hook and different types of hooks. Now that you understand your story better, spend some time honing the impact of your hook and making sure it will draw the reader into the story you are telling.

Exploring Ideas:

1. Is this the most dynamic and active opening you can write?
2. Does your story start at a point where it engages the reader?
3. Does it ask a question the reader wants to find the answer to?
4. Does your hook still reflect the story you have written?
5. Does your hook create the opening tension appropriate to start your story?
6. Is the tone and style of the story evident in the hook?
7. Write two to three possible hooks that are different from your current opening but still organic to your story.
8. Rewrite the opening until it grabs the reader and propels him into the story.

Another Look at the Ending

The end of your story will either be memorable to your reader or forgettable. If the ending is good, many readers will forgive some weaknesses in the middle of your story. There should be a resolution to this particular story, even if there is a sense that this character, or these characters, will have more stories.

Exploring Ideas:

1. By the end of the story, do readers have an answer, or the tools to find the answer within themselves, for the dramatic question asked by the story?
2. Does the ending reflect the hook?
3. Does the ending bring the story to a conclusion?
4. Does the ending leave room for a sequel, if you want to write one, without weakening the story?

Consistency in Edits and Changes

You will also want to make sure that you are consistent with whatever changes you've been making or will continue to make. You can always use "find and replace" if you've forgotten where certain changes are. I suggest making the changes one at a time and not using "replace all," or you may find you unintentionally changed something that shouldn't be changed, thus creating a new problem.

Exploring Ideas:

1. Are all name, date, and other changes consistent?

Grammar and Punctuation

An editor or an agent won't make it past the first page if the punctuation is poor. Use a good grammar book—there are lots of simple ones with basic rules to aid you in correcting as many of the problems as possible. Some software programs have grammar rules and indicate when you have a grammar or punctuation problem. The programs sometimes have a thesaurus or a synonym feature, which works quickly. If need be, you can hire a good editor to help you.

Exploring Ideas:

1. Did you punctuate properly?
2. Are your tenses consistent?
3. Do the numbers in your nouns and pronouns agree with your verbs?

Feedback

At the end of Stage 6 is a good time to give friends and family a copy of the manuscript to read and ask for feedback. (If you belong to a writer's group, you may have already been doing this all along, which has hopefully been helpful.) By now your story should be fairly complete, and this is a step that will help you see problems you may not have seen before or unexplained issues you haven't addressed. Fresh eyes will give you a fresh perspective.

Sometimes we miss strengths and weaknesses in our writing because we are too close to the work. Writers are often told that something they thought was weak was really impactful, and vice versa—that something they thought strong doesn't come across to the reader. Remember, when you give your work to readers who are not writers, they may not be able to articulate what they perceive is wrong. They may love the story because they care about you. Or they may take the job seriously and be more frank and possibly hurtful than you wanted. About the latter, I always say, "He is not the audience for this book."

For readers who are not writers, I listen for words that will give me a clue to the problem area in general. And for the people who are too kind, albeit not necessarily helpful, well, sometimes it's just nice to hear someone say how great your writing is.

When your story is as complete as you can get it, you may want to hire someone with good skills (unless you know someone qualified who'll do it for free) to line edit your work. Although I am an academic editor at a university and teach writing, I still have someone edit my work. It is very difficult to separate ourselves from our writing to see where we have made mistakes or where our eye misses the mistakes. My strength is in concepts and structure, not in line editing. Since I know my weaknesses, I know what type of editor I need. However, I also use editors who can give me feedback on concepts and structure.

In some cases, once a book or magazine publisher accepts your story, you will work with their in-house editors to help you finalize your story and prepare it for publication. Before you get to that stage, you may want to hire an editor to help you work on the final draft and make it the best it can be before you submit it. Let's spend a few minutes discussing hiring an editor.

One caution: Editors are all very different and use different approaches, even different grammar books as their guide. Some editors say they only do copy or line editing, which means they correct grammar, punctuation, and spelling, but then they proceed to interject themselves into your writing and may proceed to indicate you should make significant changes in your work. Some editors do not line edit but give you feedback on your story's strengths and weaknesses. Most editors are some sort of combination of the two. All of them have their own biases and styles. Finding the editor who is right for you is almost as challenging as writing your story.

I suggest that you find an editor who works in the same genre as your story. Ask for samples of her work to see how in-depth her editing style is, and have a conversation, in person or on the phone, to see if your personalities connect. You might even pay the editor to do a few sample pages to see if her style fits your needs. You'll also want to get quotes from editors and find out whether they charge by the page or by the project, and clarify what you are paying for. You will probably pay the editor a portion up front and the remainder before she returns the manuscript to you—odds are if you do not like the work your editor did, you are out the money. That's why it is important that you check out the editor's work and style and make sure this is someone you can work with. Check that the editor has strong credentials—it's even better if she has edited books or other materials that have been published. If another author credits the editor for her work, then that author was probably happy with the outcome. Know what it is going to cost you and what you can expect in return before you send off your manuscript.

Once you've selected an editor, take to heart her suggestions and don't automatically discount her because you don't like the edits or comments. We all get defensive when someone tells us our baby would be more attractive with green eyes instead of blue and wore orange instead of yellow. But since this isn't a living, breathing child, and we are only human, we might have made an error in judgment. Separate yourself from being the sensitive creator and become the objective writer.

What If I Don't Agree With the Editor?

As I noted before, I almost always have someone else edit my work. Because I am an editor I know that I make mistakes. Sometimes someone else sees a better way to say something that will improve my work, and I wish I'd thought of that change on my own. I also know that sometimes editors get carried away with their own voice and style. Sometimes an editor will suggest a change either because it is the correct way to write a sentence or because they believe it is a better way. However, that suggestion might change the tone or the emphasis or your voice. In that case, I do not choose to agree with the editor.

As the editor of a journal, there have been times when I have received articles and worked with the author to get them through the review process, accepted the article for publication, and then sent it out to be edited, only to be disappointed with what I got back. The editor overedited, and in correcting every flaw changed the voice of the author. Sometimes I leave a mistake in because it was intentional to make a point or to give an idea emphasis.

It is your story; you have the final say. Temper that final say with wisdom and sound judgment. Don't be offended by the editor's suggestions. If you paid him for a professional opinion, then assume he knows what he is talking about. If a change the editor suggested really does not work for you, then don't use it. If there are a lot of instances when you don't agree with the editor, then either you chose the wrong editor, or maybe you are too close to your story and not being objective. In the end, it is your story; you have to be happy with how the story is told and feel that you have kept your voice and your style. Ask yourself:

- Did the editor correct grammar mistakes and punctuation?
- Did the editor untangle words or paragraphs?
- Does the edit change your voice or style?
- Does it improve the story?
- Does your gut instinct tell you to make the suggested change?
- In the end, does it help you to tell the story you want to tell?

If not, scrap the suggestion.

TOOLS FOR STAGE 6

1. Rewrite a dynamic synopsis of the story in as many pages as you need to give a strong overview.
2. Stage 6 is the final time you will create the story map. Be aware of whether you have any holes left or have any places that are still weak. Do you have a complete story? Are the elements shown in a dynamic way that effectively expresses this story?

3. This is also your final picture map. Does the picture map reflect your story?

4. Can you feel the tension in the story?

5. Is the story shown in the strongest order? At this point in some stories, the elements could still be moved around with minor editing of transitions and by checking for consistency.

6. Is this story memorable, and will it send the reader scurrying to the bookstore for your next work? Remember, the way you present your story is important so that a literary manager, editor, agent, producer, actor, or reader will pick it up and say, "This is something new! This is exciting!"

    a. What should you change to accomplish this? List the choices you can make to create a more effective scene or story.

    b. What are all the ways you can dramatize a particular scene or add conflict to create more tension?

"The Bus Boy" Story Map

Below is a story map for the short story I mentioned earlier that I wrote called "The Bus Boy." Ollie is an aging, recovering alcoholic. It is his vulnerability and his trying to achieve his one last dream that connects the reader to his character.

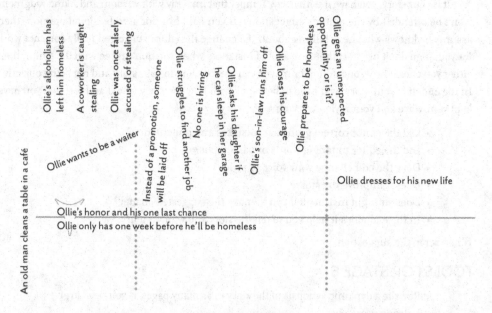

(9.1) *"The Bus Boy" Story Map*

Tools for Development

This is the last time you will return to page 88 to answer the questions. By now your answers should become specific and focused.

chapter 10

STAGE 7—EDITING
THE HARD COPY, SUBMITTING

In this stage we will discuss the final edits and getting your story ready to go out to agents, publishing editors, producers, or whoever might help you get your writing in front of an audience.

HOW MANY DRAFTS DOES IT TAKE TO FINISH A STORY?

Only you can answer that, but if you have worked through this process, your story, if not actually completed, should be at a much higher level and closer to completion. Before I started using this process, I would lose track of how many times I went through a manuscript. Now by the time I get to Stage 7, I know I've written a strong story that is ready to submit.

Will it be perfect? Never.

WHEN DO I KNOW WHETHER I'VE EDITED ENOUGH?

When you have looked at your story with a critical eye or had a professional editor go through your story and:

- There are no holes in your story
- There is a logic in the cause and effect of each event
- You have included surprises, twists, and the unexpected in your story
- Your story feels organic
- Your characters are interesting and connect the reader to the story
- Each character's motivation produces a believable outcome
- The tension and pacing fits the genre and tone of your story

- You have shown your characters and your story
- You used the strongest word choices
- You have replaced the "placeholders" with clearer, stronger writing
- You created crisp and engaging dialogue
- You corrected the grammar and punctuation errors
- You are proud of the pages and feel you have done what you can to write the best story you are capable of writing

If all of the above applies to your story, then you have probably edited enough.

WHAT'S LEFT?

At this point you should print out the final draft and find a nice quiet place to be alone and uninterrupted for a period of time. With a pen or pencil in hand, read through your final draft out loud so that you can hear what you've written. You will be more likely to catch whatever falls flat and recognize moments that don't come across the way you thought they would.

After you make your final corrections, you will want to read through to make one final check for spelling errors or punctuation and grammar mistakes or typos. It never fails that when I create my final draft I find I have made one or more of these mistakes, especially because I always retype my story at the end of each draft or sections where I have made major revisions—with retyping there are always typos. A clean manuscript is critical, or the person you submit to will not get very far in reading it. If you are sloppy with your typing or grammar, then he or she will expect you to be sloppy in your writing and figure you are an amateur. Most of the people you offer your manuscript or screenplay or play to will already be inundated. They are looking to whittle down the stack by eliminating a story in the first few pages. Typos and bad grammar are good reasons to toss yours aside quickly.

Printing Out the Final Draft

Make sure you print a clean copy on decent paper. Don't confuse the person reading your story by printing on both sides unless she specifically requests that you do. Be sure that your pages are numbered. Put your last name and a key word from the title in the header (unless you are submitting to a competition). Double-space novel and short story manuscripts. Follow the traditional accepted formatting for screenplays, plays, and television scripts.

For obvious reasons, never send out the only copy of your manuscript. And I don't care how many stamped self-addressed envelopes (SASE) you include, don't count on getting your manuscript back. Even if you do, odds are you won't reuse it. If it was read, it may contain marks or coffee stains, crimped corners, or wrinkled pages. Most stories today are stored electronically, but since computers die, always keep disks, CDs, or an external drive, and a hard copy as a backup.

Although sometimes agents and publishers and producers will allow you to submit to them electronically, most won't. They either aren't set up for that volume of email or don't have the digital storage or want to keep submissions separate or are simply concerned about viruses. Some may fear that you will later claim they manipulated your submission digitally and are now using it for a different purpose.

If you are requested to submit digitally, there will probably be a particular format requested. For screenplays and plays, I usually create a PDF of the file and submit it, since the differing software programs aren't always interchangeable, whereas Word documents have a little more flexibility.

MARKETING—MAPPING A SUBMISSION PLAN

Once you've finished writing, you have to put on the hat of a marketer. It's a very different mind-set than that of a creator/writer. Now you need to become objective and business-minded to shepherd your story through the selling and publishing or producing stage. My friend C.B. Shiepe spent years writing his story in different formats. After he decided to write a novel, he then decided to self-publish. He went from writer to entrepreneur. Taking this new position very seriously, he studied the market, studied every facet of publishing, and created a publishing company. He learned what the public preferred in cover design, studied the text on book jackets, and learned every facet of the business, from promoting online sales and the best way to ship, to paper and cover quality to distribution channels and working with bookstores, to public relations and promotional campaigns. Within a few weeks of his book's release, *Cliff Falls* became the number one book sold in a major regional bookstore and was receiving media attention. There are a number of books that can help you with marketing.

Your goal may be to find a publisher or a producer instead of self-publishing or self-producing. Publishers and producers come in all shapes and sizes, and most of the smaller ones have a niche market. Your job is to find out which publishers or producers would be interested in the genre of what you have written. It really is a waste of time to send your story off without any research. You may have written the greatest story since the beginning of storytelling, but if you are trying to tell it to the wrong audience, it will most likely be rejected. You must research who is publishing or producing what and narrow down to those who are interested in the type of story you have to offer.

Don't expect a lot of respect from any of the industries. Until you begin publishing or producing, you are a writer who nobody has ever heard of, without credentials, and you will probably feel a lot like those puppies in the puppy mills or a steer in a herd of cattle. You have to respect yourself and believe that what you have to offer stands on its own.

Every writer whose story I've heard got their work published or produced in different and generally unexpected ways. There is not one prescribed way to get your work noticed by someone who will take it to the next step.

The Submission Package

By now you should have a dynamic synopsis written in various lengths. Put together a submission packet that will include a synopsis, your resume, a brief bio, and sample chapters. The sample pages should be three chapters or up to fifty pages, as a rule of thumb. There is some disagreement over whether these pages should be the first or the most dynamic chapters. There is also a large variation in what is expected to be in the submission packet. A synopsis or summary can be from one paragraph to sixty-plus pages, depending on what the genre, agent, publisher, or producer requests, and should be written in present tense. A synopsis should emphasize the drama and conflict and your protagonist's arc throughout the story. A longer synopsis should contain actual dialogue and exposition.

When preparing your submission packet, don't make the mistake I did the first time. I made contact with the secretary of an editor at a major publishing house who encouraged me to send my manuscript. I decided to enclose the pages in a box for mailing. I found the perfect box, put my manuscript and cover letter inside, wrapped it, and sent it on its way. It was some time before I heard from the secretary. She contacted me to apologize for the delay. The box had been misplaced. I had used a box that had originally contained file folders. When the manuscript arrived at the publisher's, and the package opened, someone stuck it on a shelf of supplies, where it stayed until someone needed a file folder.

Whenever you can, prepare your package according to the requirements of the intended recipient. A producer or director may also request a character breakdown, which identifies each character's role and any particular characteristics or physical attributes that the writer deems important. However, before you submit any of these, you need to have a dynamic query letter.

Creating a Dynamic Query Letter

A strong query letter has the best chance of interesting an agent or publisher or whomever you might query. It should contain three components for fiction.

- Include an active paragraph in first person about the story—why this story fits in this journal or with this publisher or agent, possibly comparing your story to others they've published or produced.
- Add something about yourself as the author that makes you qualified to write this story or intriguing enough to follow up with. This could be your background, especially as it relates to the story you wrote: i.e., *I am the daughter of a Cherokee chief,* for a story about a Cherokee girl in contemporary America. *I spent three years in China teaching English,* for a man's search for identity in a rural Chinese village.
- Also include your level of education or experience. If you have degrees in a field that relates to your story, or your job gives you expertise for the story's background, add that information. Or include any publication information that will show you understand how to write and others have already accepted and published your work.

If you can't rely on the last two, you might want to include why this story is your passion.

All of this should be written in active language that gives a clue to your writing style and piques the interest of the person getting the query. Try to describe your story in one hundred active words or less. This is equivalent to about a paragraph in a letter. Read the backs of book jackets for the feel and the jargon of your particular genre and then write your query letter with the same enthusiasm. The book jacket is usually what sells a book. The cover entices the reader to pick it up; the blurb on the back has to convince the reader to pull out their wallet. Consider, how do these books promote themselves? Use the same strategy to entice the editor, agent, publisher, or producer to read your story.

Create a Submission List of Agents, Editors, Publishers, or Producers

Creating a list to submit to sounds simple enough, but, again, it takes research. Go to your favorite bookstore and peruse the aisles of the current books that are similar to yours and learn everything you can. Do they use particular words to attract readers—the same words attract agents and publishers. Who are their publishers? Do they give acknowledgment to particular agents or editors? These are people who might be interested in your story. The library also offers the same information, although current books, as well as books that might not interest an agent or publisher this year, will be found on the shelves, and often are missing their jacket covers, which hold valuable information. Online book sources will also have some of this information, only you won't see the prominence the bookstore gives it on the shelf or how many the bookstore is stocking (i.e., one versus five) or giving special promotions for. Online bookstores sometimes give the book's ranking in sales through their site, which may be helpful. There are books of publishers and agents and producers and what they are buying (and some lists online); you just have to ferret that information out.

Variety is a printed and online source for the entertainment industry. Look at the producers, directors, and actors of movies in the same genre of your screenplay or theaters that produce similar types of plays, You can find details about movies at www.imdb.com.

For short stories, you need to read copies of the different journals and magazines that publish them to see what they are interested in. University literary journals have a very different style, and often they are edited by college students, which means they often are looking for subjects and characters that college students are interested in or think are in vogue. Other magazines might have other interests, and you need to know who their audience is. Because most of these don't like multiple submissions, you need to be sure you are not wasting months while your submission sits in a stack in an editor's office who isn't going to be interested anyway. Sometimes you won't even hear back from editors, so you won't even know that you've been rejected. Far better to be sure your story is going to the right editor to begin with.

And speaking as an editor, I am very annoyed when I spend time reading an article by someone who obviously never read our journal and has no idea of our style or what we are looking for. I also get ticked when I've spent time on an article, and putting it through the review process, only to find out the author didn't inform me that they were also submitting it elsewhere or that another journal accepted it. You can be sure I will think twice about wasting time on that author again.

Keep a list of this information in an easily retrievable format. Use the table function in Word or a spreadsheet like Excel. This will give you an at-a-glace format where you can peruse who you've targeted and easily add new contacts. Rather than delete names, you may want to use "strikethrough" under the font function to show this is someone you've considered, but they have either rejected you or are no longer someone you can submit to. Note the reason why you are striking them out and the date you took them off the list. I find dating strikethroughs helpful, as something may later change that will cause me to reevaluate, or I might come across the same name at a later date, not realizing he was already deleted once. A date lets me know whether this is a change that occurred before or after I took them off the list, i.e., a new editor at a publishing house or new ownership, or a change in direction.

Be organized and don't let rejections hold you back. Be sure to follow through on any leads and don't drop the ball when you find interested agents and editors.

Keep Records

You've learned your craft, you've done the work, and now you are ready to submit. Present yourself professionally and with the confidence of a true artist who knows her business. As you begin submitting, keep records of who you submit to, when, a date for a follow-up, a date for sending it out again. Keep track of places you can go to meet agents, publishers, and producers, which is usually at conferences, at lectures, and sometimes at book signings. Be organized and methodical, businesslike and objective, and strategic. There are countless stories of how many rejections authors had before finally getting published or produced. In many cases, it took years for most overnight successes to get any recognition.

You can't get discouraged when you don't hear back or you get rejected. Okay, you can't help but get discouraged. Allow yourself the rest of the day for a pity party and then start the new day fresh. You might spend a little time considering why your story was rejected so that you can make corrections, or so that you understand why this might not have been the right audience after all. If you are fortunate enough to get notes on why the story was rejected, don't jump into a rewrite unless your gut tells you this editor or producer was right. Sometimes the next one has the opposite opinion, and you could find yourself rewriting after every submission for an editor or producer who has already rejected you.

The only one who can stop you is you. So keep submitting and submitting and submitting and ...

Pitch With Enthusiasm

A pitch is that few moments you have to present your story to someone who has the power to help you get it published or produced. There will be times when you will have the opportunity to give a one- or two-minute pitch. You need to rehearse and be prepared. This is when that twenty-five-word-or-fewer log line will come in handy, as will that one-paragraph synopsis you've been working on.

The first opportunity I had to pitch to an editor, I found I wasn't as prepared or practiced as I thought. I gave way too much background. The editor finally held up her hand and said something to the effect of "Move it along!" I must have looked at her horrified and embarrassed because she said, "You aren't used to pitching, are you? You need to get to the point quicker." To this day, if a good pitch tumbles out of my mouth, it's only because I've looked at my story from so many different angles, and I've learned to develop those short sound bytes about the heart of my story.

There are many great books on pitching, and several specifically for screenwriters whose main method of marketing is often pitching; novelists also get opportunities to pitch at conferences. The best way to learn to pitch is to practice—in front of a mirror, yes, but also with other writers and friends to see what excites them. Watch for telltale signs of when their eyes glaze over and they get bored or when they start shifting their weight or making small perceptible body movements; this usually means they've lost interest. You can tell when you've captivated your listener: there is either engaged silence or active interruptions to feed the story. That's when you're getting your pitch down.

A writer friend of mine, in town for a few days, told me she was having lunch with a producer she knew who was looking for a story on a small town, someplace unique. I reminded her she lived in a small town in a unique place and encouraged her to write up a few paragraphs of a story idea before her lunch date. At lunch she was to follow the producer's lead by starting with her own idea and then adapting it to the producer's interest level. When the producer started giving input, she would go with that idea. By the end of lunch they had brainstormed the story, and my friend had an assignment for a script. Note at what points of your pitch the listener is engaged and when she isn't, and adjust your tone and what you say accordingly.

Be focused, be concise, be interesting. Don't ramble on about how good your book or your play or your screenplay is. Instead show what a good writer you are by getting to the point, making sense, and presenting your most dynamic writing. Do not criticize the works of others or try to show off your own "coolness." When the person you are pitching to is interested, they will ask for more. If not, at least you got to practice and you had a chance to see when their eyes glazed over so you can tweak your pitch for the next time.

PART III

The End

LIVING A WRITER'S LIFE

chapter 11

MAPPING YOUR LIFE AS A WRITER

What does it mean to you to become a writer? At what point will you feel like a writer? What will being a writer look like in your everyday world?

NINE QUALITIES OF SUCCESSFUL WRITERS

Writers come in all shapes and sizes and personality traits. Some love to write, some hate writing but love having written. Some are compelled because they believe they have something important to say. Some just love to tell stories and create worlds and adventures. Good writers have some qualities in common. There are probably more than nine qualities of successful writers, but these are the ones I have compiled from my years of studying.

Skill

Skill is not necessarily inherent; skill is generally learned. When you read books on writing, you never know when one idea or concept will help you understand the writing process better and your work in a way that helps you ascend to a new level. Know the rules of grammar and punctuation and writing so that you can instinctively be a better writer, and then know when to break the rules to make your writing stronger. The more you know about the process of writing, the more effectively you will transfer what's in your gut to the page. Know the current writing trends so your writing won't be dated. Increase your vocabulary so you can show your story effectively by making word choices that are visual, show action, and engage the senses. Read books, short stories, plays, and screenplays and watch movies in your genre to learn techniques and how to properly format as well as the tricks of the trade for your type of stories.

Knowledge

Just as important as knowledge of your craft is knowledge of the world around you and the expansive world as a whole. Develop interests in many topics and learn something new every day. You don't have to be an expert, but every bit of information you acquire adds to the whole of what your writing can be. I find insights for both strengthening my knowledge of writing and for what I'm writing about in every subject I read and investigate. Learn about people—broaden your perceptions and build layers of depth to your understanding of others. Figure out ways in which the world works.

Writing is sometimes about telling people what they didn't know or helping them to see the world through new eyes, but it is also about telling people what they do know in a way they could not have expressed for themselves. The more you know, the better you can express ideas in new ways.

Discipline

Are you one of those people who want to convert their nine-to-five job to a writing career? Do you make as many excuses to skip a day at your job as you do to postpone the work required to succeed as a writer? We often say that writing is a priority, but then we place it far down on our list of things to do. We put it off until after the closet is cleaned, some home project is finished, right after this television program, the shopping is done, or we finish a work project so we can clear our time and minds. By then the day is over, life has gotten in the way, or we are too tired or too brain-dead to write.

Are you a serious writer or a recreational writer? There is nothing wrong with being either. The recreational writer is going to learn how to write for the pure pleasure of writing, and make writing fit into their lifestyle, without feeling guilty about either the time they take to write or the time they don't spend writing. Decide which you want to be.

Once you've made that distinction, set some writing goals and commit to them. The serious writer is compelled to write and is going to obligate her lifestyle to the demands of becoming a successful writer. If you want to be a serious writer, prioritize your writing accordingly and then be disciplined. Make a commitment to yourself that you will be consistent. Set a time of day or amount of time to spend or number of words to write or number of pages to edit—then follow through!

Discipline doesn't stop once the work is completed. Now you have to seek an agent, editor, or publisher or producer. Be organized, be consistent, be thorough. Learn the market. Get the work in the mail, and if you haven't already, start the next project.

Courage

Courage is not bravery—it is not the absence of fear! Courage is dealing with fear. Fear is agonizing over the unknown and letting it stop you from reaching your goals. Writers are usually afraid of failure, rejection, lack of talent, even success. One of the first questions every writer asks is: "Do you think I'm good enough to make it?" We all want reassurance before we begin the journey that all this hard work, all this solitude and isolation, all this commitment, all this alienation of family and friends, all this time spent, all the things not participated in are going to pay off. If you have the courage to be persistent in spite of all the obstacles, you can succeed. Talent isn't everything—the courage to persist is. This is when being determined to succeed will show in your refusal to accept defeat or setbacks. Don't allow rejections to stop you from reaching your goal. Be organized in marketing your work and persevere.

Persistence

For every acceptance there are numerous heartbreaking, gut-wrenching, soul-crushing rejections. To keep writing, to keep submitting, to keep looking for that magazine or agent or publisher or producer or director or actor or audience takes persistence. To finally say that I'm going to write the best story that I can, and because I believe in this work, I'm going to publish or produce it myself, and then to fight all the obstacles to get the work distributed, takes persistence. To get up at 4:00 A.M. when you want to sleep until 7:00 A.M., to closet yourself in an isolated spot at midnight when you'd rather be partying, is to be persistent. To struggle with that line, that scene, that dialogue, to not say *okay* is good enough, when you know in your soul it could be better—that is persistence. To endure the frustration of a sense of failure just before that breakthrough is persistence.

Sacrifice

What are you willing to sacrifice to be a writer? Before you answer, think about it—hard. Are you going to shortchange yourself when it comes to getting published? Have you prioritized your life in order to achieve your goals? There are some things that are easy to blow off because they are nonessential time wasters that we have allowed to ensnare us. Then there are those things in life that are important, but they keep us from writing. We may have to decide whether we are going to write or continue these activities. You will find that some things are too important to give up.

If you want to succeed as a writer you have to learn to evaluate your life and differentiate between what is more important and what is less important than your writing.

Passion

So many things go into writing a good story that you can't pinpoint one particular facet. However, your enthusiasm for the project is paramount to creating an exciting story. Write from your gut.

In my critique groups, workshops, and as an editor, I have worked with people who knew little about grammar and almost nothing about punctuation, but their stories were gripping. They wrote from their passion, from their love of creating a powerful story. You know a story is spellbinding when those reading or hearing it read aloud are totally silent, no paper shuffling, no squirming in their seats, no coughing or sighing, just intense concentration on listening. You can always learn or hire an editor for the technicalities, but the ability to tell an effective story comes from the gut. When you write, turn off the editor and write your story from the heart. Write with passion and tell a story about something meaningful to you and—just as important—meaningful to your audience.

Intuition

Writers must learn to develop their internal compass. They have to know when the characters are leading the story and when the vision of others has taken it over. Having a strong writing intuition means listening to that little inner voice that tweaks when you are writing. It may be telling you when you are spot-on, but most likely it is trying to tell you that something needs to be fixed.

Hear what your intuition is trying to tell you!

Don't confuse intuition with that little voice that is trying to defeat you.

Unique Style and Voice

Your work will stand out and give you an edge if you develop your own unique characters and way of describing and explaining the world. Find your authentic voice. Find your character's voice. Stand out as a storyteller.

What About Talent and Luck?

What if you don't have any of the above qualities or only some of them? Most of these are acquired qualities, not ones you were born with. I only included in this list what you can do for yourself. You note I didn't include talent. Innate talent you have to be born with, but you can substitute skill for talent if you learn your craft well.

Can I Make It As a Writer or Am I Wasting My Time?

The only thing that will stop you is you. Even bad writers have successful writing careers because they don't give up and they stick with it.

Years ago I heard editor and author Bonnie Hearn Hill in a workshop say something to the effect that there are three important keys to becoming a successful writer—persistence, talent, and luck—and if you have two of them, you can get by without the third. I usually substitute "networking" for luck. I don't usually refer to luck, since I think in terms of blessings and doing what needs to be done so that "luck" has a chance to operate—refer to the "Nine Qualities of a Successful Writer" on page 201.

These are the things I believe it takes to succeed as a writer:

- Talent or a good pitch
- Determination/persistence
- Networking

Talent or a Good Pitch

You must know talented people who are content with their life as it is, either pursuing what they are talented at as a hobby, or ignoring that talent for other priorities they have set. Talent is not everything. However, using the talent you have efficiently can take you far if others recognize it, like Shakespeare who was successful in life and continues today, and unlike Emily Dickinson or Franz Kafka, who weren't known as great writers until after their deaths.

We discussed a good pitch on previous pages. Being able to pitch a story might get you further than talent. It often takes a good pitch before anyone will read enough of your story to see whether you have talent. This is especially true in screenplays. A producer will overlook flaws in your writing if you have pitched an interesting idea. The story can always be executed by someone else, and probably will be, but you may be paid well for an idea or for the rough draft if you have convinced someone during the pitch that the story is interesting. For a novelist, the pitch at the conference or in a query letter will determine whether the writer's talent is ever seen.

Determination or Persistence

> Nothing in this world can take the place of persistence. Talent will not; nothing is more common than unsuccessful people with talent. Genius will not; unrewarded genius is almost a proverb. Education will not; the world is full of educated derelicts. Persistence and determination alone are omnipotent. The slogan "press on" has solved and always will solve the problems of the human race.

Calvin Coolidge

Neither talent nor a winning pitch will do you much good if you don't stay the course in spite of rejection and disappointment.

NETWORKING

Writing is somewhat isolating unless you connect with other writers and share your work and your experiences to encourage and commiserate with each other. (We'll talk more about writers' groups in a few pages.) However, you have to go beyond just socializing with other writers to find a network that can lead you to getting your work out there. Find opportunities to meet agents, publishers, directors, producers, and actors. If you are a playwright, volunteer at a local theater that produces the types of plays you write. If you are a screenwriter, take acting classes. Find students or actors just starting out or even character actors who have been at it a long time who might be interested in playing the roles you've created.

My first short film was produced by an actor who lived in the same apartment complex and who I sometimes ran into in the laundry room. When Kevin found out I was having a play produced, he came to support me. He was so impressed by my play that he wanted to read more of my work. One day he was using one of my plays as a cold reading to work with a student. He fell in love with the play and the main character's role, and he went out and raised the money to produce *The Hero*, a thirty-seven-minute film, and then submitted it to film festivals where we received recognition.

Workshops, conferences, and seminars are great places to do networking. Be professional in your presentation, both in your submission packet and in how you present yourself at events. Don't be afraid to meet and greet and let authors know that you enjoy their work, even letting them know particular passages or characters you've enjoyed. Go to places where professionals can be found, I don't mean to stalk or strong-arm someone, but to look for opportunities to give that thirty-second elevator pitch to someone who might be interested in what you are writing.

Find a mentor you can learn from who will be your champion. This is not easy to do, especially in the entertainment industry—most individuals in this industry are used to being accosted or stalked and are very wary of newcomers who want to suck the time and life out of them, so be respectful! And if you're snubbed, well, you are probably number 1,238 who has tried to get close to this particular individual in the last week to ask for help. This person's life is about their work, not yours. There is a fine line between being aggressive and being an aggressor. You want to be aggressive enough to seek and find opportunities, but you don't want people to hate the sight of you because they know you are trying to insinuate yourself into their lives.

I've known writers who got books published after volunteering at conferences. They weren't pushy, they didn't expect that they were going to get something out of it, they were just helpful, and when the opportunity availed itself, they had something to offer in a way that didn't say, "I'm just doing this so I can get next to you."

Most often that turning point in your writing career will come at an unexpected time from an unexpected source. But knowing how to write, writing, having your material prepared, or knowing enough to get material ready for a quick turnaround will make you available when unexpected opportunities avail themselves.

How do you know what is the right opportunity? You don't. You just keep forging ahead with your goal in mind, opening yourself up when it looks like a genuine opportunity and not being sucked into other people's agendas, schemes, or scams. Don't sit by the phone waiting for it to ring. Don't keep one hand on the keyboard hoping for an email that will catapult your career. Don't meet the mailman at the door every day. Live your life fully, participate in the world around you, write with passion and discipline, and invite opportunity into your life.

Do I Need a Writers' Group?

One of the ways to find inspiration is through interacting with other writers. Socializing with writers and forming groups can be a great personal motivation, or it can be very demoralizing. You want to avoid toxic writers who annoy you, demotivate, and overcriticize. If you are serious about getting published, you want to pick a group that is also serious. If you are interested in self-publishing, you may want to look for others who have that interest. If you want to write but aren't sure what you want the outcome to be, find a group that meets regularly and gives each other good feedback. A "group" can be one other person who you trust and share work with, or it can be several individuals. The main goal of a group should be to help its members grow as writers and to reach their goals. I was in one group where our goal was to create stories to accompany our minister's sermons. The group included both serious and recreational writers and individuals in the entertainment industry, and together we created a handful of short videos.

Although I have been in several writer's groups over the years, my current group consists of only three people. We know each other from the University of Southern California and all worked toward our Master's of Professional Writing together. We know each other's goals, problems, issues, and writing. We try to meet at least once a month, but since the three of us have very busy schedules, there have been long periods of time when we couldn't meet. However, we are a very supportive and knowledgeable writing community with very similar goals, and we have respect for each other as writers. Even after long hiatuses we continue to consider ourselves a strong writing group. We meet in an idyllic setting and have lunch, catch up on our lives, discuss any writing issues we have, and share our work. We like to share by reading aloud a limited number of pages (depending on the time we have and whether all of us have pages). We have an agreement that all feedback will be constructive and not destructive. Sometimes we just bring pages to send home for comments at the next meeting. There have been times when we didn't bring any pages but rather spent the time discussing our writing issues or our life issues and how they were impacting our writing focus.

One of the issues you will want to consider is whom you will allow in your group. I've been in groups where people will bring their work, ask to go first, and then leave soon after their work has been discussed. Or they only show up for the group when they have something to share. These people take from the group, but they bring little to nothing into the group. If you have a group of more than three or four people, or expect there may be some rotation in and out of the group, you probably will want to create some sort of charter for how your group will be run and what the group will allow and what the group's expectations of the participants are.

Because writing groups often deal with the naked you in your writing, there may be issues discussed that are quite personal at times. You may want to have confidentiality agreements signed by members stating that whatever is shared in the group stays in the group. This especially applies to your writing ideas. Unfortunately sometimes there are people in writing groups who help themselves to other people's ideas—bits and pieces from scenes and dialogues that comprise the story, if not the story idea itself.

Another type of group in which to socialize is a group of your peers who all have different talents and are all still learning. Everyone takes a different responsibility, and together you produce a play or film a story or documentary or critique each other's work and help take it to the next level. If you find you have too many leaders in a group, then agree to take turns being the lead on different projects; everyone switches up different responsibilities. Some of these people may go on to find success, and they may be the person willing to help you down the road, or you them. With the Internet, most of these projects can go online with a possibility of being seen by someone who has the power or authority to take your project to the next level. If nothing else, you may build an Internet following, which is a unique audience.

If you write plays or screenplays, it's also ideal to assemble a group who will do a table read and include actors. Make sure someone also reads the narrative (the action shots, etc.) so that you can sit back and listen. It is easier to catch places you might want to change when you hear it read out loud by others who may interpret your words differently than you thought they sounded. Everyone takes turns having their work read. Sometimes these groups work out deals to meet in local theaters.

The Ugly Truth About Hollywood

As in any industry or group, there are good, warm, sincere people who will help you. However, there are a lot of wannabes, especially in the entertainment industry, who will take you for a ride. I have made the mistake of trusting people who claimed to be producers and whose next check for their next project was only days away, only to later find out nobody would trust these individuals with lunch change, much less a movie budget of any size. In the end, I wound up spending a lot of effort to write stories that I did not own because it was based on someone else's ideas or tied to a producer who was never going to produce anything.

There's a belief in Hollywood that if the work is really good, it will find its way to be produced. I personally think that's a lot of hooey. First of all, all you have to do is look at the crap coming out of Hollywood to know that there has to be better writing than that. There are a lot of great scripts that lie at the bottom of someone's stack or that a reader didn't see any value in. The first person who reads a script is called a "reader," and these are frequently college students who are hired as interns, or for very little money, who generally have little training in storytelling. I know because a lot of them come into my class and proudly proclaim they are readers, but when we discuss their background in writing, it is minimal and does not necessarily include recognizing well-written, organic, or logical storytelling.

ENTERING WRITING COMPETITIONS

I have mixed feelings about writing competitions. Some of them are legitimate. Some of them are a way to bring income in to an organization or an individual. The fees for competitions differ, as does the quality of the judges of these competitions.

Short story and poetry competitions are one of the ways that support magazines and journals that publish them. A legitimate magazine or journal should be a legitimate competition. Fees should be reasonable and lower than for other types of competitions. However, do your research and know what they have published in the past and whether your story fits, or you are wasting your money.

Screenwriting competitions are usually more expensive and can be good or can be bogus. If you've never heard of a particular competition and can't find out much on the Internet about it, such as it's been running for a while and that winners do get the opportunities the promoters promise, then save your money.

Film festivals are a good way for screenwriters to get their work seen—both short films and feature length. Robert Rodriguez wrote a great book on how to produce a film and break into the entertainment industry called *Rebel Without a Crew*. I am a strong advocate of creating your own film your own way. If nothing else, you can distribute it through the Internet. The best way to learn filmmaking and writing screenplays is to get in the trenches and do it. There are lots of opportunities to have your short films and your full-length films shown at festivals and online sites that will host them. The budget for these is whatever you want it to be.

There are lots of full-length, ten-minute, or short play competitions. However, there is a war going on in the playwriting and theater community. In the past, playwriting competitions were free because along with poets, playwrights make very little income from their writing. But as theaters have seen their audiences dwindling, they, too, have seen playwriting competitions as a way to bring in income, as well as a way to continue promoting good playwrights. There are many in the industry who advocate boycotting competitions that charge fees to discourage that practice.

Novel competitions are rarer and are also fraught with scams. If it's not backed by a reputable publisher or agency, save your money. Almost every day I get an email for a book competition, that is called by different names and that originates from all over the country. I'm pretty sure it's a scam. If you want to enter a competition, do your homework and be selective.

SETTING GOALS THAT MAKE SENSE

By the time I decided to go to graduate school I had written a purpose statement for my life that encompasses the values I want in my writing. Whenever I get lost about my goals for my life and my writing, I go back to that statement. Just as companies and organizations write vision statements, so should every writer. Know what your values are and what you want to accomplish with your life. Take time to refine what matters to you and what you want that statement to say. Incorporate into that statement what you value and the principles you embrace. Be a writer of character, not necessarily just a character who is a writer.

Prioritizing and Balancing Your Life

Writing is very important to me, but not as important as my faith or as my family. I've had to figure out how to put it all together to make it work for my life. There is a constant juggling act between these three areas and my career as an editor and teaching and taking care of myself and having a social life. Sometimes one of these areas has to give. There are only so many hours in the day. During the semesters when I'm teaching, I have more commuting time, classes to prepare for, and papers to grade. Time for personal devotion keeps me centered but is tough on the days I have longer commutes. When the journal I edit is on deadline, I have to be more focused there. Holidays and vacations and certain hours and days are devoted more to family. Too long without being with friends makes me stale and self-focused. But because writing is one of my top priorities, I have to figure that time in as well, or this whirlwind called my life starts to feel like time is blowing past me.

Put in your priorities what's important to you in your life, and include what you are responsible for—like being the breadwinner or children or aging parents or debts you have incurred that have to be paid off. Take out of your life what is unimportant—and use that time to write.

Combining Writing With Another Career

Earlier we discussed setting life goals. Once you have determined that you want to be a writer, your goal may be to make a living as a writer, or not. Most of us have to have a source of income so that we can write. Because my career as an editor has been in graduate business schools, I've known several people who go to business school to get their MBA so that they can get rich and then quit to become full-time writers. Some of these people hate business. I can't see having a career that you hate so that someday you can do what you love. If you enjoy business, that's a great career background for a writer. If not, what are you doing to your writing soul for the sake of a buck?

Follow a career that you enjoy and make your writing part of your life, or live extremely frugally so that you can devote your time to a writing career. Even after you've had some writing success and made some money, you may find you keep your day job for the health insurance or other benefits, or because you like it, or because you want outside stimulation to feed your writing. Or because writing doesn't pay the bills or afford you certain little luxuries.

Don't put your life on hold for the day when you are a successful writer. By the time you get there, you may find your life has passed you by, and what was important in the beginning doesn't mean quite so much now.

Be a Writer of Many Talents

As noted above in the qualities of successful writers, you should expand your horizons by learning more than one form of writing. The more ways you can write, the more ways you will have to express what you want to say. All forms of writing are for the purpose of conveying information to the reader. By knowing how to write good fiction, plays, screenplays, nonfiction, and forms of poetry, you will hone your skills to be a well-rounded writer capable of finding the right word or format to reach your audience.

Develop your interest in other art forms as well. Through art you learn to better visualize and show your writing. Through music you learn how to use words to form sounds to convey meaning. Through photography you learn how to capture meaningful moments in time. Through cultural experiences you learn about people and other ways of seeing the world. Through nature you learn to develop a deeper passion for life. Fill your senses with the world around you so that you can draw deeply from your personal well-being to share your perceptions with others.

And, finally, be a writer who knows how to do more than write. Don't worry that you have to work at another job or profession for a living. In this way you are developing experiences and knowledge about more than just writing. You are learning about people from different perspectives. You are learning about life.

Quality of Writing

Writing is a journey, not a destination. When you write, think about your "quality of writing." How can you offer the best of yourself to others? One way is by continuously focusing on improving your writing skills; another is by portraying stories and characters that promote good in society.

In my opinion, people love hero stories, they love stories about the underdog overcoming the big odds, they love stories of good against evil.

When I looked at the movies on the American Film Institute's Top 100 Films for 1998 to 2007 (a list celebrating AFI's ten years in existence and one hundred years of movies), I was surprised. *Schindler's List*, 1993, was the newest film in the top 10. There are only a handful of movies listed from the 1990s and only one from the 2000s—*The Lord of the Rings*, 2001, based on a book written during the 1940s. Why aren't newer movies making this list? What is there about today's movies that is not hitting the mark?

I also believe that stories and language either build up society or they help to tear it down. The language you use in writing is important. Words are powerful and influential. Writers have become careless with words, sometimes alienating whole segments of their potential audience with extensive use of profanity, for example. What does that mean to you as a writer? How do you use words? What do your words reflect? What do you want to stand for or against as a writer? How do you want to use your words to influence the world?

What Do You Have to Say?

A couple of years ago I went through a difficult health ordeal. It took me several months to go through the treatments, with a very long recovery. During that time I wrote the short story "The Bus Boy," mentioned previously, about Ollie, an alcoholic who had lost everything. At the time of my writing this, I have only shared the story with friends and family. They still talk about Ollie and the impact the story had on them, how they were rooting for Ollie, how the story gave them hope and reminded them of people and events in their own lives. Although only a very small audience had read this story, it has had a big impact on those few people. This has been very rewarding to me. Sometimes you don't have to reach the whole wide world with your message for it to make a difference and be important. I mean, honestly, if you can touch one person's life, isn't that worth something?

> Always make a practice of provoking your own mind to think out what it accepts easily. Our position is not ours until we make it ours by suffering. The author who benefits you most is not the one who tells you something you did not know before, but the one who gives expression to the truth that has been dumbly struggling in you for utterance.

My Utmost for His Highest, Oswald Chambers

Forget the money—the average creative writer doesn't make enough to live "comfortably" anyway. If you want to write, write because you have something to say and because you want to make an impression on someone else's life. Write because you are the only one who can tell this story in just this way. Write for the love of being a storyteller.

BIBLIOGRAPHY

100 Best First Lines of Novels, http://www.infoplease.com/ipea/A0934311.html (accessed June 21, 2010).

AFI's 100 Years, http://www.afi.com/100Years/movies10.aspx (accessed September 19, 2010).

Atchity, Kenneth. (1995). *A Writer's Time*, rev. ed. New York: W. W. Norton & Company.

Begg, Alistair (Minister). "Truth for Life" Radio Series, Los Angeles Radio Station, KKLA 99.5 (March 18, 2004).

Bennis, Warren, and Thomas, Robert J. (2002). *Geeks and Geezers*. Boston, MA: Harvard Business Press, 16.

"Beware the 5 Stages of 'Grief.'" http://home.windstream.net/overbeck/grfbrf13.html (accessed September 23, 2010).

Bickham, Jack M. (1993). *Scene & Structure*. Cincinnati, OH: Writer's Digest Books.

Brislee, Jack. (April 2010). Review of "Poetics by Aristotle." http://thestorydepartment.com/reviewed-poetics-by-aristotle/.

Burnett, Hallie. (1985). *On Writing the Short Story*. New York: Barnes & Nobles Books.

Burnett, Hallie, and Burnett, Whit. (1975). *Fiction Writer's Handbook*. New York: HarperCollins Publishers, Inc.

Cameron, Julia. (1992). *The Artist's Way*. New York: G. P. Putnam's Sons.

Campbell, Joseph, and Moyers, Bill. (1988). *The Power of Myth*. (Betty Sue Flowers, ed.). New York: Doubleday.

Cather, Willa. (1994). *My Antonia*. New York: Signet Classic.

Chambers, Oswald. (1963). *My Utmost for His Highest*. Uhrichsville, OH: Barbour Publishing, Inc.

Dickens, Charles. (2004). *A Christmas Carol: A Ghost Story of Christmas*. (Original work published 1843.) http://www.gutenberg.org/files/46/46-h/46-h.htm.

Dickson, Frank A., and Smythe, Sandra, (eds.) (1973). *Handbook of Short Story Writing*. Cincinnati, OH: Writer's Digest Books.

Egri, Lajos. (1960). *The Art of Dramatic Writing*. New York: Simon & Schuster, Inc.

Epps, Preston H. (trans.) (1970). *The Poetics of Aristotle*. The University of North Carolina Press.

Epstein, Alex. (2002). *Crafty Screenwriting*. New York: Owl Books.

Epstein, Alex. (2006). *Crafty TV Writing*. New York: Owl Books.

Field, Syd. (1994). *Screenplay: The Foundations of Screenwriting*. New York: Dell Publishing.

Field, Syd. (1984). *The Screenwriter's Workbook*. New York: Dell Publishing.

Fitzgerald, F. Scott. (2008). *This Side of Paradise*. (Original work published 1920 with reprints post-1948 and 1960) http://www.gutenberg.org/files/805/805-h/805-h.htm.

Frey, James N. (1987). *How to Write a Damn Good Novel*. New York: St. Martin's Press.

Frey, James N. (1994). *How to Write a Damn Good Novel, II*. New York: St. Martin's Press.

Gardner, John. (1991). *The Art of Fiction: Notes on Craft for Young Writers*. New York: Vintage Books Edition.

Goldberg, Natalie. (1986). *Writing Down the Bones*. Boston, MA: Shambhala Publications, Inc.

Hartley, George. "Freytag's Pyramid." Posted for English 250 Textual Analysis, Ohio University. http://oak.cats.ohiou.edu/~hartleyg/250/freytag.html (accessed September 2010).

Hearn, Bonnie. (1995). *Focus Your Writing*, Redding, CA: CT Publishing Company.

Hjerter, Kathleen G. (1986). *Doubly Gifted: The Author as Visual Artist*. New York: Harry N. Abrams, Inc.

Huitt, W. (2007). Maslow's hierarchy of needs. *Educational Psychology Interactive*. Valdosta, GA: Valdosta State University. http://www.edpsycinteractive.org/topics/regsys/maslow.html (accessed September 23, 2010).

Iglesias, Karl. (2001). *The 101 Habits of Highly Successful Screenwriters*. Avon, MA: Adams Media Corporation.

Jenkins, Jerry B. (2006). *Writing for the Soul*. Cincinnati, OH: Writer's Digest Books.

Josephson Institute. "The Six Pillars of Character." http://josephsoninstitute.org/sixpillars.html (accessed October 7, 2010).

Koontz, Dean. (1981). *How to Write Best Selling Fiction*. Cincinnati, OH: Writer's Digest Books.

Kennedy, X. J. (1991). *Literature: An Introduction to Fiction, Poetry, and Drama*, Instructor's Edition, Fifth Edition. New York: HarperCollins Publishers.

Kreeft, Peter John. *C.S. Lewis & J.R.R. Tolkein on Good & Evil* (speech presented at Pepperdine University, The Thomas F. Staley Distinguished Christian Scholar Lectures, January 2002).

Kreeft, Peter (ed.). (1994). *The Shadow-Lands of C.S. Lewis*. San Francisco, CA: Ignatius Press.

L'Engle, Madeleine. (1980). *Walking on Water: Reflections on Faith & Art*. Wheaton, IL: Harold Shaw Publishers.

Mamet, David. (2008). *Bambi vs. Godzilla*. New York: Vintage Books.

Martin, Larry Jay. (1994). *Write from History*. Bakersfield, CA: Buttonwillow Books.

MacEwan, Elias J. (trans.). (1895). Dr. Gustav Freytag, *Freytag's Technique of the Drama: An Exposition of Dramatic Composition and Art*. Chicago: S. C. Griggs & Company. (trans. from the 6th ed. of *Technique of the Drama*.) http://books.google.com/books?id=2aGYPyvAEm4C&printsec=frontcover&dq=gustav+freytag+technique& hl=en&ei=CtquTLjlF4egsQOJwbmHDA&sa=X&oi=book_result&ct=result&resnum=1&ved=0CCUQ6AEw AA#v=onepage&q&f=false (accessed October 8, 2010).

MacLeod, Hugh. (2009). *Ignore Everybody: And 39 Other Keys to Creativity*. New York: Portfolio.

McManus, Barbara F. (1999, November). Outline of Aristotle's Theory of Tragedy. http://www2.cnr.edu/home/ bmcmanus/poetics.html (accessed September 27, 2010).

McManus, Barbara F. (1998, October). "Freytag's Triangle." http://www2.cnr.edu/home/bmcmanus/freytag.html (accessed October 2010).

Porter, Dee. (1996). *Anyone Can Write Fiction*, Lodi, CA: Creative Communications.

Pressfield, Steven. (2002). *The War of Art*. New York: Grand Central Publishing.

Rice, Scott (comp.). (1984). *It Was a Dark and Stormy Night*. New York: Penguin Books.

Rico, Gabriele. (2000). *Writing the Natural Way*. New York: Tarcher/Putnam Books.

Riley, Christopher. (2005). *The Hollywood Standard: The Complete & Authoritative Guide to Script Format and Style*. Ventura, CA: Michael Wiese Productions.

Rodriguez, Robert. (1995). *Rebel Without a Crew*. New York: Plume.

See, Carolyn. (2002). *Making a Literary Life*. New York: Random House.

Stebel, S. L. (1997). *Double Your Creative Power!: Make Your Subconscious Your Partner in the Writing Process*. Santa Barbara, CA: Allen A. Knoll, Publishers.

Strickland, Bill (ed.). (1989). *On Being a Writer*. Cincinnati, OH: Writer's Digest Books.

Thoene, Bodie & Thoene, Brock. (1990). *Writer to Writer*. Minneapolis, MN: Bethany House Publishers.

Trottier, David. (2005). *The Screenwriter's Bible*, 4th ed. Beverly Hills, CA: Silman-James Press.

Turner, Steve. (2001). *Imagine: A Vision for Christians in the Arts*. Downers Grove, IL: InterVarsity Press.

Valenti, F. Miguel. (2000). *More Than a Movie: Ethics in Entertainment*. Boulder, CO: Westview Press.

Vogler, Christopher. (1998). *The Writer's Journey*, 2nd ed. Studio City, CA: Michael Wiese Productions.

Wallace, Randall. (2002). *We Were Soldiers: The Screenplay*. Sherman Oaks, CA: Wheelhouse Books.

Warren, Rick. (2002). *The Purpose Driven Life*. Grand Rapids, MI: Zondervan, 312.

Wickham, Madeleine. (2009). *The Gatecrasher*. Audio CD, unabridged ed. Macmillan Audio.

Wilde, Oscar. (1995). *The Picture of Dorian Gray*. New York: Signet Classic.

Williams, Stanley D. (2006). *The Moral Premise: Harnessing Virtue & Vice for Box Office Success*. Studio City, CA: Michael Wiese Productions.

Wright, Kate. (2004). *Screenwriting Is Storytelling*. New York: Perigee Books.

INDEX

ACKNOWLEDGMENTS

There is so much that goes into a book like this and so many people who participate and from whom one learns, it is impossible to even begin acknowledging all of them. However, there are a few names of people who especially supported me in writing *The Writer's Compass* that I would like to mention. I want to thank writers, colleagues, and friends Frances Hurley Grimes, Nancy Hills, and AGS Johnson for reading the manuscript and giving me valuable feedback. A thank you to Writer's Digest editor Scott Francis for guiding me through the process and my agent Rita Rosenkranz.

I also want to thank Dave Alan Johnson and Gary R. Johnson, Velina Hasu-Houston, and Randall Wallace, who contributed pages to the book for examples of writing formats. A special thanks to writers and friends Dick Blasucci, Linnea McCord, John Struloeff, Margaret Martinello Magner, James J. Owens, C. B. Shiepe, and Ben Wilson, and students Jeffrey Doka and J. Philippe Thompson for their support in the book proposal and for their continuing encouragement. I would also like to thank all of the students who have made me a better teacher. And I especially want to thank all of the writers and teachers who have written books, given lectures, and taught classes from whom I have learned so much. A special thank you to Gwyneth Kerr Erwin and her family who gave me a base to start from as I embarked on acquiring my writing degrees.

And last, but certainly not least, my granddaughter Rachel for encouraging me to write a book that would teach her more writing skills, and my grandsons Joshua and Sean who inspire me, and my granddaughter Sophia who patiently curled up beside me while I wrote, waiting for playtime.